JUMP AT HOME

GRADE 6

NEW EDITION

Worksheets for the JUMP Math Program

JOHN MIGHTON

ANANSI

First published in 2004 by House of Anansi Press Inc.

Revised edition published in 2010 by
House of Anansi Press Inc.
www.houseofanansi.com

Some of the material in this book has previously been published by JUMP Math.

Every reasonable effort has been made to contact the holders of copyright for materials reproduced in this work. The publishers will gladly receive information that will enable them to rectify any inadvertent errors or omissions in subsequent editions.

20 19 18 17 16   6 7 8 9 10

Library and Archives Canada Cataloguing in Publication

Cataloguing data available from Library and Archives Canada

Library of Congress Control Number: 2010924083

Acknowledgements
Authors – Dr. John Mighton (Ph.D. Mathematics, Ashoka Fellow, Fellow of the Fields Institute for Research in Mathematical Sciences), Dr. Sindi Sabourin (Ph.d. Mathematics, B.Ed.), and Dr. Anna Klebanov (Ph.D. Mathematics)
Consultant – Jennifer Wyatt (M.A. Candidate, B.Ed.)
Contributors – Betony Main, Lisa Hines, and Sheila Mooney
Layout – Katie Baldwin, Rita Camacho, Tony Chen, Lyubava Fartushenko, and Pam Lostracco

This book, like the JUMP program itself, is made possible by the efforts of the volunteers and staff of JUMP Math.

 Canada Council **Conseil des Arts**
for the Arts **du Canada**

 ONTARIO ARTS COUNCIL
CONSEIL DES ARTS DE L'ONTARIO
an Ontario government agency
un organisme du gouvernement de l'Ontario

We acknowledge for their financial support of our publishing program the Canada Council for the Arts, the Ontario Arts Council, and the Government of Canada through the Canada Book Fund.

Printed and bound in Canada

Contents

Unit 2: Number Sense 1

Unit 3: Logic and Systematic Search 1

Unit 4: Patterns & Algebra 2

Unit 5: Number Sense 2

Introduction: About JUMP Math

There is a prevalent myth in our society that people are born with mathematical talent, and others simply do not have the ability to succeed. Recent discoveries in cognitive science are challenging this myth of ability. The brain is not hard-wired, but continues to change and develop throughout life. Steady, incremental learning can result in the emergence of new abilities.

The carefully designed mathematics in the JUMP Math program provide the necessary skills and knowledge to give your child the joy of success in mathematics. Through step-by-step learning, students celebrate success with every question, thereby increasing achievement and reducing math anxiety.

John Mighton: Founder of JUMP Math

"Nine years ago I was looking for a way to give something back to my local community. It occurred to me that I should try to help kids who needed help with math. Mathematicians don't always make the best teachers because mathematics has become obvious to them; they can have trouble seeing why their students are having trouble. But because I had struggled with math myself, I wasn't inclined to blame my students if they couldn't move forward."

— John Mighton, *The End of Ignorance*

JUMP Math, a national charity dedicated to improving mathematical literacy, was founded by John Mighton, a mathematician, bestselling author, and award-winning playwright. The organization grew out of John's work with a core group of volunteers in a "tutoring club"; their goal was to meet the needs of the most challenged students from local schools. Over the next three years John developed the early material — simple handouts for the tutors to use during their one-on-one teaching sessions with individual students. This period was one of experimentation in developing the JUMP Math method. Eventually, John began to work in local inner-city schools, by placing tutors in the classrooms. This led to the next period of innovation: using the JUMP Math method on small groups of students.

Teachers responded enthusiastically to the success they saw in their students and wanted to adapt the method for classroom use. In response, the needs of the teachers for curriculum-based resources were met by the development of workbooks. These started out as a series of three remedial books with limited accompanying teacher materials, released in fall 2003. The effectiveness of these workbooks led quickly to the development of grade-specific, curriculum-based workbooks. The grade-specific books were first released in 2004. Around that time, the power of teacher networks in creating learning communities was beginning to take shape.

Inspired by the work he has done with thousands of students over the past twenty years, John has systematically developed an approach to teaching mathematics that is based on fostering brain plasticity and emergent intelligence, and on the idea that children have more potential in mathematics than is generally believed. Linking new research in cognitive science to his extensive observations of students, John calls for a re-examination of the assumptions that underlie current methods of teaching mathematics.

JUMP Math, as a program and as an organization, developed in response to the needs of the students, teachers, schools, and communities where John and the volunteers were working. Recognizing the potential of all students to succeed in mathematics, and to succeed in school, was the motivation that John needed to dedicate more than ten years of his life developing a mathematics program that achieved his vision.

JUMP Math: An Innovative Approach

In only ten years, JUMP Math has gone from John's kitchen table to a thriving organization reaching more than 50,000 students with high-quality learning resources and training for 2,000 teachers. It continues to work with community organizations to reach struggling students through homework clubs and after-school programs. Through the generous support of our sponsors, JUMP Math donates resources to classrooms and homework clubs across Canada. The organization has also inspired thousands of community volunteers and teachers to donate their time as tutors, mentors, and trainers.

JUMP Math is unique; it builds on the belief that every child can be successful at mathematics by

- Promoting positive learning environments and building confidence through praise and encouragement;
- Maintaining a balanced approach to mathematics by concurrently addressing conceptual and procedural learning;
- Achieving understanding and mastery by breaking mathematics down into small sequential steps;
- Keeping all students engaged and attentive by "raising the bar" incrementally; and,
- Guiding students strategically to explore and discover the beauty of mathematics.

JUMP Math recognizes the importance of reducing math anxiety. Research in psychology has shown that our brains are extremely fallible: our working memories are poor, we are easily overwhelmed by too much new information, and we require a good deal of practice to consolidate skills and concepts. These mental challenges are compounded when we are anxious. The JUMP approach has been shown to reduce math anxiety significantly.

JUMP Math scaffolds mathematical concepts rigorously and completely. The materials were designed by a team of mathematicians and educators who have a deep understanding of and a love for mathematics. Concepts are introduced in rigorous steps, and prerequisite skills are included in the lesson. Breaking down concepts and skills into steps is often necessary even with the more able students. Math is a subject in which a gifted student can become a struggling student almost overnight, because mathematical knowledge is cumulative.

Consistent with emerging brain research, JUMP Math provides materials and methods that minimize differences between students, allowing teachers, tutors, and parents to more effectively improve student performance in mathematics. Today, parents have access to this unique innovation in mathematics learning with the revised JUMP at Home books.

JUMP Math at Home

JUMP at Home has been developed by mathematicians and educators to complement the mathematics curriculum that your child learns at school. Each grade covers core skills and knowledge to help your child succeed in mathematics. The program focuses on building number sense, pattern recognition, and foundations for algebra.

JUMP at Home is designed to boost every student's confidence, skills, and knowledge. Struggling students will benefit from practice in small steps, while good students will be provided with new ways to understand concepts that will help them enjoy mathematics even more and to exceed their own expectations.

JUMP Math in Schools

JUMP Math also publishes full curriculum-based resources — including student workbooks, teacher guides with daily lesson plans, and blackline masters — that cover all of the Ontario and the Western Canada mathematics curriculum. For more information, please visit the JUMP Math website, www.jumpmath.org, to find out how to order.

Evidence that JUMP Math Works

JUMP Math is a leader in promoting third-party research of its work. A recent study by researchers at the Ontario Institute for Studies in Education (OISE), the University of Toronto, and Simon Fraser University found that in JUMP Math classrooms conceptual understanding improved significantly for weaker students. In Lambeth, England, researchers reported that after using JUMP Math for one year, 69 percent of students who were two years behind were assessed at grade level.

Cognitive scientists from The Hospital for Sick Children in Toronto recently conducted a randomized-controlled study of the effectiveness of the JUMP math program. Studies of such scientific rigour remain relatively rare in mathematics education research in North America. The results showed that students who received JUMP instruction outperformed students who received the methods of instruction their teachers would normally use, on well-established measures of math achievement.

Using JUMP at Home

Helping your child discover the joy of mathematics can be fun and productive. You are not the teacher but the tutor. When having fun with mathematics, remember the JUMP Math T.U.T.O.R. principles:

Take responsibility for learning:
> If your child doesn't understand a concept, it can always be clarified further or explained differently. As the adult, you are responsible for helping your child understand. If they don't get it, don't get frustrated — get creative!

Use positive reinforcement:
> Children like to be rewarded when they succeed. Praise and encouragement build excitement and foster an appetite for learning. The more confidence a student has, the more likely they are to be engaged.

Take small steps:
> In mathematics, it is always possible to make something easier. Always use the JUMP Math worksheets to break down the question into a series of small steps. Practice, practice, practice!

Only indicate correct answers:
> Your child's confidence can be shaken by a lack of success. Place checkmarks for correct answers, then revisit questions that your child is having difficulty with. Never use Xs!

Raise the bar:
> When your child has mastered a particular concept, challenge them by posing a question that is slightly more difficult. As your child meets these small challenges, you will see their focus and excitement increase.

And remember: if your child is falling behind, teach the number facts! It is a serious mistake to think that students who don't know their number facts can always get by in mathematics using a calculator or other aids. Students can certainly perform operations on a calculator, but they cannot begin to solve problems if they lack a sense of numbers. Students need to be able to see patterns in numbers, and to make estimates and predictions about numbers, in order to have any success in mathematics.

Introductory Unit on Fractions

"In the twenty years that I have been teaching mathematics to children, I have never met an educator who would say that students who lack confidence in their intellectual or academic abilities are likely to do well in school. Our introductory unit has been carefully designed and tested with thousands of students to boost confidence. It has proven to be an extremely effective tool for convincing even the most challenged student that they can do well in mathematics."

— John Mighton

Cognitive scientists have discovered that in order for the brain to be "ready to learn" it cannot be distracted by anxiety. If your child struggles with mathematics or has "math anxiety," be sure to start JUMP Math with the introductory unit on Fractions found on page xxxii.

In recent years, research has shown that students are more apt to do well in subjects when they believe they are capable of doing well. It seems obvious, then, that any math program that aims to harness the potential of every student must start with an exercise that builds the *confidence* of every student. The introductory unit on Fractions was designed for this purpose. It has proven to be an extremely effective tool for convincing even the most challenged students that they can do well in mathematics.

The method used in the introductory unit can be described as *guided discovery*. The individual steps that you will follow in teaching the unit are extremely small, so even the weakest student needn't be left behind. Throughout the unit, students are expected to

- Discover or extend patterns or rules on their own;
- See what changes and what stays the same in sequences of mathematical expressions; and
- Apply what they have learned to new situations.

Students become very excited at making these discoveries and meeting these challenges as they learn the material. For many, it is the first time they have ever been motivated to pay attention to mathematical rules and patterns or to try to extend their knowledge in new cases.

How Does the Introductory Unit Build Confidence?

The introductory unit on Fractions has been specifically designed to build confidence by

- **Requiring that students possess only a few very simple skills.** To achieve a perfect score on the final test in the unit, students need only possess three skills. These skills can be taught to the most challenged students in a very short amount of time. Students must be able to do these three things:
  1) Skip count on their fingers;
  2) Add one-digit numbers; and
  3) Subtract one-digit numbers.
- **Eliminating heavy use of language.** Mathematics functions as its own symbolic language. Since the vast majority of children are able to perform the most basic operations (counting and grouping objects into sets) long before they become expert readers, mathematics is the lone subject in which the vast majority of kids are naturally equipped to excel at an early age. By removing language as a barrier, students can realize their full potential in mathematics.
- **Allowing you to continually provide feedback.** Moving on too quickly is both a hindrance to a student's confidence and an impediment to their eventual success. In the introductory unit, the mathematics are broken down into small steps so that you can quickly identify difficulties and help as soon as they arise.
- **Keeping the student engaged through the excitement of small victories.** Children respond more quickly to praise and success than to criticism and threats. If students are encouraged, they feel an incentive to learn. Students enjoy exercising their minds and showing off to a caring adult.

Since the introductory unit is about building confidence, work with your child to ensure that they are successful. Celebrate every correct answer. Take your time. Encourage your child. And, most importantly, have fun!

Work on Mental Math

Included in *JUMP at Home Grade 6* is a Mental Math unit, which will provide you with strategies and techniques for sharpening your child's math brain. Mental math is the foundation for all further study in mathematics. Students who cannot see number patterns often become frustrated and disillusioned with their work. Consistent practice in mental math allows students to become familiar with the way numbers interact, enabling them to make simple calculations quickly and effectively without always having to recall their number facts.

Mental math confronts people at every turn, making the ability to quickly calculate numbers an invaluable asset. Calculating how much change you are owed at a grocery store or deciding how much of a tip to leave at a restaurant are both real-world examples of mental math in action. For this reason, it may be the single most relevant strand of mathematics to everyday life.

How Can a Parent Best Use Math Time?

To keep your child engaged and attentive, consider breaking up your half-hour math time together into thirds:

- **First 10 Minutes:** Use this time to focus on Mental Math. This will sharpen your child's mental number skills, and they will find the remainder of the session much more enjoyable if they are not constantly struggling to remember their number facts.
- **Second 10 Minutes:** Use this time to work on grade-specific material. These worksheets have been designed by mathematicians and educators to fill gaps in learning, strengthen basic skills, and reinforce fundamental concepts.
- **Final 10 Minutes:** Save this portion of the session for math games, cards, or board games.

It is important to remember that mathematics can be fun! Liven up things by playing games and being as active as possible. If the opportunity to visually demonstrate a concept arises, JUMP at it! Have your child sort out change, look around them for geometric objects, or pace out a perimeter.

"Children will never fulfill their extraordinary potential until we remember how it felt to have so much potential ourselves. There was nothing we weren't inspired to look at or hold, or that we weren't determined to find out how to do. Open the door to the world of mathematics so your child can pass through."

— John Mighton

Mental Math Skills: Addition and Subtraction

PARENT:
If your child doesn't know their addition and subtraction facts, teach them to add and subtract using their fingers by the methods taught below. You should also reinforce basic facts using drills, games, and flash cards. There are mental math strategies that make addition and subtraction easier. Some effective strategies are taught in the next section. (Until your child knows all their facts, allow them to add and subtract on their fingers when necessary.)

To **add** $4 + 8$, Grace says the greater number (8) with her fist closed. She counts up from 8, raising one finger at a time. She stops when she has raised the number of fingers equal to the lesser number (4):

8   9   10   11   12

She said "12" when she raised her 4th finger, so: $4 + 8 = 12$

1. Add:
   a) $5 + 2 = $ _____
   b) $3 + 2 = $ _____
   c) $6 + 2 = $ _____
   d) $9 + 2 = $ _____

   e) $2 + 4 = $ _____
   f) $2 + 7 = $ _____
   g) $5 + 3 = $ _____
   h) $6 + 3 = $ _____

   i) $11 + 4 = $ _____
   j) $3 + 9 = $ _____
   k) $7 + 3 = $ _____
   l) $14 + 4 = $ _____

   m) $21 + 5 = $ _____
   n) $32 + 3 = $ _____
   o) $4 + 56 = $ _____
   p) $39 + 4 = $ _____

To **subtract** $9 - 5$, Grace says the lesser number (5) with her fist closed. She counts up from 5, raising one finger at a time. She stops when she says the greater number (9):

5   6   7   8   9

She has raised 4 fingers when she stops, so: $9 - 5 = 4$

2. Subtract:
   a) $7 - 5 = $ _____
   b) $8 - 6 = $ _____
   c) $5 - 3 = $ _____
   d) $5 - 2 = $ _____

   e) $9 - 6 = $ _____
   f) $10 - 5 = $ _____
   g) $11 - 7 = $ _____
   h) $17 - 14 = $ _____

   i) $33 - 31 = $ _____
   j) $27 - 24 = $ _____
   k) $43 - 39 = $ _____
   l) $62 - 58 = $ _____

PARENT:
To prepare for the next section (Mental Math), teach your child to add 1 to any number mentally (by counting forward by 1 in their head) and to subtract 1 from any number (by counting backward by 1).

Mental Math Skills: Addition and Subtraction *(continued)*

PARENT: Children who don't know how to add, subtract, or estimate readily are at a great disadvantage in mathematics. Children who have trouble memorizing addition and subtraction facts can still learn to mentally add and subtract numbers in a short time if they are given daily practice in a few basic skills.

SKILL 1 – Adding 2 to an Even Number

This skill has been broken down into a number of sub-skills. After teaching each sub-skill, you should give your child a short diagnostic quiz to verify that they have learned the skill. I have included sample quizzes for Skills 1 to 4.

i) *Naming the next one-digit even number:*

Numbers that have ones digit 0, 2, 4, 6, or 8 are called *even numbers*. Using drills or games, teach your child to say the sequence of one-digit even numbers without hesitation. Ask them to imagine the sequence going on in a circle so that the next number after 8 is 0 (0, 2, 4, 6, 8, 0, 2, 4, 6, 8, . . .). Then play the following game: name a number in the sequence and ask your child to give the next number in the sequence. Don't move on until they have mastered the game.

ii) *Naming the next greatest two-digit even number:*

Case 1 – Numbers that end in 0, 2, 4, or 6
Write an even two-digit number that ends in 0, 2, 4, or 6 on a piece of paper. Ask your child to name the next greatest even number. They should recognize that if a number ends in 0, then the next even number ends in 2; if it ends in 2, then the next even number ends in 4, etc. For instance, the number 54 has ones digit 4, so the next greatest even number will have ones digit 6.

QUIZ

Name the next greatest even number:

a) 52 : _____   b) 64 : _____   c) 36 : _____   d) 22 : _____   e) 80 : _____

Case 2 – Numbers that end in 8
Write the number 58 on a piece of paper. Ask your child to name the next greatest even number. Remind them that even numbers must end in 0, 2, 4, 6, or 8. But 50, 52, 54, and 56 are all less than 58, so the next greatest even number is 60. Your child should see that an even number ending in 8 is always followed by an even number ending in 0 (with a tens digit that is one higher).

QUIZ

Name the next greatest even number:

a) 58 : _____   b) 68 : _____   c) 38 : _____   d) 48 : _____   e) 78 : _____

iii) *Adding 2 to an even number:*

Point out to your child that adding 2 to any even number is equivalent to finding the next even number: e.g., $46 + 2 = 48$, $48 + 2 = 50$, etc. Knowing this, your child can easily add 2 to any even number.

Mental Math Skills: Addition and Subtraction *(continued)*

QUIZ

Add:

a) $26 + 2 =$ ___   b) $82 + 2 =$ ___   c) $40 + 2 =$ ___   d) $58 + 2 =$ ___   e) $34 + 2 =$ ___

SKILL 2 – Subtracting 2 from an Even Number

i) *Finding the preceding one-digit even number:*

Name a one-digit even number and ask your child to give the preceding number in the sequence. For instance, the number that comes before 4 is 2, and the number that comes before 0 is 8. (Remember: the sequence is circular.)

ii) *Finding the preceding two-digit even number:*

Case 1 – Numbers that end in 2, 4, 6, or 8
Write a two-digit number that ends in 2, 4, 6, or 8 on a piece of paper. Ask your child to name the preceding even number. They should recognize that if a number ends in 2, then the preceding even number ends in 0; if it ends in 4, then the preceding even number ends in 2, etc. For instance, the number 78 has ones digit 8, so the preceding even number has ones digit 6.

QUIZ

Name the preceding even number:

a) 48 : _____   b) 26 : _____   c) 34 : _____   d) 62 : _____   e) 78 : _____

Case 2 – Numbers that end in 0
Write the number 80 on a piece of paper and ask your child to name the preceding even number. They should recognize that if an even number ends in 0, then the preceding even number ends in 8 (but the ones digit is one less). So the even number that comes before 80 is 78.

QUIZ

Name the preceding even number:

a) 40 : _____   b) 60 : _____   c) 80 : _____   d) 50 : _____   e) 30 : _____

iii) *Subtracting 2 from an even number:*

Point out to your child that subtracting 2 from any even number is equivalent to finding the preceding even number: e.g., $48 - 2 = 46$, $46 - 2 = 44$, etc.

QUIZ

Subtract:

a) $58 - 2 =$ ___   b) $24 - 2 =$ ___   c) $36 - 2 =$ ___   d) $42 - 2 =$ ___   e) $60 - 2 =$ ___

Mental Math Skills: Addition and Subtraction *(continued)*

SKILL 3 – Adding 2 to an Odd Number

i) *Naming the next one-digit odd number:*

Numbers that have ones digit 1, 3, 5, 7, 9 are called *odd numbers*. Using drills or games, teach your child to say the sequence of one-digit odd numbers without hesitation. Ask them to imagine the sequence going on in a circle so that the next number after 9 is 1 (1, 3, 5, 7, 9, 1, 3, 5, 7, 9, . . .). Then play the following game: name a number in the sequence and ask your child to give the next number in the sequence. Don't move on until they have mastered the game.

ii) *Naming the next greatest two-digit odd number:*

Case 1 – Numbers that end in 1, 3, 5, or 7
Write an odd two-digit number that ends in 1, 3, 5, or 7 on a piece of paper. Ask your child to name the next greatest odd number. They should recognize that if a number ends in 1, then the next odd number ends in 3; if it ends in 3, then the next odd number ends in 5, etc. For instance, the number 35 has ones digit 5, so the next greatest odd number will have ones digit 7.

QUIZ Name the next greatest odd number:

a) 51 : _____   b) 65 : _____   c) 37 : _____   d) 23 : _____   e) 87 : _____

Case 2 – Numbers that end in 9
Write the number 59 on a piece of paper. Ask your child to name the next greatest odd number. Remind them that odd numbers must end in 1, 3, 5, 7, or 9. But 51, 53, 55, and 57 are all less than 59. The next greatest odd number is 61. Your child should see that an odd number ending in 9 is always followed by an odd number ending in 1 (with a tens digit that is one higher).

QUIZ Name the next greatest odd number:

a) 59 : _____   b) 69 : _____   c) 39 : _____   d) 49 : _____   e) 79 : _____

iii) *Adding 2 to an odd number:*

Point out to your child that adding 2 to any odd number is equivalent to finding the next odd number: e.g., $47 + 2 = 49$, $49 + 2 = 51$, etc. Knowing this, your child can easily add 2 to any odd number.

QUIZ Add:

a) $27 + 2 =$ ___   b) $83 + 2 =$ ___   c) $41 + 2 =$ ___   d) $59 + 2 =$ ___   e) $35 + 2 =$ ___

Mental Math Skills: Addition and Subtraction *(continued)*

SKILL 4 – Subtracting 2 from an Odd Number

i) *Finding the preceding one-digit odd number:*

Name a one-digit odd number and ask your child to give the preceding number in the sequence. For instance, the number that comes before 3 is 1, and the number that comes before 1 is 9. (Remember: the sequence is circular.)

ii) *Finding the preceding two-digit odd number:*

Case 1 – Numbers that end in 3, 5, 7, or 9

Write a two-digit number that ends in 3, 5, 7, or 9 on a piece of paper. Ask your child to name the preceding odd number. They should recognize that if a number ends in 3, then the preceding odd number ends in 1; if it ends in 5 then the preceding odd number ends in 3, etc. For instance, the number 79 has ones digit 9, so the preceding odd number has ones digit 7.

> **QUIZ**
>
> Name the preceding odd number:
>
> a) 49 : _____   b) 27 : _____   c) 35 : _____   d) 63 : _____   e) 79 : _____

Case 2 – Numbers that end in 1

Write the number 81 on a piece of paper and ask your child to name the preceding odd number. They should recognize that if an odd number ends in 1, then the preceding odd number ends in 9 (but the ones digit is one less). So the odd number that comes before 81 is 79.

> **QUIZ**
>
> Name the preceding odd number:
>
> a) 41 : _____   b) 61 : _____   c) 81 : _____   d) 51 : _____   e) 31 : _____

iii) *Subtracting 2 from an odd number:*

Point out to your child that subtracting 2 from any odd number is equivalent to finding the preceding odd number: e.g., $49 - 2 = 47$, $47 - 2 = 45$, etc.

> **QUIZ**
>
> Subtract:
>
> a) $59 - 2 =$ ___   b) $25 - 2 =$ ___   c) $37 - 2 =$ ___   d) $43 - 2 =$ ___   e) $61 - 2 =$ ___

SKILLS 5 and 6

Once your child can add and subtract the numbers 1 and 2, then they can easily add and subtract the number 3: Add 3 to a number by first adding 2, then adding 1 (e.g., $35 + 3 = 35 + 2 + 1$). Subtract 3 from a number by subtracting 2, then subtracting 1 (e.g., $35 - 3 = 35 - 2 - 1$).

Mental Math Skills: **Addition and Subtraction** *(continued)*

PARENT: All of the addition and subtraction tricks you teach your child should be reinforced with drills, flashcards and tests. Eventually they should memorize their addition and subtraction facts and shouldn't have to rely on the mental math tricks. One of the greatest gifts you can give your child is to teach them their number facts.

SKILLS 7 and 8

Add 4 to a number by adding 2 twice (e.g., $51 + 4 = 51 + 2 + 2$). Subtract 4 from a number by subtracting 2 twice (e.g., $51 - 4 = 51 - 2 - 2$).

SKILLS 9 and 10

Add 5 to a number by adding 4 then 1. Subtract 5 by subtracting 4 then 1.

SKILL 11

Your child can add pairs of identical numbers by doubling (e.g., $6 + 6 = 2 \times 6$). They should either memorize the 2 times table or they should double numbers by counting on their fingers by 2s.

Add a pair of numbers that differ by 1 by rewriting the larger number as 1 plus the smaller number, then use doubling to find the sum: e.g., $6 + 7 = 6 + 6 + 1 = 12 + 1 = 13$; $7 + 8 = 7 + 7 + 1 = 14 + 1 = 15$.

SKILLS 12, 13, and 14

Add a one-digit number to 10 by simply replacing the zero in 10 with the one-digit number: e.g., $10 + 7 = 17$.

Add 10 to any two-digit number by simply increasing the tens digit of the two-digit number by 1: e.g., $53 + 10 = 63$.

Add a pair of two-digit numbers (with no carrying) by adding the ones digits of the numbers and then adding the tens digits: e.g., $23 + 64 = 87$.

SKILLS 15 and 16

To add 9 to a one-digit number, subtract 1 from the number and then add 10: e.g., $9 + 6 = 10 + 5 = 15$; $9 + 7 = 10 + 6 = 16$. (Essentially, your child simply has to subtract 1 from the number and then stick a 1 in front of the result.)

To add 8 to a one-digit number, subtract 2 from the number and add 10: e.g., $8 + 6 = 10 + 4 = 14$; $8 + 7 = 10 + 5 = 15$.

SKILLS 17 and 18

To subtract a pair of multiples of ten, simply subtract the tens digits and add a zero for the ones digit: e.g., $70 - 50 = 20$.

To subtract a pair of two-digit numbers (without carrying or regrouping), subtract the ones digit from the ones digit and the tens digit from the tens digit: e.g., $57 - 34 = 23$.

Mental Math — Further Strategies

Further Mental Math Strategies

1. Your child should be able to explain how to use the strategy of "rounding the subtrahend (i.e., the number you are subtracting) up to the nearest multiple of ten."
    Examples:

    Subtrahend   Subtrahend rounded to the nearest tens

    a) $37 - 19 = 37 - 20 + 1$ You must add 1 because 20 is 1 greater than 19.
    b) $64 - 28 = 64 - 30 + 2$ You must add 2 because 30 is 2 greater than 28.
    c) $65 - 46 = 65 - 50 + 4$

    Practice Questions:

    a) $27 - 17 = 27 - \underline{\quad} + \underline{\quad}$
    b) $52 - 36 = 52 - \underline{\quad} + \underline{\quad}$
    c) $76 - 49 = 76 - \underline{\quad} + \underline{\quad}$
    d) $84 - 57 = 84 - \underline{\quad} + \underline{\quad}$
    e) $61 - 29 = 61 - \underline{\quad} + \underline{\quad}$
    f) $42 - 18 = 42 - \underline{\quad} + \underline{\quad}$

    PARENT: This strategy works well with numbers that end in 6, 7, 8, or 9.

2. Your child should be able to explain how to subtract by thinking of adding.
    Examples:

    Count by ones from 45 to the nearest tens (50).   Count from 50 until you reach the first number (62).

    a) $62 - 45 = 5 + 12 = 17$ The sum of counting up to the nearest ten and the original number is the difference.
    b) $46 - 23 = 3 + 20 = 23$
    c) $73 - 17 = 6 + 50 = 56$ What method did we use here?

    Practice Questions:

    a) $88 - 36 = \underline{\quad} + \underline{\quad} = \underline{\quad}$
    b) $58 - 21 = \underline{\quad} + \underline{\quad} = \underline{\quad}$
    c) $43 - 17 = \underline{\quad} + \underline{\quad} = \underline{\quad}$
    d) $74 - 28 = \underline{\quad} + \underline{\quad} = \underline{\quad}$
    e) $93 - 64 = \underline{\quad} + \underline{\quad} = \underline{\quad}$
    f) $82 - 71 = \underline{\quad} + \underline{\quad} = \underline{\quad}$

3. Your child should be able to explain how to "use doubles."
    Examples:

    Minuend   If you add the subtrahend to itself, and the sum is equal to the minuend, then the subtrahend is the same as the difference.

    a) $12 - 6 = 6$ $6 + 6 = 12$ Same value as minuend
    b) $8 - 4 = 4$

    Subtrahend plus itself

    Practice Questions:

    a) $6 - 3 = \underline{\quad}$
    b) $10 - 5 = \underline{\quad}$
    c) $14 - 7 = \underline{\quad}$
    d) $18 - 9 = \underline{\quad}$
    e) $16 - 8 = \underline{\quad}$
    f) $20 - 10 = \underline{\quad}$

Mental Math Exercises

PARENT: Teaching the material on these Mental Math worksheets may take several lessons. Your child will need more practice than is provided on these pages. These pages are intended as a test to be given when you are certain your child has learned the materials fully.

PARENT: Teach skills 1, 2, 3, and 4 as outlined on pages xv–xviii before you allow your child to answer Questions 1 through 12:

1. Name the <u>even</u> number that comes <u>after</u> the number. Answer in the blank provided:

   a) 32 _____ b) 46 _____ c) 14 _____ d) 92 _____ e) 56 _____

   f) 30 _____ g) 84 _____ h) 60 _____ i) 72 _____ j) 24 _____

2. Name the <u>even</u> number that comes <u>after</u> the number:

   a) 28 _____ b) 18 _____ c) 78 _____ d) 38 _____ e) 68 _____

3. Add:
   REMEMBER: Adding 2 to an even number is the same as finding the next even number.

   a) $42 + 2 =$ _____ b) $76 + 2 =$ _____ c) $28 + 2 =$ _____ d) $16 + 2 =$ _____

   e) $68 + 2 =$ _____ f) $12 + 2 =$ _____ g) $36 + 2 =$ _____ h) $90 + 2 =$ _____

   i) $70 + 2 =$ _____ j) $24 + 2 =$ _____ k) $66 + 2 =$ _____ l) $52 + 2 =$ _____

4. Name the <u>even</u> number that comes <u>before</u> the number:

   a) **38** _____ b) **42** _____ c) **56** _____ d) **72** _____ e) **98** _____

   f) **48** _____ g) **16** _____ h) **22** _____ i) **66** _____ j) **14** _____

5. Name the <u>even</u> number that comes <u>before</u> the number:

   a) **30** _____ b) **70** _____ c) **60** _____ d) **10** _____ e) **80** _____

6. Subtract:
   REMEMBER: Subtracting 2 from an even number is the same as finding the preceding even number.

   a) $46 - 2 =$ _____ b) $86 - 2 =$ _____ c) $90 - 2 =$ _____ d) $14 - 2 =$ _____

   e) $54 - 2 =$ _____ f) $72 - 2 =$ _____ g) $12 - 2 =$ _____ h) $56 - 2 =$ _____

   i) $32 - 2 =$ _____ j) $40 - 2 =$ _____ k) $60 - 2 =$ _____ l) $26 - 2 =$ _____

7. Name the <u>odd</u> number that comes <u>after</u> the number:

   a) 37 _____ b) 51 _____ c) 63 _____ d) 75 _____ e) 17 _____

   f) 61 _____ g) 43 _____ h) 81 _____ i) 23 _____ j) 95 _____

8. Name the <u>odd</u> number that comes <u>after</u> the number:

   a) 69 _____ b) 29 _____ c) 9 _____ d) 79 _____ e) 59 _____

Mental Math Exercises *(continued)*

9. Add:
   REMEMBER: Adding 2 to an odd number is the same as finding the next odd number.

   a) $25 + 2 =$ _____   b) $31 + 2 =$ _____   c) $47 + 2 =$ _____   d) $33 + 2 =$ _____

   e) $39 + 2 =$ _____   f) $91 + 2 =$ _____   g) $5 + 2 =$ _____   h) $89 + 2 =$ _____

   i) $11 + 2 =$ _____   j) $65 + 2 =$ _____   k) $29 + 2 =$ _____   l) $17 + 2 =$ _____

10. Name the <u>odd</u> number that comes <u>before</u> the number:

    a) **39** _____   b) **43** _____   c) **57** _____   d) **17** _____   e) **99** _____

    f) **13** _____   g) **85** _____   h) **79** _____   i) **65** _____   j) **77** _____

11. Name the <u>odd</u> number that comes <u>before</u> the number:

    a) **21** _____   b) **41** _____   c) **11** _____   d) **91** _____   e) **51** _____

12. Subtract:
    REMEMBER: Subtracting 2 from an odd number is the same as finding the preceding odd number.

    a) $47 - 2 =$ _____   b) $85 - 2 =$ _____   c) $91 - 2 =$ _____   d) $15 - 2 =$ _____

    e) $51 - 2 =$ _____   f) $73 - 2 =$ _____   g) $11 - 2 =$ _____   h) $59 - 2 =$ _____

    i) $31 - 2 =$ _____   j) $43 - 2 =$ _____   k) $7 - 2 =$ _____   l) $25 - 2 =$ _____

PARENT: Teach skills 5 and 6 as outlined on page xviii before you allow your child to answer Questions 13 and 14.

13. Add 3 to the number by adding 2, then adding 1 (e.g., $35 + 3 = 35 + 2 + 1$):

    a) $23 + 3 =$ _____   b) $36 + 3 =$ _____   c) $29 + 3 =$ _____   d) $16 + 3 =$ _____

    e) $67 + 3 =$ _____   f) $12 + 3 =$ _____   g) $35 + 3 =$ _____   h) $90 + 3 =$ _____

    i) $78 + 3 =$ _____   j) $24 + 3 =$ _____   k) $6 + 3 =$ _____   l) $59 + 3 =$ _____

14. Subtract 3 from the number by subtracting 2, then subtracting 1 (e.g., $35 - 3 = 35 - 2 - 1$):

    a) $46 - 3 =$ _____   b) $87 - 3 =$ _____   c) $99 - 3 =$ _____   d) $14 - 3 =$ _____

    e) $8 - 3 =$ _____   f) $72 - 3 =$ _____   g) $12 - 3 =$ _____   h) $57 - 3 =$ _____

    i) $32 - 3 =$ _____   j) $40 - 3 =$ _____   k) $60 - 3 =$ _____   l) $28 - 3 =$ _____

15. Fred has 49 stamps. He gives 2 stamps away. How many stamps does he have left?

16. There are 25 minnows in a tank. Alice adds 3 more to the tank. How many minnows are now in the tank?

Mental Math Exercises *(continued)*

PARENT: Teach skills 7 and 8 as outlined on page xix.

17. Add 4 to the number by adding 2 twice (e.g., $51 + 4 = 51 + 2 + 2$):

a) $42 + 4 =$ _____   b) $76 + 4 =$ _____   c) $27 + 4 =$ _____   d) $17 + 4 =$ _____

e) $68 + 4 =$ _____   f) $11 + 4 =$ _____   g) $35 + 4 =$ _____   h) $8 + 4 =$ _____

i) $72 + 4 =$ _____   j) $23 + 4 =$ _____   k) $60 + 4 =$ _____   l) $59 + 4 =$ _____

18. Subtract 4 from the number by subtracting 2 twice (e.g., $26 - 4 = 26 - 2 - 2$):

a) $46 - 4 =$ _____   b) $86 - 4 =$ _____   c) $91 - 4 =$ _____   d) $15 - 4 =$ _____

e) $53 - 4 =$ _____   f) $9 - 4 =$ _____   g) $13 - 4 =$ _____   h) $57 - 4 =$ _____

i) $40 - 4 =$ _____   j) $88 - 4 =$ _____   k) $69 - 4 =$ _____   l) $31 - 4 =$ _____

PARENT: Teach skills 9 and 10 as outlined on page xix.

19. Add 5 to the number by adding 4, then adding 1 (or add 2 twice, then add 1):

a) $84 + 5 =$ _____   b) $27 + 5 =$ _____   c) $31 + 5 =$ _____   d) $44 + 5 =$ _____

e) $63 + 5 =$ _____   f) $92 + 5 =$ _____   g) $14 + 5 =$ _____   h) $16 + 5 =$ _____

i) $9 + 5 =$ _____   j) $81 + 5 =$ _____   k) $51 + 5 =$ _____   l) $28 + 5 =$ _____

20. Subtract 5 from the number by subtracting 4, then subtracting 1 (or subtract 2 twice, then subtract 1):

a) $48 - 5 =$ _____   b) $86 - 5 =$ _____   c) $55 - 5 =$ _____   d) $69 - 5 =$ _____

e) $30 - 5 =$ _____   f) $13 - 5 =$ _____   g) $92 - 5 =$ _____   h) $77 - 5 =$ _____

i) $45 - 5 =$ _____   j) $24 - 5 =$ _____   k) $91 - 5 =$ _____   l) $8 - 5 =$ _____

PARENT: Teach skill 11 as outlined on page xix.

21. Add:

a) $6 + 6 =$ _____   b) $7 + 7 =$ _____   c) $8 + 8 =$ _____

d) $5 + 5 =$ _____   e) $4 + 4 =$ _____   f) $9 + 9 =$ _____

22. Add by thinking of the larger number as a sum of two smaller numbers. The first one is done for you:

a) $6 + 7 = 6 + 6 + 1$ b) $7 + 8 =$ _____   c) $6 + 8 =$ _____

d) $4 + 5 =$ _____   e) $5 + 7 =$ _____   f) $8 + 9 =$ _____

Mental Math Exercises *(continued)*

PARENT: Teach skills 12, 13, and 14 as outlined on page xix.

23. a) $10 + 3 =$ _____
    b) $10 + 7 =$ _____
    c) $5 + 10 =$ _____
    d) $10 + 1 =$ _____
    e) $9 + 10 =$ _____
    f) $10 + 4 =$ _____
    g) $10 + 8 =$ _____
    h) $10 + 2 =$ _____

24. a) $10 + 20 =$ _____
    b) $40 + 10 =$ _____
    c) $10 + 80 =$ _____
    d) $10 + 50 =$ _____
    e) $30 + 10 =$ _____
    f) $10 + 60 =$ _____
    g) $10 + 10 =$ _____
    h) $70 + 10 =$ _____

25. a) $10 + 25 =$ _____
    b) $10 + 67 =$ _____
    c) $10 + 31 =$ _____
    d) $10 + 82 =$ _____
    e) $10 + 43 =$ _____
    f) $10 + 51 =$ _____
    g) $10 + 68 =$ _____
    h) $10 + 21 =$ _____
    i) $10 + 11 =$ _____
    j) $10 + 19 =$ _____
    k) $10 + 44 =$ _____
    l) $10 + 88 =$ _____

26. a) $20 + 30 =$ _____
    b) $40 + 20 =$ _____
    c) $30 + 30 =$ _____
    d) $50 + 30 =$ _____
    e) $20 + 50 =$ _____
    f) $40 + 40 =$ _____
    g) $50 + 40 =$ _____
    h) $40 + 30 =$ _____
    i) $60 + 30 =$ _____
    j) $20 + 60 =$ _____
    k) $20 + 70 =$ _____
    l) $60 + 40 =$ _____

27. a) $20 + 23 =$ _____
    b) $32 + 24 =$ _____
    c) $51 + 12 =$ _____
    d) $12 + 67 =$ _____
    e) $83 + 14 =$ _____
    f) $65 + 24 =$ _____
    g) $41 + 43 =$ _____
    h) $70 + 27 =$ _____
    i) $31 + 61 =$ _____
    j) $54 + 33 =$ _____
    k) $28 + 31 =$ _____
    l) $42 + 55 =$ _____

PARENT: Teach skills 15 and 16 as outlined on page xix.

28. a) $9 + 3 =$ _____
    b) $9 + 7 =$ _____
    c) $6 + 9 =$ _____
    d) $4 + 9 =$ _____
    e) $9 + 9 =$ _____
    f) $5 + 9 =$ _____
    g) $9 + 2 =$ _____
    h) $9 + 8 =$ _____

29. a) $8 + 2 =$ _____
    b) $8 + 6 =$ _____
    c) $8 + 7 =$ _____
    d) $4 + 8 =$ _____
    e) $5 + 8 =$ _____
    f) $8 + 3 =$ _____
    g) $9 + 8 =$ _____
    h) $8 + 8 =$ _____

PARENT: Teach skills 17 and 18 as outlined on page xix.

30. a) $40 - 10 =$ _____
    b) $50 - 10 =$ _____
    c) $70 - 10 =$ _____
    d) $20 - 10 =$ _____
    e) $40 - 20 =$ _____
    f) $60 - 30 =$ _____
    g) $40 - 30 =$ _____
    h) $60 - 50 =$ _____

31. a) $57 - 34 =$ _____
    b) $43 - 12 =$ _____
    c) $62 - 21 =$ _____
    d) $59 - 36 =$ _____
    e) $87 - 63 =$ _____
    f) $95 - 62 =$ _____
    g) $35 - 10 =$ _____
    h) $17 - 8 =$ _____

Introduction

Mental Math (Advanced)

<u>Multiples of Ten</u>

NOTE: In the exercises below, you will learn several ways to use multiples of ten in mental addition or subtraction.

> **I** $542 + 214 = 542 + 200 + 10 + 4 = 742 + 10 + 4 = 752 + 4 = 756$
>
> $827 - 314 = 827 - 300 - 10 - 4 = 527 - 10 - 4 = 517 - 4 = 513$
>
> Sometimes you will need to carry:
>
> $545 + 172 = 545 + 100 + 70 + 2 = 645 + 70 + 2 = 715 + 2 = 717$

1. Warm up:

   a) $536 + 100 =$ _____   b) $816 + 10 =$ _____   c) $124 + 5 =$ _____   d) $540 + 200 =$ _____

   e) $234 + 30 =$ _____   f) $345 + 300 =$ _____   g) $236 - 30 =$ _____   h) $442 - 20 =$ _____

   i) $970 - 70 =$ _____   j) $542 - 400 =$ _____   k) $160 + 50 =$ _____   l) $756 + 40 =$ _____

2. Write the second number in expanded form and add or subtract one digit at a time. The first one is done for you:

   a) $564 + 215 =$ _____ $564 + 200 + 10 + 5$ _____ $=$ _____ 779 _____

   b) $445 + 343 =$ _____ $=$ _____

   c) $234 + 214 =$ _____ $=$ _____

3. Add or subtract mentally (one digit at a time):

   a) $547 + 312 =$ _____   b) $578 - 314 =$ _____   c) $845 - 454 =$ _____

> **II**   If one of the numbers you are adding or subtracting is close to a number that is a multiple of ten, add the multiple of ten and then add or subtract an adjustment factor:
>
> $645 + 99 = 645 + 100 - 1 = 745 - 1 = 744$
>
> $856 + 42 = 856 + 40 + 2 = 896 + 2 = 898$

> **III**   Sometimes in subtraction it helps to think of a multiple of ten as a sum of 1 and a number consisting entirely of 9s (e.g., $100 = 1 + 99$; $1000 = 1 + 999$). You never have to borrow or exchange when you are subtracting from a number consisting entirely of 9s.
>
> $100 - 43 = 1 + 99 - 43 = 1 + 56 = 57$ ← *Do the subtraction, using 99 instead of 100, and then add 1 to your answer.*
>
> $1000 - 543 = 1 + 999 - 543 = 1 + 456 = 457$

4. Use the tricks you've just learned:

   a) $845 + 91 =$ _____   b) $456 + 298 =$ _____   c) $100 - 84 =$ _____   d) $1000 - 846 =$ _____

Mental Math Game: Modified Go Fish

PURPOSE:

If children know the pairs of one-digit numbers that add up to particular **target numbers**, they will be able to mentally break sums into easier sums.

EXAMPLE:

As it is easy to add any one-digit number to 10, you can add a sum more readily if you can decompose numbers in the sum into pairs that add to ten. For example:

$$7 + 5 = 7 + 3 + 2 = 10 + 2 = 12$$

These numbers add to 10.

To help children remember pairs of numbers that add up to a given target number, I developed a variation of "Go Fish" that I have found very effective.

THE GAME:

Pick any target number and remove all the cards with value greater than or equal to the target number out of the deck. In what follows, I will assume that the target number is 10, so you would take all the tens and face cards out of the deck (aces count as one).

The dealer gives each player six cards. If a player has any pairs of cards that add to 10, they are allowed to place these pairs on the table before play begins.

Player 1 selects one of the cards in their hand and asks Player 2 for a card that adds to 10 with the chosen card. For instance, if Player 1's chosen card is a 3, they may ask Player 2 for a 7.

If Player 2 has the requested card, Player 1 takes it and lays it down along with the card from their hand. Player 1 may then ask for another card. If Player 2 does not have the requested card, they say, "Go fish," and Player 1 must pick up a card from the top of the deck. (If this card adds to 10 with a card in Player 1's hand, they may lay down the pair right away.) It is then Player 2's turn to ask for a card.

Play ends when one player lays down all of their cards. Players receive 4 points for laying down all of their cards first and 1 point for each pair they have laid down.

PARENT: If your child is having difficulty, I would recommend that you start with pairs of numbers that add to 5. Take all cards with value greater than 4 out of the deck. Each player should be dealt only four cards to start with.

I have worked with several children who have had a great deal of trouble sorting their cards and finding pairs that add to a target number. I have found that the following exercise helps:

Give your child only three cards, two of which add to the target number. Ask them to find the pair that adds to the target number. After your child has mastered this step with three cards, repeat the exercise with four cards, then five cards, and so on.

PARENT: You can also give your child a list of the pairs that add to the target number. As your child gets used to the game, gradually remove pairs from the list so that they learn the pairs by memory.

Hundreds Charts

1	2	3	4	5	6	7	8	9	10
11	12	13	14	15	16	17	18	19	20
21	22	23	24	25	26	27	28	29	30
31	32	33	34	35	36	37	38	39	40
41	42	43	44	45	46	47	48	49	50
51	52	53	54	55	56	57	58	59	60
61	62	63	64	65	66	67	68	69	70
71	72	73	74	75	76	77	78	79	80
81	82	83	84	85	86	87	88	89	90
91	92	93	94	95	96	97	98	99	100

1	2	3	4	5	6	7	8	9	10
11	12	13	14	15	16	17	18	19	20
21	22	23	24	25	26	27	28	29	30
31	32	33	34	35	36	37	38	39	40
41	42	43	44	45	46	47	48	49	50
51	52	53	54	55	56	57	58	59	60
61	62	63	64	65	66	67	68	69	70
71	72	73	74	75	76	77	78	79	80
81	82	83	84	85	86	87	88	89	90
91	92	93	94	95	96	97	98	99	100

1	2	3	4	5	6	7	8	9	10
11	12	13	14	15	16	17	18	19	20
21	22	23	24	25	26	27	28	29	30
31	32	33	34	35	36	37	38	39	40
41	42	43	44	45	46	47	48	49	50
51	52	53	54	55	56	57	58	59	60
61	62	63	64	65	66	67	68	69	70
71	72	73	74	75	76	77	78	79	80
81	82	83	84	85	86	87	88	89	90
91	92	93	94	95	96	97	98	99	100

1	2	3	4	5	6	7	8	9	10
11	12	13	14	15	16	17	18	19	20
21	22	23	24	25	26	27	28	29	30
31	32	33	34	35	36	37	38	39	40
41	42	43	44	45	46	47	48	49	50
51	52	53	54	55	56	57	58	59	60
61	62	63	64	65	66	67	68	69	70
71	72	73	74	75	76	77	78	79	80
81	82	83	84	85	86	87	88	89	90
91	92	93	94	95	96	97	98	99	100

How to Learn Your Times Tables in 5 Days

PARENT:

Trying to do math without knowing your times tables is like trying to play the piano without knowing the location of the notes on the keyboard. Your child will have difficulty seeing patterns in sequences and charts, solving proportions, finding equivalent fractions, decimals and percents, solving problems, etc., if they don't know their tables.

Using the method below, you can teach your child their tables in a week or so. (If you set aside five or ten minutes a day to work with them, the pay-off will be enormous.) There is really no reason for your child not to know their tables!

DAY 1: Counting by 2s, 3s, 4s, and 5s

If you have completed the JUMP Fractions unit you should already know how to count and multiply by 2s, 3s, 4s, and 5s. If you do not know how to count by these numbers, you should memorize the hands:

If you know how to count by 2s, 3s, 4s, and 5s, then you can multiply by any combination of these numbers. For instance, to find the product of 3×2, count by 2s until you have raised 3 fingers:

$$3 \times 2 = 6$$

DAY 2: The 9 Times Table

The numbers you say when you count by 9s are called the **multiples** of 9 (0 is also a multiple of 9). The first ten multiples of 9 (after 0) are 9, 18, 27, 36, 45, 54, 63, 72, 81, and 90. What happens when you add the digits of any of these multiples of 9 (such as $1 + 8$ or $6 + 3$)? The sum is always 9!

Here is another useful fact about the 9 times table: Multiply 9 by any number between 1 and 10 and look at the tens digit of the product. The tens digit is always one less than the number you multiplied by:

$9 \times 4 = 36$ $9 \times 8 = 72$ $9 \times 2 = 18$

3 is one less than 4.   7 is one less than 8.   1 is one less than 2.

You can find the product of 9 and any number by using the two facts given above. For example, to find 9×7, follow these steps:

Step 1: $9 \times 7 = $ __ __ $9 \times 7 = $ __ __

Subtract 1 from the number you are multiplying by 9: $7 - 1 = 6$ Now you know the tens digit of the product.

Step 2: $9 \times 7 = \underline{6}\ \underline{\ \ }$ $9 \times 7 = \underline{6}\ \underline{3}$

↑↗   ↑

These two digits add to 9.   So the missing digit is $9 - 6 = 3$.
(You can do the subtraction on your fingers if necesary.)

Practise these two steps for all of the products of 9: 9×2, 9×3, 9×4, and so on.

DAY 3: The 8 Times Table

There are two patterns in the digits of the 8 times table. Knowing these patterns will help you remember how to count by 8s.

<u>Step 1:</u> You can find the ones digit of the first five multiples of 8 by starting at 8 and counting backwards by 2s.

8
6
4
2
0

<u>Step 3:</u> You can find the ones digit of the next five multiples of 8 by repeating step 1.

8
6
4
2
0

<u>Step 2:</u> You can find the tens digit of the first five multiples of 8 by starting at 0 and counting up by 1s.

08
16
24
32
40

<u>Step 4:</u> You can find the remaining tens digits by starting at 4 and counting by 1s.

48
56
64
72
80

(Of course, you do not need to write the 0 in front of the 8 for the product 1×8.)

Practise writing the multiples of 8 (up to 80) until you have memorized the complete list. Knowing the patterns in the digits of the multiples of 8 will help you memorize the list very quickly. Then you will know how to multiply by 8.

$8 \times 6 = 48$

Count by 8 until you have 6 fingers up: 8, 16, 24, 32, 40, 48.

How to Learn Your Times Tables in 5 Days *(continued)*

DAY 4: The 6 Times Table

If you have learned the 8 and 9 times tables, then you already know 6×9 and 6×8.

And if you know how to multiply by 5 up to 5×5, then you also know how to multiply by 6 up to 6×5! That is because you can always calculate 6 times a number by calculating 5 times the number and then adding the number itself to the result. The pictures below show how this works for 6×4:

$$6 \times 4 = 5 \times 4 + 4 = 20 + 4 = 24$$

Similarly: $6 \times 2 = 5 \times 2 + 2$; $6 \times 3 = 5 \times 3 + 3$; $6 \times 5 = 5 \times 5 + 5$.

Knowing this, you only need to memorize 2 facts:

$$6 \times 6 = 36 \qquad 6 \times 7 = 42$$

Or, if you know 6×5, you can find 6×6 by calculating $6 \times 5 + 6$.

DAY 5: The 7 Times Table

If you have learned the 6, 8, and 9 times tables, then you already know 6×7, 8×7, and 9×7.

And since you also already know $1 \times 7 = 7$, you only need to memorize 5 facts:

$$2 \times 7 = 14 \qquad 3 \times 7 = 21 \qquad 4 \times 7 = 28 \qquad 5 \times 7 = 35 \qquad 7 \times 7 = 49$$

If you are able to memorize your own phone number, then you can easily memorize these 5 facts!

NOTE: You can use doubling to help you learn the facts above: 4 is double 2, so 4×7 (28) is double 2×7 (14); 6 is double 3, so 6×7 (42) is double 3×7 (21).

Try this test every day until you have learned your times tables.

1. $\quad 3 \times 5 = $ _____	2. $\quad 8 \times 4 = $ _____	3. $\quad 9 \times 3 = $ _____	4. $\quad 4 \times 5 = $ _____
5. $\quad 2 \times 3 = $ _____	6. $\quad 4 \times 2 = $ _____	7. $\quad 8 \times 1 = $ _____	8. $\quad 6 \times 6 = $ _____
9. $\quad 9 \times 7 = $ _____	10. $\quad 7 \times 7 = $ _____	11. $\quad 5 \times 8 = $ _____	12. $\quad 2 \times 6 = $ _____
13. $\quad 6 \times 4 = $ _____	14. $\quad 7 \times 3 = $ _____	15. $\quad 4 \times 9 = $ _____	16. $\quad 2 \times 9 = $ _____
17. $\quad 9 \times 9 = $ _____	18. $\quad 3 \times 4 = $ _____	19. $\quad 6 \times 8 = $ _____	20. $\quad 7 \times 5 = $ _____
21. $\quad 9 \times 5 = $ _____	22. $\quad 5 \times 6 = $ _____	23. $\quad 6 \times 3 = $ _____	24. $\quad 7 \times 1 = $ _____
25. $\quad 8 \times 3 = $ _____	26. $\quad 9 \times 6 = $ _____	27. $\quad 4 \times 7 = $ _____	28. $\quad 3 \times 3 = $ _____
29. $\quad 8 \times 7 = $ _____	30. $\quad 1 \times 5 = $ _____	31. $\quad 7 \times 6 = $ _____	32. $\quad 2 \times 8 = $ _____

Base Ten Blocks

1 cm {

Hundreds Block

1 cm {

Tens Blocks

1 cm {

1 cm {

Ones Blocks

Introduction

Fractions

1. Name the following fractions.

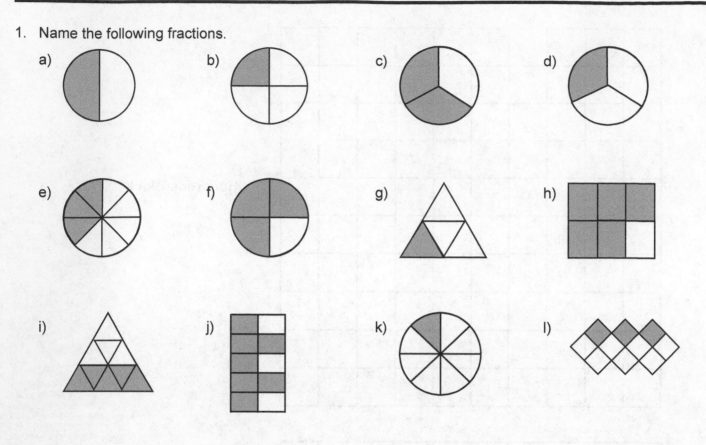

2. Shade the fractions named.

a) $\frac{1}{2}$

b) $\frac{1}{3}$

c) $\frac{3}{4}$

d) $\frac{3}{6}$

e) $\frac{2}{5}$

f) $\frac{5}{9}$

Fractions *(continued)*

3. Add.

a) $\frac{1}{3} + \frac{1}{3}$

b) $\frac{2}{7} + \frac{3}{7}$

c) $\frac{2}{11} + \frac{1}{11}$

d) $\frac{2}{5} + \frac{2}{5}$

e) $\frac{2}{11} + \frac{3}{11}$

f) $\frac{3}{8} + \frac{4}{8}$

g) $\frac{3}{17} + \frac{2}{17}$

h) $\frac{1}{21} + \frac{4}{21}$

i) $\frac{4}{9} + \frac{3}{9}$

4. Subtract.

a) $\frac{3}{5} - \frac{1}{5}$

b) $\frac{2}{7} - \frac{1}{7}$

c) $\frac{4}{11} - \frac{2}{11}$

d) $\frac{5}{8} - \frac{2}{8}$

e) $\frac{6}{17} - \frac{2}{17}$

f) $\frac{5}{9} - \frac{1}{9}$

5. **Advanced:** Add or Subtract.

a) $\frac{1}{7} + \frac{1}{7} + \frac{1}{7}$

b) $\frac{1}{7} + \frac{2}{7} + \frac{3}{7}$

c) $\frac{1}{15} + \frac{2}{15} + \frac{5}{15}$

BONUS:

d) $\frac{16}{21} - \frac{5}{21} - \frac{3}{21}$

e) $\frac{7}{9} - \frac{4}{9} + \frac{2}{9}$

f) $\frac{2}{11} + \frac{5}{11} - \frac{3}{11}$

Fractions (continued)

6. Write times signs beside the fractions.

Example: $\dfrac{1}{5} + \dfrac{1}{3} \longrightarrow \dfrac{\times}{\times}\,\dfrac{1}{5} + \dfrac{1}{3}\,\dfrac{\times}{\times}$

$\dfrac{1}{2} + \dfrac{1}{3}$	$\dfrac{1}{2} + \dfrac{1}{5}$	$\dfrac{1}{3} + \dfrac{1}{5}$

7. Switch the bottom numbers.

Example: $\dfrac{1}{5} + \dfrac{1}{3} \longrightarrow \dfrac{3 \times}{3 \times}\,\dfrac{1}{5} + \dfrac{1}{3}\,\dfrac{\times\, 5}{\times\, 5}$

$\dfrac{\times}{\times}\,\dfrac{1}{2} + \dfrac{1}{3}\,\dfrac{\times}{\times}$	$\dfrac{\times}{\times}\,\dfrac{1}{2} + \dfrac{1}{5}\,\dfrac{\times}{\times}$	$\dfrac{\times}{\times}\,\dfrac{1}{3} + \dfrac{1}{5}\,\dfrac{\times}{\times}$

8. Write times signs and switch the numbers.

Example: $\dfrac{1}{5} + \dfrac{1}{3} \longrightarrow \dfrac{3 \times}{3 \times}\,\dfrac{1}{5} + \dfrac{1}{3}\,\dfrac{\times\, 5}{\times\, 5}$

$\dfrac{1}{2} + \dfrac{1}{3}$	$\dfrac{1}{2} + \dfrac{1}{5}$	$\dfrac{1}{3} + \dfrac{1}{5}$
$\dfrac{2}{3} + \dfrac{1}{2}$	$\dfrac{2}{3} + \dfrac{1}{5}$	$\dfrac{2}{5} + \dfrac{1}{3}$

9. Perform the multiplications.

Example: $\dfrac{1}{5} + \dfrac{1}{3} \longrightarrow \dfrac{3 \times}{3 \times}\,\dfrac{1}{5} + \dfrac{1}{3}\,\dfrac{\times\, 5}{\times\, 5}$

$$= \dfrac{3}{15} + \dfrac{5}{15}$$

$\dfrac{3 \times}{3 \times}\,\dfrac{1}{2} + \dfrac{1}{3}\,\dfrac{\times\, 2}{\times\, 2}$	$\dfrac{5 \times}{5 \times}\,\dfrac{1}{2} + \dfrac{1}{5}\,\dfrac{\times\, 2}{\times\, 2}$	$\dfrac{5 \times}{5 \times}\,\dfrac{1}{3} + \dfrac{1}{5}\,\dfrac{\times\, 3}{\times\, 3}$
$= \underline{\quad} + \underline{\quad}$	$= \underline{\quad} + \underline{\quad}$	$= \underline{\quad} + \underline{\quad}$

Fractions *(continued)*

$$\frac{2}{2} \times \frac{2}{3} + \frac{1}{2} \times \frac{3}{3}$$

$$= \frac{}{} + \frac{}{}$$

$$\frac{5}{5} \times \frac{2}{3} + \frac{1}{5} \times \frac{3}{3}$$

$$= \frac{}{} + \frac{}{}$$

$$\frac{3}{3} \times \frac{2}{5} + \frac{1}{3} \times \frac{5}{5}$$

$$= \frac{}{} + \frac{}{}$$

10. Perform the additions.

Example: $\frac{1}{5} + \frac{1}{3} \longrightarrow \frac{3}{3} \times \frac{1}{5} + \frac{1}{3} \times \frac{5}{5}$

$$= \frac{3}{15} + \frac{5}{15} = \mathbf{\frac{8}{15}}$$

$$\frac{3}{3} \times \frac{1}{2} + \frac{1}{3} \times \frac{2}{2}$$

$$= \frac{3}{6} + \frac{2}{6} = \underline{\ \ }$$

$$\frac{5}{5} \times \frac{1}{2} + \frac{1}{5} \times \frac{2}{2}$$

$$= \frac{5}{10} + \frac{2}{10} = \underline{\ \ }$$

$$\frac{5}{5} \times \frac{1}{3} + \frac{1}{5} \times \frac{3}{3}$$

$$= \frac{5}{15} + \frac{3}{15} = \underline{\ \ }$$

$$\frac{2}{2} \times \frac{2}{3} + \frac{1}{2} \times \frac{3}{3}$$

$$= \frac{4}{6} + \frac{3}{6} = \underline{\ \ }$$

$$\frac{5}{5} \times \frac{2}{3} + \frac{1}{5} \times \frac{3}{3}$$

$$= \frac{10}{15} + \frac{3}{15} = \underline{\ \ }$$

$$\frac{3}{3} \times \frac{2}{5} + \frac{1}{3} \times \frac{5}{5}$$

$$= \frac{6}{15} + \frac{5}{15} = \underline{\ \ }$$

11. Perform the multiplications and the additions.

Example: $\frac{1}{5} + \frac{1}{3} \longrightarrow \frac{3}{3} \times \frac{1}{5} + \frac{1}{3} \times \frac{5}{5}$

$$= \frac{3}{15} + \frac{5}{15} = \mathbf{\frac{8}{15}}$$

$$\frac{3}{3} \times \frac{1}{2} + \frac{1}{3} \times \frac{2}{2}$$

$$= \frac{}{} + \frac{}{} = \frac{}{}$$

$$\frac{5}{5} \times \frac{1}{2} + \frac{1}{5} \times \frac{2}{2}$$

$$= \frac{}{} + \frac{}{} = \frac{}{}$$

$$\frac{5}{5} \times \frac{1}{3} + \frac{1}{5} \times \frac{3}{3}$$

$$= \frac{}{} + \frac{}{} = \frac{}{}$$

$$\frac{2}{2} \times \frac{2}{3} + \frac{1}{2} \times \frac{3}{3}$$

$$= \frac{}{} + \frac{}{} = \frac{}{}$$

$$\frac{5}{5} \times \frac{2}{3} + \frac{1}{5} \times \frac{3}{3}$$

$$= \frac{}{} + \frac{}{} = \frac{}{}$$

$$\frac{3}{3} \times \frac{2}{5} + \frac{1}{3} \times \frac{5}{5}$$

$$= \frac{}{} + \frac{}{} = \frac{}{}$$

Fractions *(continued)*

12. Add.

a) $\dfrac{1}{2} + \dfrac{1}{3}$

b) $\dfrac{1}{3} + \dfrac{1}{5}$

c) $\dfrac{1}{2} + \dfrac{1}{5}$

13. Advanced: Add or Subtract.

a) $\dfrac{2}{5} + \dfrac{1}{3}$

b) $\dfrac{3}{5} + \dfrac{1}{2}$

c) $\dfrac{2}{3} + \dfrac{1}{2}$

d) $\dfrac{1}{5} + \dfrac{2}{3}$

d) $\dfrac{4}{5} + \dfrac{1}{2}$

f) $\dfrac{2}{3} + \dfrac{2}{5}$

BONUS:

a) $\dfrac{1}{2} - \dfrac{1}{3}$

b) $\dfrac{2}{3} - \dfrac{1}{2}$

c) $\dfrac{3}{5} - \dfrac{1}{2}$

Introduction

Fractions *(continued)*

14. Write how many times the lesser denominator goes into the greater denominator.

Example: $\dfrac{1}{2} + \dfrac{1}{10} \longrightarrow \dfrac{5}{5} \times \dfrac{1}{2} + \dfrac{1}{10}$

$\dfrac{1}{2} + \dfrac{1}{10}$	$\dfrac{1}{5} + \dfrac{1}{10}$	$\dfrac{1}{2} + \dfrac{1}{8}$
$\dfrac{1}{3} + \dfrac{1}{6}$	$\dfrac{1}{5} + \dfrac{1}{20}$	$\dfrac{1}{2} + \dfrac{1}{6}$
$\dfrac{2}{5} + \dfrac{1}{25}$	$\dfrac{3}{5} + \dfrac{1}{15}$	$\dfrac{1}{2} + \dfrac{7}{8}$

15. Change the fraction with the lesser denominator and keep the other fraction the same.

Example: $\dfrac{1}{2} + \dfrac{1}{10} \longrightarrow \dfrac{5}{5} \times \dfrac{1}{2} + \dfrac{1}{10}$

$$= \dfrac{5}{10} + \dfrac{1}{10}$$

$\dfrac{1}{2} + \dfrac{1}{10}$	$\dfrac{1}{5} + \dfrac{1}{10}$	$\dfrac{1}{2} + \dfrac{1}{8}$
$\dfrac{1}{3} + \dfrac{1}{6}$	$\dfrac{1}{5} + \dfrac{1}{20}$	$\dfrac{1}{2} + \dfrac{1}{6}$
$\dfrac{2}{5} + \dfrac{1}{25}$	$\dfrac{3}{5} + \dfrac{1}{15}$	$\dfrac{1}{2} + \dfrac{7}{8}$

Fractions *(continued)*

16. Add. (Remember to change only one denominator.)

a) $\dfrac{1}{2} + \dfrac{1}{10}$

b) $\dfrac{1}{5} + \dfrac{1}{10}$

c) $\dfrac{1}{2} + \dfrac{1}{8}$

d) $\dfrac{1}{3} + \dfrac{1}{6}$

e) $\dfrac{1}{5} + \dfrac{1}{20}$

f) $\dfrac{1}{2} + \dfrac{1}{6}$

17. **Advanced:** Add or Subtract.

a) $\dfrac{2}{3} + \dfrac{1}{15}$

b) $\dfrac{2}{5} + \dfrac{1}{10}$

c) $\dfrac{3}{5} + \dfrac{2}{15}$

d) $\dfrac{2}{3} + \dfrac{1}{12}$

e) $\dfrac{1}{4} + \dfrac{3}{8}$

f) $\dfrac{1}{4} + \dfrac{3}{12}$

g) $\dfrac{3}{4} + \dfrac{1}{2}$

h) $\dfrac{4}{25} + \dfrac{1}{5}$

i) $\dfrac{3}{15} + \dfrac{4}{5}$

BONUS:

j) $\dfrac{7}{20} - \dfrac{1}{5}$

k) $\dfrac{3}{8} - \dfrac{1}{4}$

l) $\dfrac{1}{2} - \dfrac{3}{10}$

Introduction

Fractions *(continued)*

18. Write **yes** beside the number in bold if you say the number when counting by 2s.
    If you don't, write **no**.

    a) **6** _____   b) **3** _____   c) **9** _____   d) **8** _____

    e) **10** _____   f) **4** _____   g) **5** _____   h) **7** _____

19. Write **yes** beside the given number if you say the number when counting by 3s.
    If you don't, write **no**.

    a) **9** _____   b) **4** _____   c) **12** _____   d) **13** _____

    e) **6** _____   f) **5** _____   g) **8** _____   h) **14** _____

20. Write **yes** beside the given number if you say the number when counting by 5s.
    If you don't, write **no**.

    a) **10** _____   b) **12** _____   c) **15** _____   d) **8** _____

    e) **20** _____   f) **9** _____   g) **14** _____   h) **11** _____

21. Circle the smaller denominator. The first one has been done for you.

    a) $\dfrac{1}{②} + \dfrac{1}{3}$ b) $\dfrac{1}{3} + \dfrac{1}{5}$ c) $\dfrac{2}{6} + \dfrac{1}{2}$

    d) $\dfrac{1}{4} + \dfrac{1}{8}$ e) $\dfrac{3}{5} + \dfrac{1}{2}$ f) $\dfrac{1}{2} + \dfrac{1}{8}$

22. Count by the lesser denominator, and write **yes** if you say the greater denominator.
    Write **no** if you don't. The first one has been done for you.

    a) _no_ $\dfrac{1}{②} + \dfrac{1}{3}$ b) _____ $\dfrac{1}{③} + \dfrac{1}{5}$ c) _____ $\dfrac{2}{6} + \dfrac{1}{②}$

    d) _____ $\dfrac{1}{4} + \dfrac{1}{8}$ e) _____ $\dfrac{3}{5} + \dfrac{1}{2}$ f) _____ $\dfrac{1}{2} + \dfrac{1}{8}$

    g) _____ $\dfrac{1}{2} + \dfrac{1}{8}$ h) _____ $\dfrac{3}{15} + \dfrac{1}{3}$ i) _____ $\dfrac{1}{5} + \dfrac{1}{9}$

Fractions *(continued)*

23. Count by the lesser denominator until you reach the greater denominator. Write the number of fingers you have raised beside the times signs.

a) ___yes___

$$\times \dfrac{1}{2} + \dfrac{1}{6}$$
$$\times$$

b) ___yes___

$$\times \dfrac{1}{5} + \dfrac{1}{10}$$
$$\times$$

c) ___yes___

$$\times \dfrac{1}{3} + \dfrac{1}{9}$$
$$\times$$

24. Complete the first step of addition by multiplying each fraction by the opposite denominator.

a) ___no___

$$\times \dfrac{1}{2} + \dfrac{1}{6} \times$$
$$\times \qquad \times$$

b) ___no___

$$\times \dfrac{1}{5} + \dfrac{1}{10} \times$$
$$\times \qquad \times$$

c) ___no___

$$\times \dfrac{1}{3} + \dfrac{1}{9} \times$$
$$\times \qquad \times$$

25. Write **yes** or **no** above the following fractions. If you wrote **yes**, then complete the first step of addition as in Question 23 above. If you wrote **no**, complete the first step as in Question 24.

a) _____

$$\dfrac{1}{3} + \dfrac{1}{5}$$

b) _____

$$\dfrac{3}{5} + \dfrac{1}{10}$$

c) _____

$$\dfrac{1}{2} + \dfrac{1}{4}$$

d) _____

$$\dfrac{1}{3} + \dfrac{1}{4}$$

BONUS:

e) _____

$$\dfrac{3}{15} + \dfrac{1}{5}$$

f) _____

$$\dfrac{1}{10} + \dfrac{1}{5}$$

26. Add or Subtract. Change *one* denominator or change *both*. (For each question you have to decide what to do. Start by writing **yes** or **no** above the fraction.)

a) _____

$$\dfrac{1}{4} + \dfrac{1}{5}$$

b) _____

$$\dfrac{2}{3} + \dfrac{1}{5}$$

c) _____

$$\dfrac{2}{5} + \dfrac{1}{20}$$

BONUS:

d) _____

$$\dfrac{3}{20} + \dfrac{4}{5}$$

e) _____

$$\dfrac{2}{15} + \dfrac{3}{5}$$

f) _____

$$\dfrac{1}{16} + \dfrac{1}{4}$$

Introduction

Fractions *(continued)*

27. **Advanced:** Add or Subtract. (Change *one* denominator or change *both*.)

a) $\dfrac{1}{3} + \dfrac{1}{9}$

b) $\dfrac{2}{3} + \dfrac{1}{5}$

c) $\dfrac{1}{5} + \dfrac{1}{20}$

d) $\dfrac{1}{2} + \dfrac{1}{3}$

e) $\dfrac{1}{4} + \dfrac{1}{5}$

f) $\dfrac{1}{4} + \dfrac{5}{16}$

g) $\dfrac{1}{2} - \dfrac{1}{10}$

h) $\dfrac{3}{4} - \dfrac{1}{3}$

i) $\dfrac{7}{20} - \dfrac{1}{4}$

28. If the denominators are the same, write **same**. Otherwise change *one* denominator or change *both*. Then complete all the questions.

a) $\dfrac{1}{3} + \dfrac{1}{12}$

b) $\dfrac{1}{4} + \dfrac{3}{5}$

c) $\dfrac{1}{7} + \dfrac{1}{7}$

d) $\dfrac{2}{3} + \dfrac{1}{2}$

e) $\dfrac{10}{11} - \dfrac{6}{11}$

f) $\dfrac{4}{5} - \dfrac{3}{20}$

Introduction

Fractions *(continued)*

Example: $\frac{1}{2} + \frac{1}{3} + \frac{1}{6}$ $\longrightarrow$ $\frac{\mathbf{3}}{\mathbf{3}} \times \frac{1}{2} + \frac{\mathbf{2}}{\mathbf{2}} \times \frac{1}{3} + \frac{1}{6}$

$\frac{1}{2} + \frac{1}{3} + \frac{1}{6}$	$\frac{1}{3} + \frac{1}{5} + \frac{1}{15}$
$\frac{1}{2} + \frac{1}{4} + \frac{3}{8}$	$\frac{1}{4} + \frac{1}{5} + \frac{1}{20}$
$\frac{2}{3} + \frac{1}{4} + \frac{1}{12}$	$\frac{1}{5} + \frac{3}{10} + \frac{2}{20}$

30. Write times signs and numbers, and carry out multiplication as needed.

Example: $\frac{1}{2} + \frac{1}{3} + \frac{1}{6}$ $\longrightarrow$ $\frac{\mathbf{3}}{\mathbf{3}} \times \frac{1}{2} + \frac{\mathbf{2}}{\mathbf{2}} \times \frac{1}{3} + \frac{1}{6}$

$$= \frac{\mathbf{3}}{\mathbf{6}} + \frac{\mathbf{2}}{\mathbf{6}} + \frac{\mathbf{1}}{\mathbf{6}}$$

$\frac{1}{2} + \frac{1}{3} + \frac{1}{6}$	$\frac{1}{3} + \frac{1}{5} + \frac{1}{15}$
$\frac{1}{2} + \frac{1}{4} + \frac{3}{8}$	$\frac{1}{4} + \frac{1}{5} + \frac{1}{20}$
$\frac{2}{3} + \frac{1}{4} + \frac{1}{12}$	$\frac{1}{5} + \frac{3}{10} + \frac{2}{20}$

Fractions *(continued)*

31. Solve completely.

a) $\dfrac{1}{2} + \dfrac{1}{3} + \dfrac{3}{6}$

b) $\dfrac{1}{3} + \dfrac{1}{5} + \dfrac{1}{15}$

c) $\dfrac{1}{2} + \dfrac{1}{4} + \dfrac{3}{8}$

d) $\dfrac{1}{4} + \dfrac{1}{5} + \dfrac{5}{20}$

e) $\dfrac{2}{3} + \dfrac{1}{4} + \dfrac{1}{12}$

f) $\dfrac{1}{5} + \dfrac{3}{10} + \dfrac{2}{20}$

BONUS:

g) $\dfrac{17}{20} - \dfrac{1}{4} - \dfrac{1}{5}$

h) $\dfrac{3}{4} - \dfrac{1}{8} - \dfrac{1}{2}$

i) $\dfrac{1}{2} - \dfrac{1}{6} + \dfrac{1}{3}$

j) $\dfrac{2}{3} + \dfrac{1}{4} - \dfrac{5}{12}$

A The number is even.	B The number is odd.	C You can count to the number by 2s.
D You can count to the number by 3s.	E You can count to the number by 5s.	F You can count to the number by 10s.
G The number is greater than 15.	H The number is less than 25.	I The number has 1 digit.
J The number has 2 digits.	K The number has two digits that are the same.	L The number has a zero in it.
M The number is 7.	N The number is less than 7.	O You can see the number on the face of a clock.
P The ones digit is smaller than 6.	Q The sum of its digits is less than 9.	R The number is divisible by 2.

1. Write a number that statement **A** applies to. _____

2. Statements **B**, **D**, **H**, and **J** all apply to the number 15.
   Which other statements apply to the number 15 as well? _____

3. Choose a number between 1 and 25 (besides 15).
   Find all the statements that apply to that number.

   Your number: _____ Statements that apply to that number: _____

4. a) Which statements apply to both 3 and 18? _____

   b) Which statements apply to both 7 and 11? _____

5. a) Can you find a number that statements **A**, **E**, **J**, **L**, and **R** apply to?
   (**NOTE:** There may be more than one answer.)

   _____

   b) Can you find a number that statements **B**, **D**, **H**, and **Q** apply to?

   _____

   c) Can you find a number that statements **C**, **K**, **H**, and **P** apply to?

   _____

Define a Number *(continued)*

PARENT: You should only assign a few questions on this page at a time.

6. a) Is it possible for statements **A** and **B** to both apply to a number? Explain.

   _____

   _____

   b) Is it possible for statements **D** and **E** to both apply to a number? _____

   c) Is it possible for statements **C** and **R** to both apply to a number? _____

7. a) Can you think of a number where statements **E** and **F** apply, but not **H**? _____

   b) Can you think of a number where statements **H** and **K** apply, but not **G**? _____

8. a) If statement **N** applies to a number, does statement **O** always have to apply? _____

   b) If statement **O** applies to a number, does statement **N** always have to apply? _____

9. Fill out the chart below by writing in a number for each statement. Don't use the same number more than once.

A	B	C
D	E	F
G	H	I
J	K	L
M	N	O
P	Q	R

 Games, Activities, and Puzzles

Models of Fractions

1. Give your child a ruler and ask them to solve the following puzzles:

   a. Draw a line 1 cm long. If the line, represents $\frac{1}{4}$, show what a whole line what look like.

   b. Line: 1 cm long. The line represents $\frac{1}{6}$. Show the whole.

   c. Line: 2 cm long. The line represents $\frac{1}{3}$. Show the whole.

   d. Line: 3 cm long. The line represents $\frac{1}{4}$. Show the whole.

   e. Line: $1\frac{1}{2}$ cm long. The line represents $\frac{1}{2}$. Show the whole.

   f. Line: $1\frac{1}{2}$ cm long. The line represents $\frac{1}{4}$. Show the whole.

   g. Line: 3 cm long. The line represents $\frac{1}{4}$. Show $\frac{1}{2}$.

   h. Line: 2 cm long. The line represents $\frac{1}{8}$. Show $\frac{1}{4}$.

2. Give your child counters to make a model of the following problem:
   Postcards come in packs of 4. How many packs would you need to buy to send 15 postcards?
   Write a mixed and improper fraction for the number of packs you would use.

   Your child could use a counter of a particular colour to represent the postcards they have used and
   a counter of a different colour to represent the postcards left over. After they have made their model,
   they could fill in the following chart:

Number of postcards	15
Number of packs of 4 postcards (improper fraction)	$\frac{15}{4}$
Number of packs of 4 postcards (mixed fraction)	$3\frac{3}{4}$

   Model:

   4 postcards in each package

   one left over

   Here is another sample problem your child could try:

   Juice cans come in boxes of 6. How many boxes would you bring if you needed 20 cans?
   What fraction of the boxes would you use?

3. Give your child blocks of 2 colours and have them make models of fractions of whole numbers using
   the method described at the top of the worksheet. Here are some fractions they might try:

   a) $\frac{3}{4}$ of 15   b) $\frac{3}{4}$ of 16   c) $\frac{3}{5}$ of 20   d) $\frac{2}{7}$ of 21

Models of Fractions *(continued)*

4. Ask your child to draw 4 boxes of equal length on grid paper and shade 1 box:

Point out to them that $\frac{1}{4}$ of the area of the boxes is shaded. Now ask them to draw the same set of boxes, but in each box to draw a line dividing the box into 2 parts:

Now $\frac{2}{8}$ of the area is shaded. Repeat the exercise, dividing the boxes into 3 equal parts, (roughly: the sketch doesn't have to be perfectly accurate), then 4 parts, then five parts:

$\frac{3}{12}$ of the area is shaded.

$\frac{4}{16}$ of the area is shaded.

$\frac{5}{20}$ of the area is shaded.

Point out to your child that while the appearance of the fraction changes, the same amount of area is represented:

$\frac{1}{4}$, $\frac{2}{8}$, $\frac{3}{12}$, $\frac{4}{16}$, and $\frac{5}{20}$ all represent the same amount; they are equivalent fractions.

Ask your child how each of the denominators in the fractions above can be generated from the initial fraction of $\frac{1}{4}$:

Answer:

Each denominator is a multiple of the denominator 4 in the original fraction:

$$8 = 2 \times 4 \qquad 12 = 3 \times 4 \qquad 16 = 4 \times 4 \qquad 20 = 5 \times 4$$

Then ask them how each fraction could be generated from the original fraction.

Answer:

Multiplying the numerator and denominator of the original fraction by the same number:

$$\frac{1}{4}\begin{smallmatrix}\times 2\\ \times 2\end{smallmatrix} = \frac{2}{8} \qquad \frac{1}{4}\begin{smallmatrix}\times 3\\ \times 3\end{smallmatrix} = \frac{3}{12} \qquad \frac{1}{4}\begin{smallmatrix}\times 4\\ \times 4\end{smallmatrix} = \frac{4}{16} \qquad \frac{1}{4}\begin{smallmatrix}\times 5\\ \times 5\end{smallmatrix} = \frac{5}{20}$$

Models of Fractions *(continued)*

Point out that multiplying the top and bottom of the original fraction by any given number, say 5, corresponds to cutting each box into that number of pieces:

$\dfrac{1}{4}$ × 5 ← ———— There are 5 pieces in each box.

× 5 ← ———— There are 4 × 5 pieces altogether.

5 pieces in each box

4 × 5 = pieces altogether.

The fractions $\dfrac{1}{4}$, $\dfrac{2}{8}$, $\dfrac{3}{12}$, $\dfrac{4}{16}$, . . . form a **family of equivalent fractions**. Notice that no whole number greater than 1 will divide into both the numerator and denominator of $\dfrac{1}{4}$: $\dfrac{1}{4}$ is said to be reduced to lowest terms. By multiplying the top and bottom of a reduced fraction by various whole numbers, you can generate an entire fraction family. For instance, $\dfrac{2}{5}$ generates this family:

$$\dfrac{2}{5} \begin{smallmatrix} \times 2 \\ \times 2 \end{smallmatrix} = \dfrac{4}{10} \qquad \dfrac{2}{5} \begin{smallmatrix} \times 3 \\ \times 3 \end{smallmatrix} = \dfrac{6}{15} \qquad \dfrac{2}{5} \begin{smallmatrix} \times 4 \\ \times 4 \end{smallmatrix} = \dfrac{8}{20}$$

Games, Activities, and Puzzles

Elimination Game

Find the special number in each square by reading the clues and eliminating.
REMEMBER: Zero is an even number.

1. Cross out numbers that are…

a)

4	3	9
7	9	8
1	6	5

• Odd
• Less than 4
• Greater than 5
What number is left? ☐

b)

4	2	3
5	1	7
0	9	8

• Even
• Less than 4
• Greater than 6
What number is left? ☐

c)

4	20	9
11	6	16
5	3	18

• Even
• Multiples of 3
• Greater than 10
What number is left? ☐

d)

4	20	9
15	6	16
5	3	18

• Multiples of 2
• Multiples of 3
• Multiples of 4
What number is left? ☐

2. **BONUS:** Cross out numbers **with**…

a)

42	31	92
27	99	88
21	66	52

• Ones digit 2
• Tens digit 2
• Both digits are the same
What number is left? ☐

b)

24	3	9
7	89	83
1	6	52

• One digit
• Tens digit 8
• Ones digit 2
What number is left? ☐

JUMP at Home Grade 6   No unauthorized copying   **Games, Activities, and Puzzles**

Battleship and Secret Squares

Once your child understands the game, they can play in pairs.

Battleship

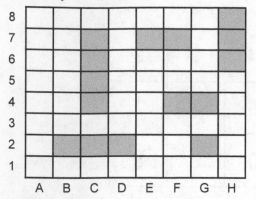

Player 1 and Player 2 each draw a grid as shown. Each player shades:

1 battleship   2 cruisers   2 destroyers   1 submarine

(See grid for an example: no square of a ship may be adjacent to a square of another ship, including diagonally.)

Players try to sink all their partner's battleships by guessing their coordinates. If a player's ship is in a square that is called out, the player must say "hit." Otherwise they say "miss."

Each player should keep track of the squares they have guessed on a blank grid by marking hits with ✗'s and misses with ✓'s. The game ends when all of one player's ships are sunk. A ship is sunk when <u>all</u> its squares are hit.

Secret Squares

Player 1 draws a 4 × 4 grid as shown and picks a square. Player 2 tries to guess the square by giving its coordinates.

Each time Player 2 guesses, Player 1 writes the distance between the guessed square and the hidden square.

For instance, if Player 1 has chosen square A2 (✓) and Player 2 guesses C4, Player 1 writes 3 in the guessed square. (Distances on the grid are counted horizontally and vertically, <u>never</u> diagonally.)

The game ends when Player 2 guesses the correct square.

PARENT: As a warm-up for the Secret Squares game above, have your child try to guess the locations of each hidden square from the information given in the grids below. In 2 grids, not enough information is given (have your child mark all possible locations for the hidden square) and in one grid too much information is given (have your child identify one piece of redundant information):

Models of Decimals

Children often make mistakes in comparing decimals where one of the decimals is expressed in tenths and the other in hundredths. (For instance, they will say that .17 is greater than .2.) The following activity will help your child understand the relation between tenths and hundredths.

Give your child a set of play-money dimes and pennies. Explain that a dime is a tenth of a dollar (which is why it is written as $0.10) and a penny is a hundredth of a dollar (which is why it is written as $0.01).

Ask your child to make models of the amounts in the left-hand column of the chart below and to write as many names for the amounts as they can think of in the right-hand columns (sample answers are provided in italics):

Amount	Amount in Pennies	Decimal Names (in words)	Decimal Names (in numbers)
2 dimes	*20 pennies*	*2 tenths (of a dollar)* *20 hundredths*	*.2* *.20*
3 pennies	*3 pennies*	*3 hundredths*	*.03*
4 dimes and 3 pennies	*43 pennies*	*4 tenths and 3 hundredths* *43 hundredths*	*.43* *.43*

You should also write various amounts of money on a sheet of paper and have your child make models of the amounts (e.g., make models of .3 dollars, .27 dollars, .07 dollars, etc.). Also challenge them to make models of amounts that have 2 different decimal representations (e.g., 2 dimes can be written as .2 dollars or .20 dollars).

When you feel your child is able to translate between money and decimal notation, ask them to say whether they would rather have .2 dollars or .17 dollars. In their answer, they should say exactly how many pennies each amount represents (e.g., they must articulate that .2 represents 20 pennies and so it is actually the larger amount).

Amount (in dollars)	Amount (in pennies)
.2	
.15	

For extra practice, ask your child to fill in the right-hand column of the chart and then circle the greater amount. (Create several charts of this sort for them.)

Magic Squares and Number Pyramids

1. In a magic square, the numbers in each row, column, and diagonal all add up to the same number (the "magic number" for the square):

   What is the magic number for this square? _____

2	9	4
7	5	3
6	1	8

2. Complete the magic squares:

   a)

1		5
8	4	
3	2	

   b)

	8	
9	4	11

   c)

		9
	11	
13		17

3. Here are some number pyramids:

   Can you find the rule by which the patterns in the pyramids were made? Describe it here:

4. Using the rule you described in Question 3, find the missing numbers:

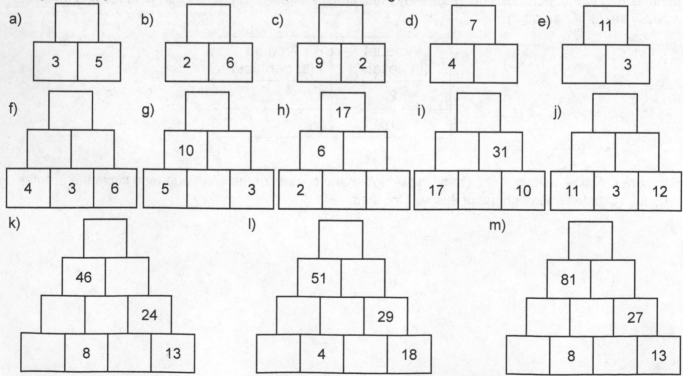

Magic Trick (Algebra)

In the magic trick below, the magician can always predict the result of a sequence of operations performed on any chosen number. Try the trick with your child, then encourage them to figure out how it works using a block to stand in for the mystery number (give lots of hints).

The Trick

Pick any number.

Add 4.

Multiply by 2.

Subtract 2.

Divide by 2.

Subtract the mystery number.

The answer is 3!

The Algebra

Use a square block to represent the mystery number.

Use 4 circles to represent the 4 ones that were added.

Create 2 sets of blocks to show the doubling.

Take away 2 circles to show the subtraction.

Remove one set of blocks to show the division.

Remove the square.

No matter what number you choose, after performing the operations in the magic trick, you will always get the number 3. The model above shows why the trick works.

Encourage your child to make up their own trick of the same type.

JUMP at Home Grade 6   No unauthorized copying   **Games, Activities, and Puzzles**

In an **increasing sequence**, each number is greater than the one before it.

Deborah wants to continue the number pattern:

6 , 8 , 10 , 12 , _?_

She finds the **difference** between the first two numbers:

6 , 7 , 8

②
6 , 8 , 10 , 12 , _?_

She finds that the difference between the other numbers in the pattern is also 2. So the pattern was made by adding 2:

② ② ②
6 , 8 , 10 , 12 , _?_

To continue the pattern, Deborah adds 2 to the last number in the sequence.

The final number in the pattern is 14:

② ② ② ②
6 , 8 , 10 , 12 , 14

----

1. Extend the following patterns. Start by finding the gap between the numbers.

a) 2 , 5 , 8 , ___ , ___ , ___

b) 1 , 7 , 13 , ___ , ___ , ___

c) 2 , 7 , 12 , ___ , ___ , ___

d) 4 , 8 , 12 , ___ , ___ , ___

e) 1 , 6 , 11 , ___ , ___ , ___

f) 4 , 10 , 16 , ___ , ___ , ___

g) 2 , 12 , 22 , ___ , ___ , ___

h) 7 , 15 , 23 , ___ , ___ , ___

i) 31 , 34 , 37 , ___ , ___ , ___

j) 92 , 98 , 104 , ___ , ___ , ___

k) 12 , 23 , 34 , ___ , ___ , ___

l) 0 , 8 , 16 , ___ , ___ , ___

2. A plant that is 17 cm high grows 2 cm each day.

a) How high will the plant be after three days? _____

b) In how many days will the plant be 27 cm high? _____

Patterns & Algebra 1

In a **decreasing sequence**, each number is less than the one before it.

Inder wants to continue the number pattern:

25 , 23 , 21 , _?_

She finds the **difference**
between the first two numbers:

25   **24**   **23**

(-2)
25 , 23 , 21 , _?_

She finds that the difference between the other numbers in the pattern
is also 2. So the pattern was made by subtracting 2.

(-2) (-2)
25 , 23 , 21 , ?

The final number in the pattern is 19:

(-2) (-2) (-2)
25 , 23 , 21 , _19_

----

1.   Extend the following patterns:

a) 18 , 15 , 12 , ___ , ___ , ___

b) 32 , 26 , 20 , ___ , ___ , ___

c) 52 , 47 , 42 , ___ , ___ , ___

d) 34 , 30 , 26 , ___ , ___ , ___

e) 51 , 46 , 41 , ___ , ___ , ___

f) 84 , 80 , 76 , ___ , ___ , ___

g) 62 , 51 , 40 , ___ , ___ , ___

h) 97 , 89 , 81 , ___ , ___ , ___

i) 71 , 64 , 57 , ___ , ___ , ___

j) 62 , 58 , 54 , ___ , ___ , ___

k) 82 , 73 , 64 , ___ , ___ , ___

l) 84 , 72 , 60 , ___ , ___ , ___

Use decreasing sequences to solve these problems:

2.   Judi has saved $49. She spends $8 each day.
     How much money does she have left after 5 days?

3.   Yen has a roll of 74 stamps. She uses 7 each day for 4 days.
     How many are left?

Patterns & Algebra 1

1. Continue the following sequences by <u>adding</u> the number given:

   a) (add 4)   41, 45, _____, _____, _____

   b) (add 8)   60, 68, _____, _____, _____

   c) (add 3)   74, 77, _____, _____, _____

   d) (add 11) 20, 31, _____, _____, _____

   e) (add 8)   61, 69, _____, _____, _____

   f) (add 11) 31, 42, _____, _____, _____

2. Continue the following sequences by <u>subtracting</u> the number given:

   a) (subtract 3)   25, 22, _____, _____, _____

   b) (subtract 2)   34, 32, _____, _____, _____

   c) (subtract 6)   85, 79, _____, _____, _____

   d) (subtract 12) 89, 77, _____, _____, _____

   e) (subtract 8)   57, 49, _____, _____, _____

   f) (subtract 7)   57, 50, _____, _____, _____

BONUS

3. Create a pattern of your own. After writing the pattern in the blanks, say what you added or subtracted each time:

   _____ , _____ , _____ , _____ , _____   My rule: _____

4. Which one of the following sequences was made by adding 7? Circle it:
   HINT: Check all the numbers in the sequence.

   a) 4, 10, 18, 21   b) 4, 11, 16, 21   c) 3, 10, 17, 24

5.   **72, 61, 50, 39, 28, ...**

   Brenda says this sequence was made by subtracting 12 each time.
   Sanjukta says it was made by subtracting 11.
   Who is right?

   _____

   _____

PA6-4: Identifying Pattern Rules

1. What number was added to make the sequence?

   a) 12, 17, 22, 27   add ____   b) 32, 35, 38, 41   add ____

   c) 28, 34, 40, 46   add ____   d) 50, 57, 64, 71   add ____

   e) 101, 106, 111, 116   add ____   f) 269, 272, 275, 278   add ____

2. What number was subtracted to make the sequence?

   a) 58, 56, 54, 52   subtract ____   b) 75, 70, 65, 60   subtract ____

   c) 320, 319, 318, 317   subtract ____   d) 191, 188, 185, 182   subtract ____

   e) 467, 461, 455, 449   subtract ____   f) 939, 937, 935, 933   subtract ____

3. State the rules for the following patterns:

   a) 419, 412, 405, 398, 391   subtract ____   b) 311, 319, 327, 335, 343, 351   add ____

   c) 501, 505, 509, 513   _____   d) 210, 199, 188, 177,   _____

   e) 653, 642, 631, 620, 609   _____   f) 721, 730, 739, 748, 757, 766   _____

   g) 807, 815, 823, 831   _____   h) 1731, 1725, 1719, 1713,   _____

4. Use the first three numbers in the pattern to find the rule. Then fill in the blanks:

   a) 52, 57, 62, __67__, _____, _____   The rule is: ___Start at 52 and add 5___

   b) 78, 75, 72, _____, _____, _____   The rule is: _____

   c) 824, 836, 848, _____, _____, _____   The rule is: _____

   d) 1 328, 1 319, 1 310, _____, _____, _____   The rule is: _____

5.   **5, 11, 17, 23, 29, ...**

   Tim says the pattern rule is: "Start at 5 and subtract 6 each time."

   Jack says the rule is: "Add 5 each time."

   Hannah says the rule is: "Start at 5 and add 6 each time."

   a) Whose rule is correct? _____

   b) What mistakes did the others make? _____

   _____

Patterns & Algebra 1

Claude creates an **increasing pattern** with squares. He records the number of squares in each figure in a chart or T-table. He also records the number of squares he adds each time he makes a new figure:

| Figure 1 | Figure 2 | Figure 3 |

Figure	# of Squares	
1	4	
2	6	② Number of squares
3	8	② added each time

The number of squares in the figures are 4, 6, 8, …

Claude writes a rule for this number pattern:

RULE: Start at 4 and add 2 each time.

----

1. Claude makes other <u>increasing patterns</u> with squares.

    How many squares does he add to make each new figure?

    Write your answer in the circles provided. Then write a rule for the pattern:

a)

Figure	Number of Squares
1	2
2	8
3	14

Rule:

b)

Figure	Number of Squares
1	3
2	9
3	15

Rule:

c)

Figure	Number of Squares
1	1
2	6
3	11

Rule:

d)

Figure	Number of Squares
1	1
2	8
3	15

Rule:

e)

Figure	Number of Squares
1	5
2	13
3	21

Rule:

f)

Figure	Number of Squares
1	11
2	22
3	33

Rule:

Patterns & Algebra 1

g)

Figure	Number of Squares
1	3
2	12
3	21

Rule:

h)

Figure	Number of Squares
1	6
2	13
3	20

Rule:

i)

Figure	Number of Squares
1	7
2	13
3	19

Rule:

2. Extend the number pattern. How many squares would be used in Figure 6?

a)

Figure	Number of Squares
1	2
2	10
3	18

b)

Figure	Number of Squares
1	4
2	9
3	14

c)

Figure	Number of Squares
1	7
2	11
3	15

3. After making Figure 3, Claude only has 35 squares left. Does he have enough squares to complete Figure 4?

a)

Figure	Number of Squares
1	4
2	13
3	22

YES   NO

b)

Figure	Number of Squares
1	6
2	17
3	28

YES   NO

c)

Figure	Number of Squares
1	9
2	17
3	25

YES   NO

4. In your notebook, make a T-table to show how many shapes will be needed to make the fifth figure in each pattern:

a)   b)

1. Count the number of line segments (lines that join pairs of dots) in each set of figures by marking each line segment as you count, as shown in the example:
   HINT: Count around the outside of the figure first.

Example:

a) _____   b) _____   c) _____

2. Continue the pattern below, then complete the chart:

Figure 1

Figure 2

Figure 3

Figure	Number of Line Segments
1	
2	
3	

a) How many line segments would Figure 4 have? _____

b) How many line segments would you need to make a figure with 5 triangles? _____

3. Continue the pattern below, then complete the chart:

Figure 1

Figure 2

Figure 3

Figure 4

Figure	Number of Triangles	Number of Line Segments

a) How many line segments would Figure 5 have? _____

b) How many triangles would Figure 6 have? _____

4. The snow is 17 cm deep at 5 pm.
    4 cm of snow falls each hour.
    How deep is the snow at 9 pm?

Hour	Depth of Snow	
5 pm	17 cm	

5. Philip has $42 in savings by the end of July.
    Each month he saves $9. How much will he have by the end of October?

Month	Savings	
July	$42	

6. Sarah's fish tank is leaking.
    At 6 pm, there are 21 L of water in the tank.
    At 7 pm, there are 18 L and at 8 pm, there are 15 L.

    a) How many litres of water leak out each hour?
    _____

    b) How many litres will be left in the tank at 10 pm?
    _____

    c) How many hours will it take for all the water
        to leak out?
    _____

Hour	Amount of water in the tank	
6 pm	21 L	
7 pm	18 L	
8 pm	15 L	
9 pm		
10 pm		

7. A store rents snowboards at $7 for the first hour and $5 for every hour after that.
    How much does it cost to rent a snowboard for 6 hours?

8. a) How many triangles would April need to make
        a figure with 10 squares?

    b) April says that she needs 15 triangles to make the sixth figure. Is she correct?

9. Merle saves $55 in August. She saves $6 each month after that.
    Alex saves $42 in August. He saves $7 each month after that.
    Who has saved the most money by the end of January?

Patterns & Algebra 1

PA6-7: T-Tables (Advanced)

The **terms** of a sequence are the numbers or items in the sequence.

A **term number** gives the position of each item.

*This is **term number 4** since it is in the fourth position.*

↓

4, 7, 10, 13, 16

---

1. Draw a T-table for each sequence to find the given term:

   a) Find the 5th term: 3, 8, 13, 18, … b) Find the 7th term: 42, 46, 50, 54,…

2. Ben says that the 6th term of the sequence 7, 13, 19,… is 53. Is he correct? Explain.

3. Find the missing terms in each sequence.

   a) 8, 12, _____, 20

   b) 11, _____, _____, 26

   c) 15, _____, _____, 24, _____

   d) 59, _____, _____, _____, 71

4.

Term Number	Term
1	13
2	15
3	18
4	19
5	21

Term Number	Term
1	25
2	29
3	34
4	37
5	41

Each T-Table was made by adding a number repeatedly.

Find and correct any mistakes in the tables.

5. Rita made an ornament using a hexagon (shaded figure), pentagons (dotted) and triangles.

   a) How many pentagons does she need to make 7 ornaments?

   b) Rita used 6 hexagons to make ornaments.
      How many triangles and pentagons did she use?

   c) Rita used 36 pentagons. How many triangles did she use?

6. A newborn Siberian Tiger cub weighs 1 300 g. It gains 100 g a day.
   A newborn baby weighs 3 300 g. It gains 200 g every week.

   a) A cub and a baby are born on the same day. Who weighs more after…

   i) 2 weeks?   ii) 6 weeks?

   b) After how many weeks would the cub and the baby have the same weight?

JUMP at Home Grade 6   No Unauthorized Copying

Patterns & Algebra 1

Jacqui is on a bicycle tour 300 km from home. She can cycle 75 km each day.

If she starts riding towards home on Tuesday morning,
how far away from home will she be by Thursday evening?

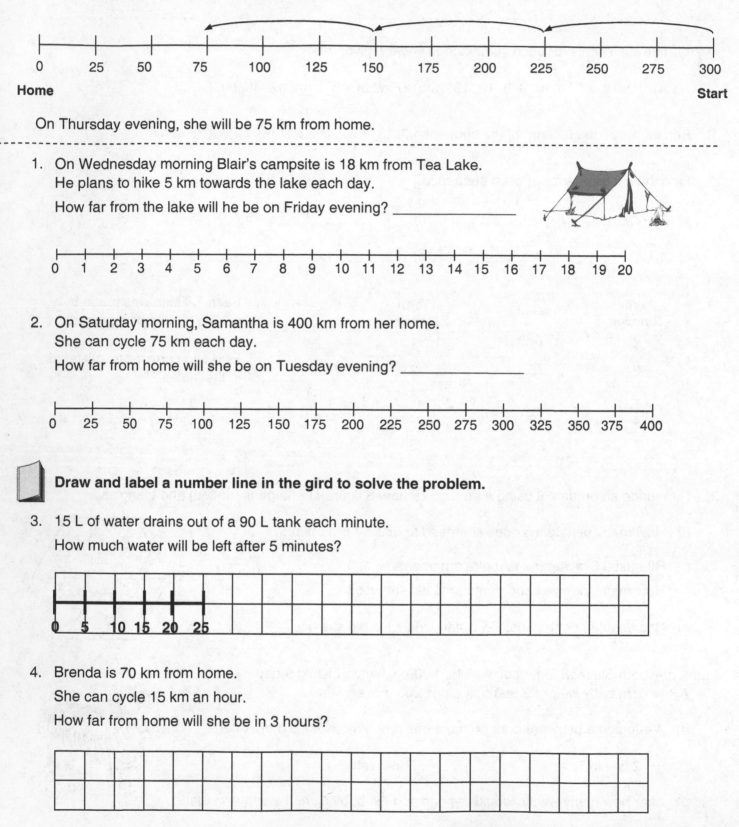

On Thursday evening, she will be 75 km from home.

1. On Wednesday morning Blair's campsite is 18 km from Tea Lake.
    He plans to hike 5 km towards the lake each day.

    How far from the lake will he be on Friday evening? _____

2. On Saturday morning, Samantha is 400 km from her home.
    She can cycle 75 km each day.

    How far from home will she be on Tuesday evening? _____

Draw and label a number line in the gird to solve the problem.

3. 15 L of water drains out of a 90 L tank each minute.

    How much water will be left after 5 minutes?

4. Brenda is 70 km from home.

    She can cycle 15 km an hour.

    How far from home will she be in 3 hours?

PA6-8: Number Lines

5. A grade six class is on a field trip 250 km from home.

   Their bus travels at a speed of 75 km each hour.

   How far from home will they be after 3 hours?

6. Paul plants 5 trees in a row.

   The nearest tree is 5 metres from his house. The farthest tree is 17 metres from his house.

   The trees are equally spaced.

   How far apart are the trees?

   HINT: Put Paul's house at zero on the number line.

7. Michael's house is 18 metres from the ocean.

   He is sleeping in a chair 3 metres away from his house (toward the ocean).

   The tide rises 5 metres every hour. How long will it take before his feet get wet?

8. Robert's bookcase has 5 shelves.

   The top shelf is 150 cm above the floor and the bottom shelf is 30 cm above the floor.

   How far apart are the shelves?

9. Aaron is training for football.

   He runs 5 metres forward and 2 metres back every 4 seconds.

   How far from where he started will he be after 16 seconds?

Patterns & Algebra 1

The multiples of 2 and 3 are marked with Xs on the number lines below:

The **lowest common multiple** (**LCM**) of 2 and 3 is 6: 6 is the least non-zero number that 2 and 3 both divide into evenly.

1. Mark the multiples of the given numbers on the number lines. What is the lowest common multiple of the pair?

    a) 3:

        4:   LCM = _____

    b) 4:

        6:   LCM = _____

2. Find the lowest common multiple of each pair of numbers. The first one has been done for you:
    HINT: Count up by the largest number until you find a number that both numbers divide into with no remainder.

    a) 3 and 5   b) 4 and 10   c) 3 and 9   d) 2 and 6

        3: 3, 6, 9, 12, **15**, 18

        5: 5, 10, **15**, 20

        LCM = __15__   LCM = _____   LCM = _____   LCM = _____

    e) 2 and 10   f) 3 and 6   g) 3 and 12   h) 4 and 8   i) 8 and 10

    j) 5 and 15   k) 6 and 10   l) 3 and 10   m) 6 and 8   n) 6 and 9

3. Paul visits the library every <u>fourth</u> day in January (beginning on January 4th).
    Werda visits every sixth day (beginning on January 6th)
    Nigel visits every 8th day (beginning on January 8th).

    On what day of the month will they all visit the library together?

Patterns & Algebra 1

PA6-10: 2-Dimensional Patterns

TEACHER: Review ordinal numbers before beginning this page.

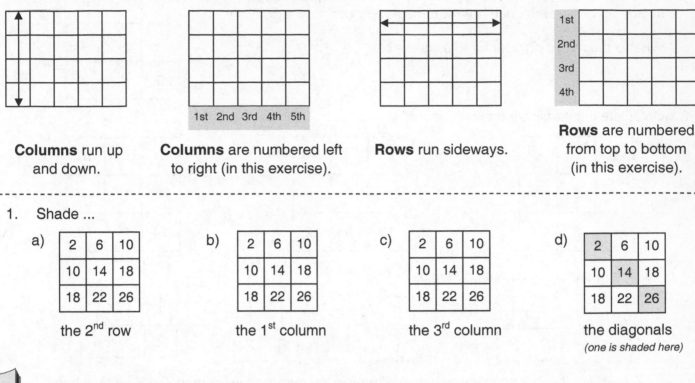

Columns run up and down.

Columns are numbered left to right (in this exercise).

Rows run sideways.

Rows are numbered from top to bottom (in this exercise).

----

1. Shade ...

   a)
2	6	10
10	14	18
18	22	26

   the 2nd row

   b)
2	6	10
10	14	18
18	22	26

   the 1st column

   c)
2	6	10
10	14	18
18	22	26

   the 3rd column

   d)
2	6	10
10	14	18
18	22	26

   the diagonals
   (one is shaded here)

2. Describe the pattern in the numbers you see in each chart below:
   NOTE: You should use the words "rows", "columns", and "diagonals" in your answer.

   a)
1	3	5
5	7	9
9	11	13

   b)
6	12	18	24
12	18	24	30
18	24	30	36
24	30	36	42

   c)
16	20	24	28
12	16	20	24
8	12	16	20
4	8	12	16

3. Make up your own pattern and describe it:

4. Place the letters X and Y so that each row and each column has two Xs and two Ys in it:

5. a) Which row of the chart has a decreasing pattern (looking left to right)?

   b) Which column has a repeating pattern?

   c) Write pattern rules for the first and second column.

   d) Describe the relationship between the numbers in the third and fourth columns.

   e) Describe one other pattern in the chart.

   f) Name a row or column that does not appear to have any pattern.

0	4	8	6	2
5	6	7	5	9
10	8	6	4	2
15	10	5	3	9
20	12	4	2	2

Patterns & Algebra 1

1. In a magic square, the numbers in each row, column, and diagonal all add up to the same number (the "magic number" for the square):

   What is the magic number for this square? _____

2	9	4
7	5	3
6	1	8

2. Complete the magic squares:

a)

2		6
9	5	
4	3	

b)

	9	
10	5	12

c)

		10
	12	
14		18

3. Here are some number pyramids:

   Can you find the rule by which the patterns in the pyramids were made? Describe it here:

4. Using the rule you described in Question 3, find the missing numbers:

Andre makes a garden path using 6 triangular stones for every 1 square stone.

He writes an equation that shows how to calculate the number of triangles from the number of squares:

squares × 6 = triangles

or (for short):   **6 × s = t**

Squares (s)	6 × s = t	Triangles (t)
1	6 × [1] = 6	6
2	6 × [2] = 12	12
3	6 × [3] = 18	18

1. Each chart represents a different design for a path. Complete the charts:

a)

Squares (s)	4 × s = t	Triangles (t)
1	4 × [1] = 4	4
2	4 × [ ] = 8	
3	4 × [ ] = 12	

b)

Squares (s)	3 × s = t	Triangles (t)
1	3 × [ ] = 3	
2	3 × [ ] = 6	
3	3 × [ ] = 9	

2. Write a rule that tells you how to calculate the number of triangles from the number of squares:

a)

Squares	Triangles
1	4
2	8
3	12

b)

Squares	Triangles
1	5
2	10
3	15

c)

Squares	Triangles
1	2
2	4
3	6

d)

Squares	Triangles
1	6
2	12
3	18

3. Wendy makes broaches using squares (s), rectangles (r), and triangles (t). Complete the chart.
Write an equation (such as **4 × s = t**) for each design:

a)

Squares (s)	Rectangles (r)
1	
2	
3	

b)

Rectangles (r)	Triangles (t)
1	
2	
3	

Patterns & Algebra 1

c)

Squares (s)	Rectangles (t)

d)

Squares (s)	Triangles (t)

e)

Squares (s)	Triangles (t)

f)

Squares (s)	Triangles (t)

4. Wendy has 39 triangles.

   Does she have enough triangles to make 7 broaches using the design here?

   How can you tell without making a chart?

5. Create a design using squares (s) and triangles (t) to go with each equation:

   a) $6 \times s = t$

   b) $5 \times s = t$

6. Create a design with squares and triangles and then write an equation for your design:

In the auditorium, the number of chairs in each row is always 4 greater than the row number.

Kelly writes an equation that shows how to calculate the number of chairs from the row number:

row number + 4 = number of chairs (or **r + 4 = c** for short)

Row	r + 4 = c	Chairs
1	[1] + 4 = 5	5
2	[2] + 4 = 6	6
3	[3] + 4 = 7	7

----

7. Each chart represents a different arrangement of chairs. Complete the charts:

a)

Row	r + 6 = c	Chairs
1	[1] + 6 = 7	7
2	[ ] + 6 =	
3	[ ] + 6 =	

b)

Row	r + 9 = c	Chairs
1	[ ] + 9 =	
2	[ ] + 9 =	
3	[ ] + 9 =	

8. Say what number you must add to the row number to get the number of chairs.
Write an equation using **r** for the row number and **c** for the number of chairs:

a)

Row	Chairs
1	5
2	6
3	7

Add 4

r + 4 = c

b)

Row	Chairs
1	8
2	9
3	10

c)

Row	Chairs
1	9
2	10
3	11

d)

Row	Chairs
7	12
8	13
9	14

9. Complete the charts. Then, in the box provided, write an equation for each arrangement of chairs:

a)

Row	Chairs

b)

Row	Chairs

10. Apply the given rule to the numbers in the input column. Write your answer in the output column:

a)

INPUT	OUTPUT
1	
2	
3	

Rule:

Add 4 to the input.

b)

INPUT	OUTPUT
5	
6	
7	

Rule:

Subtract 4 from the input.

c)

INPUT	OUTPUT
3	
5	
6	

Rule:

Multiply the input by 6.

d)

INPUT	OUTPUT
32	
8	
40	

Rule:

Divide each input by 4.

e)

INPUT	OUTPUT
18	
19	
20	

Rule:

Add 10 to the input.

f)

INPUT	OUTPUT
4	
5	
6	

Rule:

Multiply the input by 8.

11. For each chart, give a rule that tells you how to make the output numbers from the input numbers.

a)

INPUT	OUTPUT
2	6
3	7
4	8

Rule:

b)

INPUT	OUTPUT
3	8
5	10
7	12

Rule:

c)

INPUT	OUTPUT
1	7
2	14
3	21

Rule:

d)

INPUT	OUTPUT
3	15
2	10
1	5

Rule:

e)

INPUT	OUTPUT
2	16
4	32
6	48

Rule:

f)

INPUT	OUTPUT
19	16
15	12
21	18

Rule:

Complete the T-table for each pattern.
Then write a rule that tells you how to calculate the second number from the first number.

1.

Number of Vertical Lines	Number of Horizontal Lines	Rule:

2.

Number of Crosses	Number of Triangles	Rule:

3.

Number of Suns	Number of Moons	Rule:

4.

Number of Light Hexagons	Number of Dark Hexagons	Rule:

5.

Number of Diamonds	Number of Stars	Rule:

6. Make a T-table and write a rule for the number of hexagons and triangles:

 Figure 1   Figure 2   Figure 3

7. How many triangles are needed for 9 hexagons in the pattern in Question 6? How do you know?

Fill in the chart and write a rule for the number of blocks in each figure, as shown in part a).

1. a)

Figure 1   Figure 2   Figure 3

Rule: __3 × Figure Number__

Figure Number	Number of Blocks
1	
2	
3	

b)

Figure 1   Figure 2   Figure 3

Rule: _____

Figure Number	Number of Blocks

c)

Figure 1   Figure 2   Figure 3

Rule: _____

Figure Number	Number of Blocks

d)

Figure 1   Figure 2   Figure 3

Rule: _____

Figure Number	Number of Blocks

> In each example above, you can find the **total number of blocks** by *multiplying* the **Figure Number** by the **number of blocks in the first figure**.
>
> In such cases, **the number of blocks** is said to vary <u>directly</u> with the <u>Figure Number</u>.

2. Circle the sequences where the number of blocks varies <u>directly</u> with the Figure Number:

a)

Figure Number	Number of Blocks
1	3
2	6
3	9

b)

Figure Number	Number of Blocks
1	4
2	7
3	10

c)

Figure Number	Number of Blocks
1	6
2	12
3	18

d)

Figure Number	Number of Blocks
1	5
2	10
3	16

Patterns & Algebra 1

1. In each pattern below, the number of *shaded* blocks increases <u>directly</u> with the Figure Number.
   The *total* number of blocks, however, <u>does not</u> increase directly.

   i) Write a rule for the number of *shaded* blocks in each sequence.
   ii) Write a rule for the *total number* of blocks in each sequence.

a)

Figure 1   Figure 2   Figure 3

Rule for the number of shaded blocks:

_____2 × Figure Number_____

Rule for the total number of blocks:

_____2 × Figure Number + 1_____

b)

Figure 1   Figure 2   Figure 3

Rule for the number of shaded blocks:

_____

Rule for the total number of blocks:

_____

c)

Figure 1   Figure 2   Figure 3

Rule for the number of shaded blocks:

_____

Rule for the total number of blocks:

_____

d)

Figure 1   Figure 2   Figure 3

Rule for the number of shaded blocks:

_____

Rule for the total number of blocks:

_____

e) Rule for the number of shaded blocks:

_____

Rule for the total number of blocks:

_____

Figure 1   Figure 2   Figure 3

2. Draw or build a sequence of figures that might go with the following tables.
   Shade the part of each figure that varies directly with the Figure Number:

a)

Figure Number	Number of Blocks
1	5
2	7
3	9

b)

Figure Number	Number of Blocks
1	6
2	10
3	14

c)

Figure Number	Number of Blocks
1	7
2	10
3	13

Patterns & Algebra 1

1. Fill in the chart using the rule.

   a) Rule: <u>Multiply by 4 and add 3</u>

INPUT	OUTPUT
1	
2	
3	

   Gap: _____

   b) Rule: <u>Multiply by 2 and add 3</u>

INPUT	OUTPUT
1	
2	
3	

   Gap: _____

   c) Rule: <u>Multiply by 5 and add 4</u>

INPUT	OUTPUT
1	
2	
3	

   Gap: _____

   d) Rule: <u>Multiply by 10 and add 1</u>

INPUT	OUTPUT
1	
2	
3	

   Gap: _____

   e) Compare the **gap** in each pattern above to the rule for the pattern. What do you notice?

   _____

   _____

2. For each pattern below, make a T-table as shown.

   Fill in the total number of blocks (shaded and unshaded) and the gap.

   Can you predict what the gap will be for each pattern before you fill in the chart?

Figure Number	Number of Blocks
1	
2	
3	

   Figure 1   Figure 2   Figure 3

   Can you write a rule for each pattern that tells how to find the number of blocks from the figure number?

In the T-table shown here, the output is calculated from the input by two operations:

To find the rule:

INPUT	OUTPUT
1	5
2	8
3	11

Step 1:
Find the step (or gap) between the numbers in the OUTPUT column.

INPUT	INPUT x GAP	OUTPUT
1		5
2		8
3		11

Step 2:
Multiply the INPUT numbers by the gap.

INPUT	INPUT x GAP	OUTPUT
1	3	5
2	6	8
3	9	11

Step 3:
What must you add to each number in the second column?

INPUT	INPUT x GAP	OUTPUT
1	3	5
2	6	8
3	9	11

Add 2

Step 4:
Write a rule for the T-table – **Rule:** _Multiply the input by 3 and add 2_

1. Use the steps above to find the rule that tells you how to calculate the OUTPUT from the INPUT:

a)

INPUT	INPUT x GAP	OUTPUT
1		9
2		13
3		17

Add ____

Rule: Multiply by _____ then add _____.

b)

INPUT	INPUT x GAP	OUTPUT
1		3
2		5
3		7

Add ____

Rule: Multiply by _____ then add _____.

c)

INPUT	INPUT x GAP	OUTPUT
1		7
2		10
3		13

Add ____

Rule: Multiply by _____ then add _____.

d)

INPUT	INPUT x GAP	OUTPUT
1		6
2		8
3		10

Add ____

Rule: Multiply by _____ then add _____.

2. Write a rule that tells you how to calculate the OUTPUT from the INPUT:

a)

INPUT	INPUT x GAP	OUTPUT
1		9
2		14
3		19

Multiply by _____ then add _____.

b)

INPUT	INPUT x GAP	OUTPUT
1		12
2		18
3		24

Multiply by _____ then add _____.

c)

INPUT	INPUT x GAP	OUTPUT
1		6
2		10
3		14

Multiply by _____ then add _____.

d)

INPUT	INPUT x GAP	OUTPUT
1		6
2		11
3		16

Multiply by _____ then add _____.

3. Write the rule that tells you how to calculate the OUTPUT from the INPUT:
   NOTE: In this case you will have to subtract rather than add.

a)

INPUT	INPUT x GAP	OUTPUT
1		4
2		9
3		14

Multiply by _____ then subtract _____.

b)

INPUT	INPUT x GAP	OUTPUT
1		1
2		4
3		7

Multiply by _____ then subtract _____.

c)

INPUT	INPUT x GAP	OUTPUT
1		2
2		6
3		10

Multiply by _____ then subtract _____.

d)

INPUT	INPUT x GAP	OUTPUT
1		5
2		11
3		17

Multiply by _____ then subtract _____.

Patterns & Algebra 1

4. Write a rule that tells you how to make the Output from the Input:
   Each rule may involve either one or two operations.

a)

Input	Output
1	2
2	7
3	12
4	17

Rule:

b)

Input	Output
1	3
2	9
3	15
4	21

Rule:

c)

Input	Output
1	5
2	6
3	7
4	8

Rule:

d)

Input	Output
1	7
2	9
3	11
4	13

Rule:

e)

Input	Output
0	4
1	8
2	12
3	16

Rule:

f)

Input	Output
1	4
2	8
3	12
4	16

Rule:

BONUS
5. Find the rule by guessing and checking.

a)

Input	Output
5	27
6	32
7	37
8	42

Rule:

b)

Input	Output
4	7
5	9
6	11
7	13

Rule:

c)

Input	Output
57	63
58	64
59	65
60	66

Rule:

d)

Input	Output
2	7
4	13
6	19
8	25

Rule:

e)

Input	Output
10	31
9	28
3	10
1	4

Rule:

f)

Input	Output
8	13
4	5
3	3
7	11

Rule:

1. For each, draw Figure 4 and fill in the T-table.
    Then write a rule that tells you how to calculate the input from the output:

a)
Figure	Number of Triangles
1	
2	
3	
4	

Rule for T-table: _____

Use your rule to predict how many triangles will be needed for Figure 9: _____

b)
Figure	Perimeter
1	
2	
3	
4	

Rule for T-table: _____

Use your rule to predict the number of line segments in Figure 11: _____

c)
Figure	Number of Squares
1	
2	
3	
4	

Rule for T-table: _____

Use your rule to predict the number of squares needed for Figure 10: _____

d)
Figure	Perimeter
1	
2	
3	
4	

Rule for T-table: _____

Use your rule to predict the perimeter of Figure 23: _____

NS6-1: Introduction to Place Value

1. Write the place value of the underlined digit.

REMEMBER:

hundred thousands | ten thousands | thousands

millions — {8 3 1 7 5 2 4

hundreds | tens | ones

a) 56 2<u>3</u>6   `tens`

b) <u>1</u> 956 336

c) 8 <u>2</u>56 601

d) 6 453 <u>1</u>56   e) 7 103 25<u>6</u>

f) 2 5<u>8</u>9 143   g) 92<u>3</u> 156

2. Give the place value of the number 5 in each of the numbers below.
   HINT: First underline the 5 in each question.

a) 35 689   b) 5 308 603   c) 36 905

d) 215   e) 2 542   f) 3 451 628

g) 43 251   h) 152 776   i) 1 543 001

3. You can also write numbers using a place value chart.

   Example:

   4 672 953 would be:

millions	hundred thousands	ten thousands	thousands	hundreds	tens	ones
4	6	7	2	9	5	3

Write the following numbers into the place value chart.

	millions	hundred thousands	ten thousands	thousands	hundreds	tens	ones
a) 2 316 953	2	3	1	6	9	5	3
b) 62 507							
c) 5 604 891							
d) 1 399							
e) 17							
f) 998 260							

The number 684 523 is a **6-digit number**.

* The **digit** 6 stands for 600 000 – the **value** of the digit 6 is 600 000

* The **digit** 8 stands for 80 000 – the **value** of the digit 8 is 80 000

* The **digit** 4 stands for 4 000 – the **value** of the digit 4 is 4 000

* The **digit** 5 stands for 500 – the **value** of the digit 5 is 500

* The **digit** 2 stands for 20 – the **value** of the digit 2 is 20

* The **digit** 3 stands for 3 – the **value** of the digit 3 is 3

---

1. Write the **value** of each digit.

a)

6	5	4	8	7	2

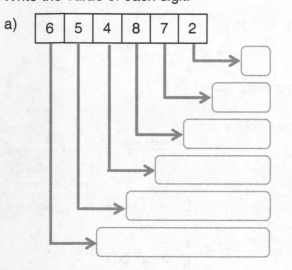

b)

1	2	8	5	3	7

2. What does the digit 7 stand for in each number? The first one is done for you.

a)   8 476

    70

b)   38 725

c)   93 726

d)   730 025

e)   7 250

f)   64 297

g)   43 075

h)   382 457

3. Fill in the blanks.

a) In the number 4 523, the <u>digit</u> 5 stands for _____ .

b) In the number 34 528, the <u>digit</u> 3 stands for _____ .

c) In the number 420 583, the <u>value</u> of the digit 8 is _____ .

d) In the number 75 320, the <u>value</u> of the digit 7 is _____ .

e) In the number 723 594, the digit _____ is in the <u>ten thousands place</u>.

PARENT: Model the two kinds of expanded form for your child (see page 32, Question 6 for details).

1. Write each number in expanded form.
    (numerals and words).

Example:

__1__ thousands + __2__ hundreds + __3__ tens + __3__ ones = [1 233]

REMEMBER:

= 1000   = 100   = 10   □ = 1

a)

___ thousands + ___ hundreds + ___ tens + ___ ones = [   ]

b)

___ thousands + ___ hundreds + ___ tens + ___ ones = [   ]

c)

_____ = [   ]

Steps for drawing a thousands block:

Step 1:
Draw a square:

Step 2:
Draw lines from
its 3 vertices:

Step 3:
Join the lines:

2. Represent the given numbers with the base ten blocks in the place value chart. The first one has been started for you.

	Number	Thousands	Hundreds	Tens	Ones
a)	3 468				
b)	1 542				
c)	2 609				

3. Write the numbers for the given base ten blocks.

	Thousands	Hundreds	Tens	Ones	Number
a)					_____
b)					_____

NS6-4: Representation in Expanded Form

1. Expand the following numbers using <u>numerals</u> and <u>words</u>. The first one is done for you.

 a) 2 536 784 = _2_ millions + _5_ hundred thousands + _3_ ten thousands + _6_ thousands + _7_ hundreds + _8_ tens + _4_ ones

 b) 6 235 401 = _____

 c) 3 056 206 = _____

2. Write the number in expanded form (using <u>numerals</u>). The first one is done for you.

 a) 72 613 = _70 000 + 2 000 + 600 + 10 + 3_   b) 36 = _____

 c) 526 = _____   d) 12 052 = _____

 e) 2 382 = _____   f) 56 384 = _____

 g) 3 082 385 = _____

3. Write the number for each sum.

 a) 6 000 + 700 + 40 + 7 = _____   b) 800 + 60 + 8 = _____   c) 3 000 + 30 + 2 = _____

 d) 50 000 + 6 000 + 400 + 90 + 3 = _____   e) 10 000 + 6 000 + 200 + 30 + 4 = _____

 f) 30 000 + 2 000 + 500 = _____   g) 90 000 + 3 000 + 600 + 7 = _____

BONUS
 h) 300 000 + 2 000 000 + 5 + 70 000 + 200 = _____

4. Find the missing numbers.

 a) 2 000 + 600 + _____ + 5 = 2 645   b) 4 000 + 200 + _____ + 5 = 4 285

 c) 40 000 + 3 000 + _____ + 10 + 5 = 43 715   d) 80 000 + 5 000 + _____ + 60 + 3 = 85 263

 e) 20 000 + 6 000 + 300 + _____ = 26 302   f) _____ + 400 = 9 400

 g) 6 000 + _____ = 6 080   h) 80 000 + _____ + _____ = 87 005

 i) 300 000 + 90 000 + _____ + _____ = 390 702

5. Write each number in expanded form. Then draw a base ten model.

    Example: 3 152 = | 3 000 + 100 + 50 + 2 |

    a) 4 354 = [   ]

    b) 2 604 = [   ]

6. Represent the number 8 564 in four different ways – by sketching a base ten model, with number words, and in expanded form (2 ways).

    Example: 234 – Two hundred thirty-four

    234 = 2 hundreds + 3 tens + 4 ones   *expanded form (using number words)*

    234 = 200 + 30 + 4   *expanded form (using numerals)*

7. In the number 38 562, what is the sum of the tens digit and the thousands digit?

8. How many two-digit numbers have digits that add to twelve?

9. Using 5 blocks make (or draw) a model of a number such that...

    • The number is odd   • There are twice as many thousands blocks as hundreds blocks

10. How many thousands blocks would you need to represent a million?

1. Write the **value** of each digit. Then complete the sentence.

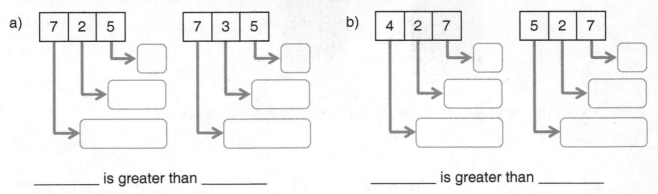

a)

| 7 | 2 | 5 |

| 7 | 3 | 5 |

b)

| 4 | 2 | 7 |

| 5 | 2 | 7 |

_____ is greater than _____   _____ is greater than _____

2. Circle the pair of digits that are different in each pair of numbers.
    Then write the greater number in the box.

a) 83 7(5)2
    83 7(6)2
    [83 762]

b) 273 605
    272 605
    [   ]

c) 614 852
    614 858
    [   ]

d) 383 250
    483 250
    [   ]

e) 812 349
    813 349
    [   ]

f) 569 274
    579 274
    [   ]

g) 323
    324
    [   ]

h) 195 385
    196 385
    [   ]

3. Read the numbers from left to right. Circle the first pair of digits you find that are different.
    Then write the greater number in the box.

a) 641 5(8)3
    641 5(9)7
    [641 597]

b) 384 207
    389 583
    [   ]

c) 576 986
    603 470
    [   ]

d) 621 492
    621 483
    [   ]

4. The inequality sign ">" in **7 > 5** is read "seven is greater than five."
    The sign "<" in **8 < 10** is read "eight is less than ten."
    Write the correct inequality sign in the box.

a) 8 653 [>] 8 486   b) 15 332 [ ] 16 012   c) 9 000 [ ] 7 999

d) 323 728 [ ] 323 729   e) 648 175 [ ] 648 123   f) 72 382 [ ] 8 389

g) 24 489 [ ] 38 950   h) 85 106 [ ] 83 289   i) 1 572 306 [ ] 1 573 306

NS6-6: Differences from 10 to 10 000

1. Write "10 more," "10 less," "100 more," or "100 less" in the blanks.

   a) 70 is _____ than 60   b) 500 is _____ than 600

   c) 40 is _____ than 30   d) 100 is _____ than 90

2. Write "100 more," "100 less," "1 000 more," or "1 000 less" in the blanks.

   a) 1 000 is _____ than 2 000   b) 14 000 is _____ than 15 000

   c) 5 900 is _____ than 6 000   d) 70 000 is _____ than 69 000

3. Write "1 000 more," "1 000 less," "10 000 more," or "10 000 less" in the blanks.

   a) 7 000 is _____ than 6 000   b) 13 000 is _____ than 14 000

   c) 40 000 is _____ than 50 000   d) 60 000 is _____ than 50 000

   e) 8 000 is _____ than 7 000   f) 40 000 is _____ than 39 000

4. Write "10 000 more," "10 000 less," "100 000 more," or "100 000 less" in the blanks.

   a) 200 000 is _____ than 100 000   b) 70 000 is _____ than 80 000

   c) 160 000 is _____ than 150 000   d) 400 000 is _____ than 500 000

   e) 19 000 is _____ than 200 000   f) 800 000 is _____ than 900 000

5. Circle the pair of digits that are different. Then fill in the blanks.

   a) 385 237
      395 237

   385 237 is ___10 000 less___
   than 395 237.

   b) 291 375
      291 475

   291 375 is _____
   than 291 475.

   c) 143 750
      133 750

   143 750 is _____
   than 133 750.

   d) 522 508
      532 508

   522 508 is _____
   than 532 508.

   e) 96 405
      96 415

   96 405 is _____
   than 96 415.

   f) 3 752 582
      3 751 582

   3 752 582 is _____
   than 3 751 582.

6. Fill in the blanks.

a) _____ is 10 more than 3 782

b) _____ is 100 less than 39 927

c) _____ is 100 more than 3 782

d) _____ is 1 000 less than 15 023

e) _____ is 10 000 more than 287 532

f) _____ is 1 000 less than 23 685

g) _____ is 10 000 more than 8 305

h) _____ is 100 000 more than 4 253

i) _____ is 100 000 less than 273 528

j) _____ is 10 000 less than 178 253

7. Fill in the blanks.

a) $226 + 10 =$ _____

b) $28 573 + 10 =$ _____

c) $39 035 + 10 =$ _____

d) $42 127 + 100 =$ _____

e) $63 283 + 1 000 =$ _____

f) $58 372 + 10 000 =$ _____

g) $2 873 - 10 =$ _____

h) $485 - 10 =$ _____

i) $837 - 100 =$ _____

j) $32 487 - 1 000 =$ _____

k) $81 901 - 100 =$ _____

l) $25 836 - 10 000 =$ _____

m) $382 507 + 10 000 =$ _____

n) $1 437 652 - 100 000 =$ _____

8. Fill in the blanks.

a) $685 +$ _____ $= 695$

b) $302 +$ _____ $= 402$

c) $2 375 +$ _____ $= 2 385$

d) $2 617 +$ _____ $= 2 717$

e) $43 210 +$ _____ $= 44 210$

f) $26 287 +$ _____ $= 26 387$

g) $1 287 -$ _____ $= 1 187$

h) $6 325 -$ _____ $= 6 315$

i) $14 392 -$ _____ $= 14 292$

j) $386 053 -$ _____ $= 376 053$

k) $1 260 053 + 1 000 =$ _____

BONUS

9. Continue the number patterns.

a) 6 407, 6 417, 6 427, _____ , _____

b) 46 640, 47 640, 48 640, _____ , _____

c) 624 823, 624 833, _____ , 624 853

d) _____ , 28 393, 28 403, 28 413

10. Circle the pair of digits that are different. Then fill in the blanks.

a) 827 3②5
   827 3③5

   <u>827 325</u> is <u>10</u>

   less than <u>827 335</u>

b) 382 305
   482 305

   _____ is _____

   greater than _____

c) 925 778
   915 778

   _____ is _____

   less than _____

Number Sense 1

1. Write the number represented by the base ten materials in each box. Then circle the greater number in each pair.

    HINT: If there is the same number of thousands, count the number of hundreds or tens.

2. Circle the greater number in each pair.

    a) 47 or forty-eight   b) three thousand, five hundred seven or 3508   c) ninety-four or 88

    d) six hundred fifty-five or 662   e) 60 385 or sixty thousand four hundred twenty-five

3. List all the two-digit numbers you can make using the digits provided (using each digit only once). Then circle the greatest one.

    a) 6, 7 and 8   b) 2, 9 and 4   c) 5, 2, and 0

4. Create the greatest possible <u>four-digit</u> number using the digits given. Only use each digit once.

    a) 4, 3, 2, 6 _____   b) 7, 8, 9, 4 _____   c) 0, 4, 1, 2 _____

5. Create the greatest possible number using these digits. Only use each digit once.

    a) 3, 4, 1, 2, 8 _____   b) 2, 8, 9, 1, 5 _____   c) 3, 6, 1, 5, 4 _____

6. Use the digits to create the greatest number, the least number and a number in between.

	Digits	Greatest Number	Number in Between	Least Number
a)	8 5 7 2 1			
b)	2 1 5 3 9			
c)	3 0 1 5 3			

7. Arrange the numbers in order, starting with the <u>least</u> number.

    a) 683 759, 693 238, 693 231

    _____ , _____ , _____

    b) 473 259, 42 380, 47 832

    _____ , _____ , _____

    c) 385 290, 928 381, 532 135

    _____ , _____ , _____

    d) 2 575, 38 258, 195

    _____ , _____ , _____

8. What is the greatest number less than 10 000 whose digits are all the same? _____

9. Identify the greater number by writing > or <.

    a) 63 752 [ ] 63 750

    b) 927 385 [ ] 928 303

    c) 572 312 [ ] 59 238

    d) 1 230 075 [ ] 1 230 123

10.

City	Population
Ottawa	774 072
Hamilton	662 401
Kitchener	414 284

a) Which city has a population greater than 670 000?

    _____

b) Write the populations in order from least to greatest.

    _____

11. What is the greatest possible number you can create that has …

    a) 3 digits? _____

    b) 4 digits? _____

    c) 5 digits? _____

12. Using the digits 0, 1, 2, 3, 4, create an even number greater than 42 000 and less than 43 000.

13. Using the digits 4, 5, 6, 7, 8, create an odd number greater than 64 000 and less than 68 000.

14. What digit can be substituted for [ ] to make each statement true?

    a) 54 [ ] 21 is between 54 348 and 54 519.

    b) 76 [ ] 99 is between 76 201 and 76 316.

Nancy has 3 hundreds blocks, 14 tens blocks, and 8 ones blocks.
She exchanges 10 tens blocks for a hundreds block.

3 hundreds + 14 tens + 8 ones   =   4 hundreds + 4 tens + 8 ones

----

1. Regroup 10 ones as 1 tens block.

    a)

    ___ tens + ___ ones = ___ tens + ___ ones

    b)

    ___ tens + ___ ones = ___ tens + ___ ones

2. Exchange ones for tens.

    a) 53 ones = ___ tens + ___ ones   b) 85 ones = ___ tens + ___ ones   c) 14 ones = ___ tens + ___ ones

    d) 27 ones = ___ tens + ___ ones   e) 32 ones = ___ tens + ___ ones   f) 16 ones = ___ tens + ___ ones

    g) 11 ones = ___ tens + ___ ones   h) 82 ones = ___ tens + ___ ones   i) 93 ones = ___ tens + ___ ones

3. Complete the charts by regrouping 10 tens as 1 hundred.

    a)

hundreds	tens
7	28
7 + 2 = 9	8

    b)

hundreds	tens
6	24

    c)

hundreds	tens
3	15

    d)

hundreds	tens
6	36

    e)

hundreds	tens
8	19

    f)

hundreds	tens
2	20

4. Exchange tens for hundreds or ones for tens. The first one has been done for you.

    a) 6 hundreds + 7 tens + 19 ones = _6 hundreds + 8 tens + 9 ones_____

    b) 2 hundreds + 6 tens + 15 ones = _____

    c) 8 hundreds + 28 tens + 9 ones = _____

Rupa has 1 thousands block, 12 hundreds blocks, 1 tens block, and 2 ones blocks.

She regroups 10 hundreds blocks as a thousands block.

1 thousand + 12 hundreds + 1 ten + 2 ones   =   2 thousands + 2 hundreds + 1 ten + 2 ones

---

5. Complete the charts by regrouping 10 hundreds as 1 thousand.

a)
thousands	hundreds
5	25
5 + 2 = 7	5

b)
thousands	hundreds
3	12

c)
thousands	hundreds
8	20

6. Exchange 10 hundreds for a thousand. The first one has been done for you.

   a) 5 thousands + 23 hundreds + 2 tens + 5 ones = __7__ thousands + __3__ hundreds + __2__ tens + __5__ ones

   b) 1 thousands + 54 hundreds + 2 tens + 6 ones = ____ thousands + ____ hundreds + ____ tens + ____ ones

   c) 8 thousands + 15 hundreds + 3 tens + 0 ones = _____

   _____

7. Exchange thousands for ten thousands, hundreds for thousands, tens for hundreds, or ones for tens.

   a) 2 thousands + 13 hundreds + 2 tens + 5 ones = ____ thousands + ____ hundreds + ____ tens + ____ ones

   b) 5 thousands + 2 hundreds + 3 tens + 56 ones = _____

   _____

   c) 3 ten thousands + 27 thousands + 2 hundreds + 37 tens + 8 ones = _____

   _____

8. Teresa wants to build a model of 6 thousand, 5 hundred and ninety.
   She has 5 thousands blocks, 14 hundreds blocks and 30 tens blocks.

   Can she build the model?

   Use diagrams and numbers to explain your answer.

1. Add the numbers below by drawing a picture and by adding the digits. Use base ten materials to show how to combine the numbers and how to regroup. (The first one has been done for you.)

a) **26 + 36**

	with base ten materials		with numerals	
	tens	ones	tens	ones
26			2	6
36			3	6
sum		regroup 10 ones as ten	5	12
		after regrouping	6	2

b) **57 + 27**

	with base ten materials		with numerals	
	tens	ones	tens	ones

2. Add the ones digits. Show how you would regroup 10 ones as 1 ten. The first question has been done for you.

tens go here

a)
```
  1
  1 6
+ 1 7
  3
```
ones go here

b)
```
  2 4
+ 3 6
```

c)
```
  5 7
+ 1 9
```

d)
```
  7 3
+ 1 9
```

e)
```
  5 7
+ 3 5
```

3. Add the numbers by regrouping. The first one has been done for you.

a)
```
  1
  4 6
+ 2 5
  7 1
```

b)
```
  3 3
+ 4 8
```

c)
```
  7 2
+ 1 9
```

d)
```
  8 5
+ 1 7
```

e)
```
  4 7
+ 2 6
```

f)
```
  3 8
+ 4 3
```

g)
```
  6 9
+   9
```

h)
```
  7 4
+ 1 9
```

i)
```
  4 3
+ 3 9
```

j)
```
  6 8
+ 2 9
```

Simon adds **363 + 274** using base ten materials.

363 = 3 hundreds + 6 tens + 3 ones

+ 274 = 2 hundreds + 7 tens + 4 ones

= 5 hundreds + 13 tens + 7 ones

Then, to get the final answer, Simon regroups 10 tens as 1 hundred.

= 6 hundreds + 3 tens + 7 ones

1. Add the numbers below, either by using base ten materials or by drawing a picture in your notebook. Record your work here.

   483 = _____ hundreds + _____ tens + _____ ones

   + 245 = _____ hundreds + _____ tens + _____ ones

   = _____ hundreds + _____ tens + _____ ones

   after regrouping = _____ hundreds + _____ tens + _____ ones

2. Add. You will need to regroup. The first one is started for you.

   a) [1]
       3 6 4
       + 2 5 3
       _____
           1 7

   b) 5 7 1
       + 2 5 5

   c) 6 5 2
       +   9 4

   d) 3 6 4
       + 4 8 2

   e) 4 4 7
       + 1 7 2

3. Add, regrouping where necessary.

   a) 1 6 8
       + 3 2 3

   b) 2 5 5
       + 3 6 2

   c) 2 9 5
       + 1 2 3

   d) 4 6 5
       + 1 5 9

   e) 4 5 7
       + 3 0 3

   f) 4 6 5
       + 2 6 4

4. Add by lining the numbers up correctly in the grid. The first one has been started for you.

   a) 449 + 346

	4	4	9
+	3	4	6

   b) 273 + 456

   c) 832 + 109

   d) 347 + 72

Samuel adds **2 974 + 2 313** using base ten materials.

2 974 = 2 thousands + 9 hundreds + 7 tens + 4 ones

+ 2 313 = 2 thousands + 3 hundreds + 1 tens + 3 ones

= 4 thousands + 12 hundreds + 8 tens + 7 ones

Then, to get the final answer, Samuel exchanges 10 hundreds for 1 thousand.

= 5 thousands + 2 hundreds + 8 tens + 7 ones

---

1. Add the numbers below, either by using base ten materials or by drawing a picture in your notebook. Record your work here.

          5 486 = _____ thousands + _____ hundreds + _____ tens + _____ ones

      + 3 713 = _____ thousands + _____ hundreds + _____ tens + _____ ones

                = _____ thousands + _____ hundreds + _____ tens + _____ ones

   after regrouping = _____ thousands + _____ hundreds + _____ tens + _____ ones

2. Add. (You will need to regroup.) The first one is started for you.

a)   4 6 8 3   b)   2 5 3 7   c)   8 6 5 4   d)   3 1 7 4   e)   5 9 4 6
     + 2 7 1 2   + 4 6 2 1   +   7 2 4   + 4 9 2 3   + 2 4 3 2
        3 9 5

3. Add. You will need to regroup tens as hundreds.

a)   8 5 6 3   b)   4 4 8 7   c)   3 6 8 3   d)   2 4 7 8   e)   9 5 9 3
     + 1 3 5 1   + 2 3 5 1   + 3 1 3 2   +   2 7 1   +   2 5 2

4. Add the following, regrouping or carrying where necessary.

a)
```
  5 8 4 6
+ 1 1 3 5
```

b)
```
  3 5 6 4
+ 2 8 1 3
```

c)
```
  6 5 3 4
+ 3 2 9 4
```

d)
```
  8 8 5 4
+ 1 0 6 3
```

e)
```
  2 4 4 3
+ 5 9 3 5
```

f)
```
  6 7 5 2
+ 2 3 3 4
```

g)
```
  3 4 7 3
+ 5 2 4 3
```

h)
```
  5 6 7 5
+   9 2 3
```

i)
```
  8 2 3 0
+ 1 4 8 8
```

j)
```
  2 5 4 8
+ 3 4 8 1
```

5. Add by lining the digits up correctly in the grid. In some questions you may have to regroup twice.

a) 2 468 + 7 431

b) 8 596 + 1 235

c) 6 650 + 2 198

d) 8 359 + 48

6. Add, regrouping where necessary.

a)
```
  5 4 5 5
+ 1 2 7 3
```

b)
```
  7 3 2 4 6
+ 1 8 3 8 2
```

c)
```
  1 4 5 6 8 3
+ 3 2 9 2 3 4
```

d)
```
  2 3 5 2 7 5
+ 5 1 2 9 1 3
```

e) 5 326 + 1 234 + 6 762   f) 3 658 + 6 343 + 4 534   g) 389 + 3247 + 712 + 52

7. A **palindrome** is a number (or word) that reads the same forward and backward.

   For instance: 363, 51 815, and 2 375 732 are all palindromes.

   For each number below, follow the steps shown here for the number 124.

   Step 1:   Reverse the digits.   124 → 421

   Step 2:   Add the two numbers.   124 + 421 = 545

   Step 3:   If the number you create is *not* a palindrome, repeat Steps 1 and 2 with the new number. Most numbers will eventually become palindromes if you keep repeating these steps.

   Create palindromes from the following numbers.

   a) 216   b) 154   c) 651   d) 23153   e) 371   f) 258   g) 1385

Mark subtracts **54 – 17** using base ten materials.

Step 1:
Mark represents 54 with base ten materials...

Step 2:
7 (the ones digit of 17) is greater than 4 (the ones digit of 54) so Mark regroups a tens block as 10 ones...

Step 3:
Mark subtracts 17 (he takes away 1 tens block and 7 ones)...

Here is how Mark uses numerals to show his work:

54
– 17

Here is how Mark shows the regrouping:

4 14
5̶4̶
– 1 7

And now Mark can subtract 14 – 7 ones and 4 – 1 tens:

4 14
5̶4̶
– 1 7
3 7

----

1. In these questions, Mark doesn't have enough ones to subtract. Help him by regrouping a tens block as 10 ones. Show how he would rewrite his subtraction statement.

a) **53 – 36**

b) **65 – 29**

c) **45 – 27**

d) **53 – 48**

Number Sense 1

2. Subtract by regrouping. The first one is done for you.

a)
	7	12
	8̸	2̸
−	3	7
	4	5

b)
	5	4
−	2	6

c)
	7	5
−	3	8

d)
	4	1
−	2	3

e)
	6	7
−	4	9

3. For the questions where you need to regroup, write "Help!" in the space provided.

How do you know when you need to regroup? Write an answer in your notebook. If you are working with a partner, discuss.

a)
```
   58     Help!
 − 19   8 is less than 9
```

b)
```
   34   _____
 − 13
```

c)
```
   85   _____
 − 27
```

d)
```
   48   _____
 − 42
```

e)
```
   68   _____
 − 35
```

f)
```
   91   _____
 − 25
```

g)
```
   85   _____
 − 24
```

h)
```
   66   _____
 −  8
```

i)
```
   25   _____
 − 16
```

j)
```
   93   _____
 − 47
```

k)
```
   56   _____
 −  9
```

l)
```
   85   _____
 − 12
```

4. To subtract 425 −182, Rita regroups a hundreds block for 10 tens blocks.

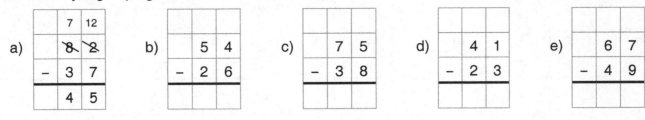

hundreds	tens	ones
4	2	5

hundreds	tens	ones
3	12	5

hundreds	tens	ones
2	4	3

Subtract by regrouping <u>hundreds</u> as tens. The first one has been started for you.

a)

	5	13	
	6̸	3̸	8
−	4	5	3

b)
	8	5	4
−	3	7	2

c)
	7	5	5
−	3	8	2

d)
	4	2	3
−	1	8	2

5. Subtract by regrouping <u>tens</u> as ones. The first one has been started for you.

a)
```
      7  14
   7  8̸  4̸
-  2  4  8
```

b)
```
   3  4  3
-  2  1  9
```

c)
```
   8  2  5
-  5  1  7
```

d)
```
   6  7  1
-  3  1  6
```

6. For the questions below, you will have to regroup *twice*.

Example:

Step 1:
```
      2 16
   8  3̸  6̸
-  3  5  8
```

Step 2:
```
      2 16
   8  3̸  6̸
-  3  5  8
         8
```

Step 3:
```
      12
   7  2̸ 16
   8̸  3̸  6̸
-  3  5  8
         8
```

Step 4:
```
      12
   7  2̸ 16
   8̸  3̸  6̸
-  3  5  8
      7  8
```

Step 5:
```
      12
   7  2̸ 16
   8̸  3̸  6̸
-  3  5  8
   4  7  8
```

a)
```
   9  3  4
-  4  5  6
```

b)
```
   7  4  7
-  2  6  9
```

c)
```
   5  3  2
-     5  9
```

d)
```
   8  9  2
-  4  9  5
```

7. To subtract 5 267 – 3 415, Laura regroups a thousands block as 10 hundreds blocks.

thousands	hundreds	tens	ones
5	2	6	7

thousands	hundreds	tens	ones
4	12	6	7

thousands	hundreds	tens	ones
1	8	5	2

Subtract by regrouping thousands as hundreds. The first one has been done for you.

a)
```
   3 13
   4̸  3̸  5  8
-  1  5  2  6
   2  8  3  2
```

b)
```
   6  5  3  5
-  3  8  1  4
```

c)
```
   7  3  6  2
-  4  5  1  2
```

d)
```
   9  0  6  3
-  2  7  0  2
```

Number Sense 1

8. In some of the questions below, you will need to regroup.

a)

	3	6	4	8
− 1		9	3	4

b)

	9	1	2	4
− 6		0	6	2

c)

	8	5	4	2
− 3		4	6	1

d)

3	2	8	3	9
− 4	6	2	8	

9. In the questions below, you will have to regroup *three* times (i.e., regroup a ten as 10 ones, a hundred as 10 tens, and a thousand as 10 hundreds).

Example:

Step 1:	Step 2:	Step 3:	Step 4:	Step 5:
1 13 6 4 2̶ 3̶ − 3 7 4 6	1 13 6 4 2̶ 3̶ − 3 7 4 6 7	11 3 ̶4̶ 13 6 4̶ 2̶ 3̶ − 3 7 4 6 7 7	11 3 ̶4̶ 13 6 4̶ 2̶ 3̶ − 3 7 ̶4̶ 6 6 7 7	13 11 3 ̶4̶ 13 5 ̶4̶ 2̶ 3̶ − 3 7 4 6̶ 2 6 7 7

a)

	9	5	4	2
− 1		7	6	3

b)

	6	4	3	7
− 2		6	7	8

c)

	4	5	6	3
− 1		7	9	5

d)

	7	8	4	3
− 4		8	6	5

10. In the questions below, you will have to regroup *two*, *three*, or *four* times.

Example:

Step 1:	Step 2:	Step 3:	Step 4:
0 10 1̶ 0̶ 0 0 − 7 5 6	9 0 1̶0̶ 10 1̶ 0̶ 0̶ 0 − 7 5 6	9 9 0 1̶0̶ 1̶0̶ 10 1̶ 0̶ 0̶ 0̶ − 7 5 6	9 9 0 1̶0̶ 1̶0̶ 10 1̶ 0̶ 0̶ 0̶ − 7 5 6 2 4 4

a)

	1	0	0	0
−		4	6	8

b)

	1	0	0
−		3	2

c)

1	0	0	0	0
−	6	4	8	6

d)

1	0	0	0	0
−		5	1	1	1

1. A school has 150 students.
   80 of the students are boys.

   How many are girls?

2. Raj has 150 stamps.
   Sharif has 12 fewer stamps than Raj.
   Cedric has 15 more stamps than Raj.

   How many stamps do the children have altogether?

3. Camile cycled 2 357 km one year
   and 5 753 km the next.

   How many km did she
   cycle altogether?

4. Two nearby towns have populations
   of 442 670 and 564 839 people.

   What is the total population of both towns?

5. A grocery store had 480 cans of soup.

   In one week they sold:

   • 212 cans of tomato soup
   • 57 cans of chicken soup
   • 43 cans of mushroom soup

   How many cans were left?

6. A box turtle can live 100 years.
   A rabbit can live 15 years.

   How much longer than a rabbit can a box
   turtle live?

7. In the number 432...

   • The 100s digit is one more than the tens digit
   • The 10s digit is one more than the ones digit

   Make up your own number with this property.

   ——— ——— ———

   Now write the number backwards.

   ——— ——— ———

   Next write these two numbers in a grid and
   subtract them (be sure to put the greater number
   on top).

   Try this again with several other numbers. You
   will always get 198!

   BONUS
   Can you explain why this works?

8. The shoreline of Lake Ontario is 1 146 km.

   The shoreline of Lake Erie is 1 402 km.

   How much longer is the shoreline of Lake Erie
   than the shoreline of Lake Ontario?

9. The Nile River is about 6 690 km long and
   the Amazon River is 6 440 km long.

   How much longer is the Nile River than the
   Amazon River?

Answer the questions below in your notebook.

1. The chart below gives the area of some of the largest islands in Canada.

Island	Area in km²
Baffin Island	507 450
Ellesmere Island	196 240
Newfoundland	108 860
Vancouver Island	31 290

   a) Write the area of the islands in order from least to greatest.

   b) How much greater than the area of the smallest island is the area of the largest island?

   c) How much greater is the area of Ellesmere Island than Newfoundland?

   d) The area of Greenland is 2 166 086 km².

   Do Baffin Island and Vancouver Island *together* have an area greater than Greenland?

2. Use each of the digits 4, 5, 6, 7, 8 once to create…

   a) the greatest odd number possible.

   b) a number between 56 700 and 57 000.

   c) an even number whose tens digit and hundreds digit add to 12.

   d) a number as close to 70 000 as possible (explain how you know your answer is correct).

3. There are 390 000 species of plants and 1 234 400 species of animals.

   How many more species of animals are there than plants?

4. Use the numbers 1, 2, 3, 4 once in each question.

5. Here are some important dates in the history of science.

   - In 1543, Copernicus published a book claiming the sun is the center of our solar system.
   - In 1610, Galileo Galilei used his newly invented telescope to discover the moons of Jupiter.
   - In 1667, Isaac Newton announced his law of gravity.

   a) How long ago did Copernicus publish his book?

   b) How many years passed between each pair of dates given?

When you multiply a pair of numbers, the result is called the **product** of the numbers. You can represent a product using an **array**.

row → [array of dots: 5, 10, 15] Sue counts the dots by skip counting by 5s.

Sue writes a multiplication statement for the array: $3 \times 5 = 15$ (3 and 5 are called **factors** of 15)

-----

1. Write a multiplication statement for each array.

a) _____3_____ rows

_____4_____ dots in each row

_____3 × 4 = 12_____

b) _____ rows

_____ dots in each row

_____

c) _____

_____

_____

2. Write a product for each array.

a) ____4 × 3____
   rows   dots in each row

b) _____

c) _____

d) _____

3. Draw arrays for these products.

a) 2 × 5   b) 3 × 7   c) 4 × 6   d) 1 × 8   e) 4 × 2

4. There are only *three* ways to arrange 4 dots in an array.
   So there are only 3 ways to write 4 as a product of two factors.

   • • • • 1 × 4 = 4   2 × 2 = 4   4 × 1 = 4

   How many ways can you write each number as a product of two factors? (Draw arrays to help.)

   a) 6   b) 8   c) 9   d) 10   e) 12

5. The numbers that appear beside the arrays in Question 4 are called the **factors** of 4.
   The factors of 4 are the numbers 1, 2, and 4.

   Write a list of factors for the numbers 6, 8, 9, 10, and 12.

A **prime** number has <u>two</u> distinct factors (no more, no less): itself and 1.

A **composite** number has <u>more than two</u> factors: at least one number **other than** itself and 1.

---

1. a) How many <u>distinct</u> factors does the number 1 have? _____   b) Is 1 a prime number? _____

2. List all the prime numbers less than 10: _____

3. List all the composite numbers between 10 and 20: _____

4. What is the greatest prime number less than 30? _____

5. Circle the prime numbers.

    1   25   14   13   17   20   27   15   12   18   29   33

6.   Eratosthenes was a Libyan scholar who lived over 2000 years ago.
     He developed a method to systematically identify prime numbers.
     It is called **Eratosthenes' Sieve**.

     Follow the directions below to identify the prime numbers from 1 to 100.

     a) Cross out the number 1 (it is not prime).

     b) Circle 2, and cross out all the multiples of 2.

     c) Circle 3, and cross out all the multiples of 3
        (that haven't already been crossed out).

     d) Circle 5, and cross out all the multiples of 5
        (that haven't already been crossed out).

     e) Circle 7, and cross out all the multiples of 7
        (that haven't already been crossed out).

     f) Circle all remaining numbers.

     You've just used **Eratosthenes' Sieve** to find
     all the prime numbers from 1 to100!

1	2	3	4	5	6	7	8	9	10
11	12	13	14	15	16	17	18	19	20
21	22	23	24	25	26	27	28	29	30
31	32	33	34	35	36	37	38	39	40
41	42	43	44	45	46	47	48	49	50
51	52	53	54	55	56	57	58	59	60
61	62	63	64	65	66	67	68	69	70
71	72	73	74	75	76	77	78	79	80
81	82	83	84	85	86	87	88	89	90
91	92	93	94	95	96	97	98	99	100

7. The prime numbers 3 and 5 differ by 2.
   Find three pairs of prime numbers less than 20 that differ by 2.

Number Sense 1

1. List all the factors of each number (the first one is done for you).

    a) 25: ____1, 5, 25_____   b) 8: _____

    c) 12: _____   d) 16: _____

    e) 9: _____   f) 18: _____

    g) 50: _____   h) 45: _____

    i) 60: _____   j) 42: _____

2. Put a check mark in front of the numbers that are composite numbers.

    ____ 30   ____ 31   ____ 32   ____ 33   ____ 34   ____ 35   ____ 36   ____ 37

3. Write a number between 0 and 20 that has ...

    a) two factors: _____   b) four factors: _____   c) five factors _____

4. Cross out any number that is *not* a multiple of 4. | 12   19   34   20   50   40 |

5. Write the three numbers less than 40 that have 2 and 5 as factors: _____ _____ _____

ADVANCED
6. Write three consecutive composite numbers.   ☐ ☐ ☐

7. Write five odd multiples of 3 between 10 and 40: _____ _____ _____ _____ _____

8. I am a prime number less than 10.
    If you add 10 or 20 to me, the result is a prime number.
    What number am I?

9. Which number is neither prime nor composite? Explain.

10. Find the **sum** of the first five composite numbers. Show your work.

11. How many prime numbers are there between 30 and 50? Explain how you know.

NS6-18: Prime Factorizations

Any composite number can be written as a product of prime numbers.
This product is called the **prime factorization** of the original number.

>*Example:* Find a prime factorization of 20.
>
>It can't be 10 × 2 (because the number 10 is a composite number).
>
>**5 × 2 × 2** is a prime factorization of 20.

---

1. You can find a prime factorization for a number by using a **factor tree**. Here is how you can make a factor tree for the number 20.

    Step 1:
    Find any pair of numbers (not including one) that multiply to give 20.

    Step 2:
    Repeat Step 1 for the numbers on the "branches" of the tree.

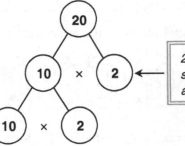

2 is a prime number, so you can leave it as is.

Complete the factor tree for the numbers below.

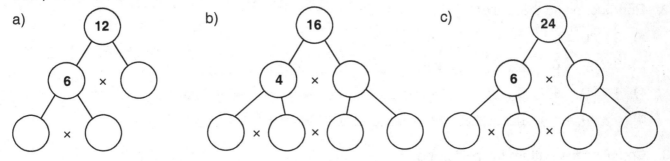

a)   b)   c)

2. Write a prime factorization for each number below. The first one is started for you.
    HINT: It helps to first find any factorization and then factor any composite numbers in the factorization.

    a) 30 = 20 × 3 =   b) 18 =

    c) 8 =   d) 14 =

3. Using a factor tree, find prime factorizations for:
    a) 30   b) 36   c) 27   d) 28   e) 75

4. Here are some branching patterns for factor trees.
    Can you find a factor tree for the number 24 that looks different from the tree in Question 1 c)?

JUMP at Home Grade 6   No Unauthorized Copying

Number Sense 1

To multiply **4 × 20**, Allen makes 4 groups containing 2 <u>tens</u> blocks (20 = 2 tens).

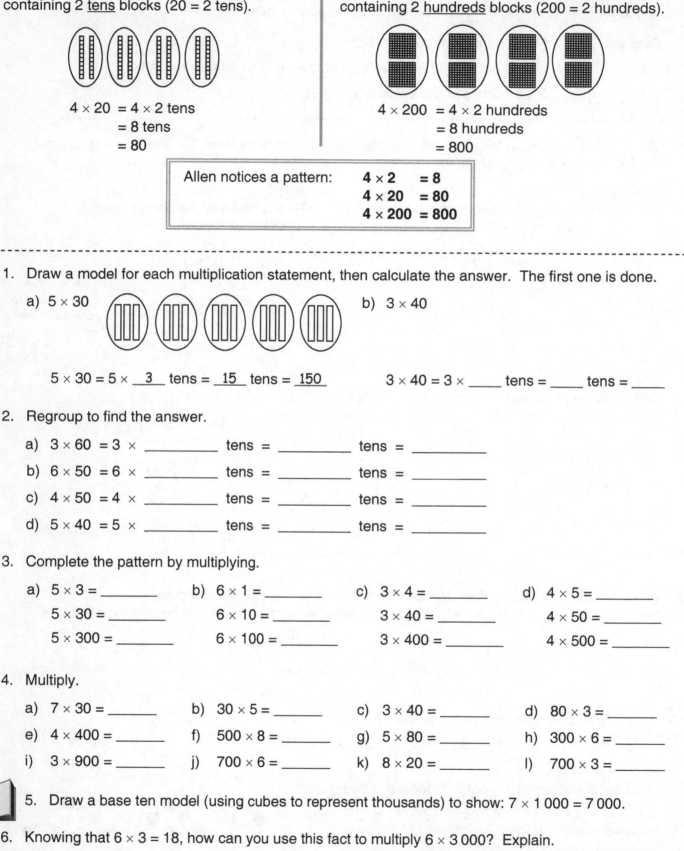

$4 \times 20 = 4 \times 2$ tens
$\quad\quad\quad = 8$ tens
$\quad\quad\quad = 80$

To multiply **4 × 200**, Allen makes 4 groups containing 2 <u>hundreds</u> blocks (200 = 2 hundreds).

$4 \times 200 = 4 \times 2$ hundreds
$\quad\quad\quad\; = 8$ hundreds
$\quad\quad\quad\; = 800$

Allen notices a pattern:
4 × 2	**= 8**
4 × 20	**= 80**
4 × 200	**= 800**

---

1. Draw a model for each multiplication statement, then calculate the answer. The first one is done.

   a) 5 × 30

   b) 3 × 40

   $5 \times 30 = 5 \times \underline{\;3\;}$ tens = $\underline{\;15\;}$ tens = $\underline{\;150\;}$

   $3 \times 40 = 3 \times \underline{\quad}$ tens = $\underline{\quad}$ tens = $\underline{\quad}$

2. Regroup to find the answer.

   a) $3 \times 60 = 3 \times \underline{\qquad}$ tens = $\underline{\qquad}$ tens = $\underline{\qquad}$

   b) $6 \times 50 = 6 \times \underline{\qquad}$ tens = $\underline{\qquad}$ tens = $\underline{\qquad}$

   c) $4 \times 50 = 4 \times \underline{\qquad}$ tens = $\underline{\qquad}$ tens = $\underline{\qquad}$

   d) $5 \times 40 = 5 \times \underline{\qquad}$ tens = $\underline{\qquad}$ tens = $\underline{\qquad}$

3. Complete the pattern by multiplying.

   a) $5 \times 3 = \underline{\qquad}$
      $5 \times 30 = \underline{\qquad}$
      $5 \times 300 = \underline{\qquad}$

   b) $6 \times 1 = \underline{\qquad}$
      $6 \times 10 = \underline{\qquad}$
      $6 \times 100 = \underline{\qquad}$

   c) $3 \times 4 = \underline{\qquad}$
      $3 \times 40 = \underline{\qquad}$
      $3 \times 400 = \underline{\qquad}$

   d) $4 \times 5 = \underline{\qquad}$
      $4 \times 50 = \underline{\qquad}$
      $4 \times 500 = \underline{\qquad}$

4. Multiply.

   a) $7 \times 30 = \underline{\qquad}$
   b) $30 \times 5 = \underline{\qquad}$
   c) $3 \times 40 = \underline{\qquad}$
   d) $80 \times 3 = \underline{\qquad}$

   e) $4 \times 400 = \underline{\qquad}$
   f) $500 \times 8 = \underline{\qquad}$
   g) $5 \times 80 = \underline{\qquad}$
   h) $300 \times 6 = \underline{\qquad}$

   i) $3 \times 900 = \underline{\qquad}$
   j) $700 \times 6 = \underline{\qquad}$
   k) $8 \times 20 = \underline{\qquad}$
   l) $700 \times 3 = \underline{\qquad}$

5. Draw a base ten model (using cubes to represent thousands) to show: $7 \times 1\,000 = 7\,000$.

6. Knowing that $6 \times 3 = 18$, how can you use this fact to multiply $6 \times 3\,000$? Explain.

NS6-20: Mental Math

To multiply **4 × 22**,
Leela rewrites 22 as a sum: 22 = 20 + 2

She first multiplies 4 by 20:   4 × 20 = 80

Next she multiplies 4 by 2:   4 × 2 = 8

Finally she adds the two results: 80 + 8 = 88

So Leela can conclude that **4 × 22 = 88**.

This picture shows why Leela's method works:

4 × 22

4 × 20 = 80   4 × 2 = 8

4 × 22 = (4 × 20) + (4 × 2) = 80 + 8 = 88

----

1. Use the picture to write the multiplication statement as a sum. The first one is started for you.

    a) **2 × 25**

    2 × 20   2 ×

    2 × 25 = (2 × ____) + (2 × ____)

    b) **3 × 15**

    3 × 15 = (_____) + (_____)

2. Multiply using Leela's method. The first one has been done for you.

    a) 5 × 13 = ___5 × 10___ + ___5 × 3___ = ___50 + 15___ = ___65___

    b) 4 × 21 = _____ + _____ = _____ = _____

    c) 3 × 43 = _____ + _____ = _____ = _____

    d) 2 × 432 = ___2 × 400___ + ___2 × 30___ + ___2 × 2___ + 800 + 60 + 4 = ___864___

    e) 3 × 312 = _____

    f) 4 × 321 = _____

3. Multiply in your head by multiplying the digits separately.

    a) 3 × 12 = _____   b) 3 × 52 = _____   c) 6 × 31 = _____   d) 7 × 21 = _____

    e) 5 × 31 = _____   f) 3× 43 = _____   g) 6 × 51 = _____   h) 2 × 44 = _____

    i) 4 × 521 = _____   j) 3 × 621 = _____   k) 5 × 411 = _____   l) 2 × 444 = _____

    m) 3 × 632 = _____   n) 4 × 422 = _____   o) 4 × 212 = _____   p) 2 × 421 = _____

4. a) Stacy placed 821 books in each of 4 bookshelves.
        How many books did she place altogether?

    b) Nickalo put 723 pencils in each of 3 boxes.
        How many pencils did he put in the boxes?

Number Sense 1

NS6-21: The Standard Method for Multiplication

Clara uses a chart to multiply 3 × 42:

Step 1:
She multiplies the ones digit of 42 by 3 (3 × 2 = 6).

	4	2
×		3
		6

Step 2:
She multiplies the tens digit of 42 by 3 (3 × 4 tens = 12 tens).

She regroups 10 tens as 1 hundred.

	4	2
×		3
1	2	6

hundreds   tens

1. Use Clara's method to find the products.

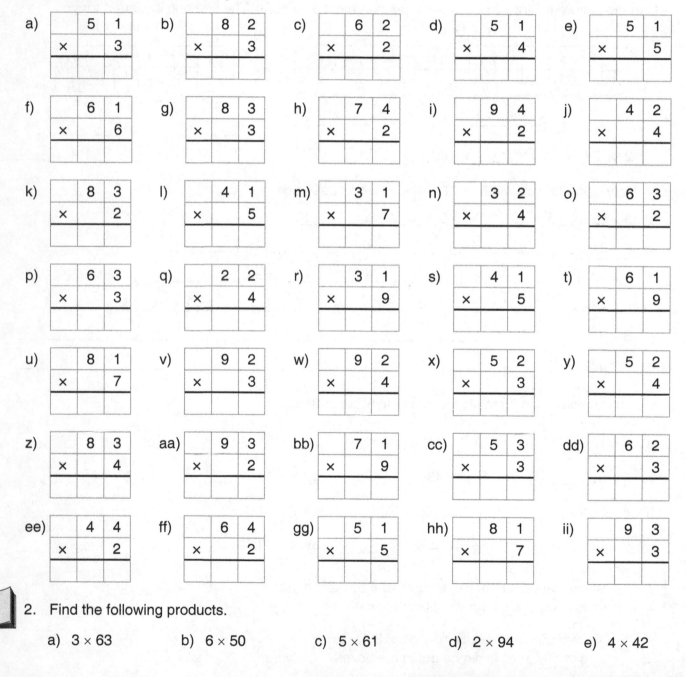

a)
	5	1
×		3

b)
	8	2
×		3

c)
	6	2
×		2

d)
	5	1
×		4

e)
	5	1
×		5

f)
	6	1
×		6

g)
	8	3
×		3

h)
	7	4
×		2

i)
	9	4
×		2

j)
	4	2
×		4

k)
	8	3
×		2

l)
	4	1
×		5

m)
	3	1
×		7

n)
	3	2
×		4

o)
	6	3
×		2

p)
	6	3
×		3

q)
	2	2
×		4

r)
	3	1
×		9

s)
	4	1
×		5

t)
	6	1
×		9

u)
	8	1
×		7

v)
	9	2
×		3

w)
	9	2
×		4

x)
	5	2
×		3

y)
	5	2
×		4

z)
	8	3
×		4

aa)
	9	3
×		2

bb)
	7	1
×		9

cc)
	5	3
×		3

dd)
	6	2
×		3

ee)
	4	4
×		2

ff)
	6	4
×		2

gg)
	5	1
×		5

hh)
	8	1
×		7

ii)
	9	3
×		3

2. Find the following products.

a) 3 × 63   b) 6 × 50   c) 5 × 61   d) 2 × 94   e) 4 × 42

Number Sense 1

Jane uses a chart to multiply 3 × 24:

Step 1:
She multiples 4 ones by 3 (4 × 3 = 12).

She regroups 10 ones as 1 ten.

Step 2:
She multiples 2 tens by 3 (3 × 2 tens = 6 tens).

She adds 1 ten to the result (6 + 1 = 7 tens).

1. Using Alicia's method, complete the <u>first</u> step of the multiplication. The first one has been done.

a) b) c) d) e)

2. Using Alicia's method, complete the <u>second</u> step of multiplication.

a) b) c) d) e)

f) g) h) i) j)

3. Using Alicia's method, complete the <u>first</u> and <u>second</u> steps of the multiplication.

a) b) c) d) e)

f) g) h) i) j)

Dillon multiplies **2 × 213** in <u>three</u> different ways.

1. With a **chart**:

hundreds	tens	ones
2	1	3
×		2
4	2	6

2. In **expanded form**:

$$200 + 10 + 3$$
$$\times\ 2$$
$$= 400 + 20 + 6$$
$$= 426$$

3. With **base ten materials**:

× 2

---

1. Rewrite the multiplication statement in expanded notation. Then perform the multiplication.

a)
```
  234
×   2
```
_____ + _____ + _____
× 2

= _____ + _____ + _____

= _____

b)
```
  133
×   3
```
_____ + _____ + _____
× 3

= _____ + _____ + _____

= _____

2. Multiply.

a)
```
    4 1
×     4
```

b)
```
  4 3 4
×     2
```

c)
```
  3 1 2
×     3
```

d)
```
  1 2 4
×     2
```

e)
```
  3 2 3
×     3
```

3. Multiply by regrouping ones as tens.

a)
```
  2 2 7
×     2
```

b)
```
  2 1 6
×     4
```

c)
```
  2 2 4
×     3
```

d)
```
  4 3 6
×     2
```

e)
```
  1 1 6
×     6
```

4. Multiply by regrouping tens as hundreds. In the last question, you will also regroup ones as tens.

a)
```
  3 6 4
×     2
```

b)
```
  1 5 1
×     6
```

c)
```
  2 4 2
×     4
```

d)
```
  1 7 1
×     5
```

e)
```
  2 5 6
×     3
```

5. Multiply.

a) 5 × 134   b) 7 × 421   c) 6 × 132   d) 9 × 134   e) 8 × 124   f) 6 × 135

6. Draw a picture in your notebook to show the result of the multiplication.

a) _____ × 2

b) _____ × 4

c) _____ × 3

NS6-24: Multiplying by 10, 100 and 1000

1. a) Skip count by 10 fifteen times. What number did you reach? _____

   b) What is the product: $10 \times 15 =$ _____

   c) Skip count by 100 fifteen times. What number did you reach? _____

   d) What is the product: $100 \times 15 =$ _____

2. How many zeroes do you add to a number when you multiply the number by…

   a) 10? You add ___ zero.   b) 100? You add ____ zeroes.   c) 1000? You add ____ zeroes.

3. Continue the pattern.

   a) $10 \times 6 =$ _____

      $100 \times 6 =$ _____

      $1000 \times 6 =$ _____

      $10\,000 \times 6 =$ _____

   b) $10 \times 36 =$ _____

      $100 \times 36 =$ _____

      $1000 \times 36 =$ _____

      $10\,000 \times 36 =$ _____

   c) $10 \times 85 =$ _____

      $100 \times 85 =$ _____

      $1000 \times 85 =$ _____

      $10\,000 \times 85 =$ _____

4. Find the products.

   a) $19 \times 10 =$ _____

   b) $10 \times 56 =$ _____

   c) $10 \times 83 =$ _____

   d) $42 \times 100 =$ _____

   e) $80 \times 100 =$ _____

   f) $13 \times 100 =$ _____

   g) $100 \times 40 =$ _____

   h) $10 \times 23 =$ _____

   i) $1\,000 \times 6 =$ _____

   j) $572 \times 10 =$ _____

   k) $1\,000 \times 28 =$ _____

   l) $93 \times 1\,000 =$ _____

5. Round each number to the **leading digit**.

   Then find the product of the rounded numbers.

   > The first (non-zero) digit in a number – that is, the furthest to the left – is called the **leading digit**.

   leading digit

   a) 12×29

10×30
$= 300$

   b) 11×23

   c) 12×58

   d) 13×74

   e) 68×110

   f) 61×120

6. Al works 38 hours a week. He earns $12 per hour.
   About how much is his weekly income?
   How did you find your answer?

7. How many hundred dollar bills would you need to make …

   a) one hundred thousand dollars?

   b) one million dollars? Explain.

8. Which amount is worth more: 25 723 dimes or 231 524 pennies?

No Unauthorized Copying   **Number Sense 1**

Erin wants to multiply **20 × 32**.

She knows how to find 10 × 32, so she rewrites 20 × 32 as <u>double</u> 10 × 32.

$$20 \times 32 = 2 \times \mathbf{10 \times 32}$$
$$= 2 \times 320$$
$$= 640$$

This picture shows why this works:

A 20 by 32 array contains the same number of squares as two 10 by 32 arrays.

1. Write each number as a product of two factors (where one of the factors is 10).

   a) 30 = _3 × 10_   b) 40 = _____   c) 70 = _____   d) 50 = _____

2. Write an equivalent product for each array. The first one is done for you.

   a)   b)   c)

   20 × 33 = 2 × 10 × 33

   20 × 21 = _____

   30 × 17 = _____

3. Find each product in two stages.

   <u>Step 1</u>: Multiply the second number by 10
   <u>Step 2</u>: Multiply the result by the tens digit of the first number

   a) 20 × 24 = _2 × 240_   b) 30 × 32 = _____   c) 40 × 12 = _____   d) 50 × 41 = _____

       = _____   = _____   = _____   = _____

4. Find each product mentally.

   a) 30 × 33 = _____   b) 20 × 60 = _____   c) 20 × 80 = _____   d) 40 × 34 = _____

   e) 20 × 42 = _____   f) 30 × 83 = _____   g) 64 × 20 = _____   h) 30 × 74 = _____

   i) 40 × 42 = _____   j) 30 × 53 = _____   k) 60 × 51 = _____   l) 91 × 50 = _____

   m) 60 × 30 = _____   n) 80 × 40 = _____   o) 52 × 90 = _____   p) 18 × 30 = _____

5. Estimate each product. (Round each fator to the leading digit.)

   a) 36 × 58 ≈ _40 × 60 = 2 400_   b) 33 × 72 ≈ _____   c) 28 × 82 ≈ _____

   d) 63 × 48 ≈ _____   e) 71 × 32 ≈ _____   f) 21 × 16 ≈ _____

Ed multiplies **20 × 37** by splitting the product into a sum of two smaller products.

$$20 \times 37 = (20 \times 7) + (20 \times 30)$$
$$= 140 + 600$$
$$= 740$$

He keeps track of the steps of the multiplication in a chart.

Step 1:
Ed multiplies 2 × 7 = 14. He is really multiplying **20 × 7** so he first writes a zero in the ones place.

Step 2:
Next, since 2 × 7 = 14, Ed writes the 4 in the tens place and the 1 at the top of the hundreds column.

Step 3:
Ed then multiplies **20 × 30** (= 600). As a short cut, he multiplies 2 × 3 = 6 and then he adds the 1 from the top of the hundreds column: 6 + 1 = 7 (= 700).

----

1. Practise the first two steps of the multiplication (given above). The first one is done for you.
   NOTE: In one of the questions you will not need to regroup the hundreds.

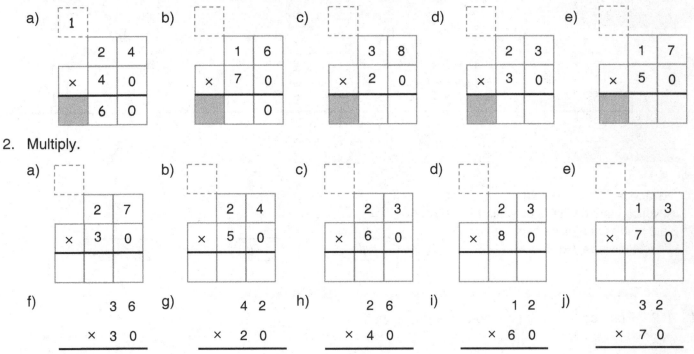

2. Multiply.

3. Rewrite each product as a sum then find the answer.

   a) 20 × 14 = __(20 × 10) + (20 × 4) = 200 + 80 = 280__

   b) 30 × 23 = _____

   c) 40 × 32 = _____

Number Sense 1

NS6-27: Multiplying – 2-Digit by 2-Digit

Grace multiplies **26 × 28** by splitting the product into a sum of two smaller products.

$$26 \times 28 = (6 \times 28) + (20 \times 28)$$
$$= 168 + 560$$
$$= 728$$

She keeps track of the steps of the multiplication using a chart.

1. Practise the first step of the multiplication.

2. Practise the second step of the multiplication.

3. Practise the first two steps of the multiplication.

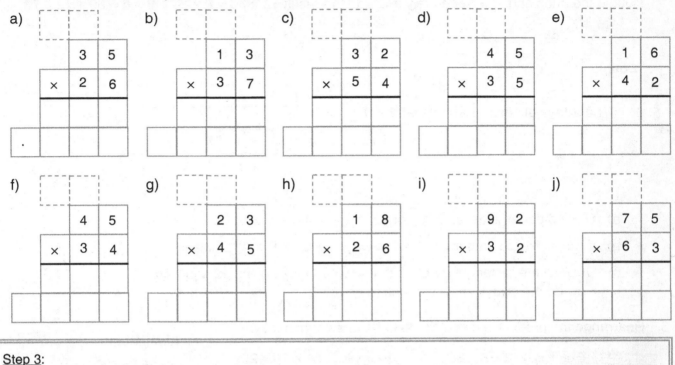

a)
```
      3   5
×     2   6
```

b)
```
      1   3
×     3   7
```

c)
```
      3   2
×     5   4
```

d)
```
      4   5
×     3   5
```

e)
```
      1   6
×     4   2
```

f)
```
      4   5
×     3   4
```

g)
```
      2   3
×     4   5
```

h)
```
      1   8
×     2   6
```

i)
```
      9   2
×     3   2
```

j)
```
      7   5
×     6   3
```

Step 3:
Grace completes the multiplication by adding the products of **6 × 28** and **20 × 28**

4. Complete the multiplication by adding the numbers in the last two rows of the chart.

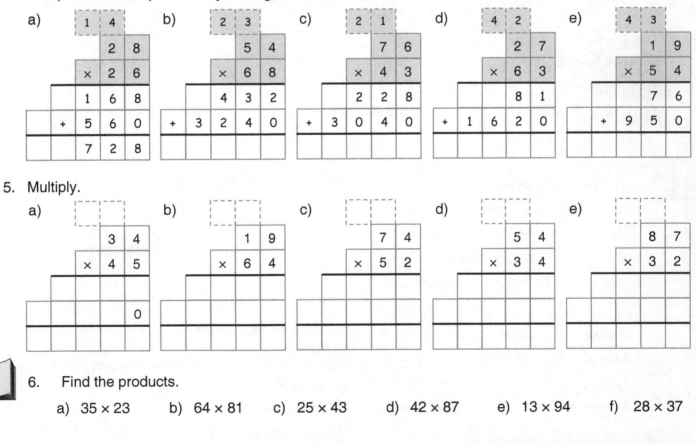

a)
```
   1   4
       2   8
×      2   6
─────────────
       1   6   8
+      5   6   0
─────────────
       7   2   8
```

b)
```
   2   3
       5   4
×      6   8
─────────────
       4   3   2
+  3   2   4   0
```

c)
```
   2   1
       7   6
×      4   3
─────────────
       2   2   8
+  3   0   4   0
```

d)
```
   4   2
       2   7
×      6   3
─────────────
       8   1
+  1   6   2   0
```

e)
```
   4   3
       1   9
×      5   4
─────────────
       7   6
+  9   5   0
```

5. Multiply.

a)
```
      3   4
×     4   5
─────────────


          0
─────────────
```

b)
```
      1   9
×     6   4
```

c)
```
      7   4
×     5   2
```

d)
```
      5   4
×     3   4
```

e)
```
      8   7
×     3   2
```

6. Find the products.

   a) 35 × 23　　b) 64 × 81　　c) 25 × 43　　d) 42 × 87　　e) 13 × 94　　f) 28 × 37

1. Double the ones and tens separately and add the result: $2 \times 36 = 2 \times 30 + 2 \times 6 = 60 + 12 = 72$.

	25	45	16	28	18	17	35	55	39
Double									

2. The arrays of squares show that $2 \times 3 = 3 \times 2$:

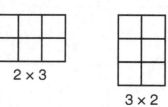

2×3

3×2

   a) On grid paper, draw an array of squares to show that $7 \times 5 = 5 \times 7$

   b) If A and B are numbers, is $A \times B$ always equal to $B \times A$? Explain.

   c) Draw all the rectangular arrays that you can make using 12 squares. How do the arrays show the factors of 12?

3. Rearrange the products so you can find the answer mentally.

   Example: $2 \times 8 \times 35$
   $= 2 \times 35 \times 8$
   $= 70 \times 8$
   $= 560$

   Example: $4 \times 18 \times 25$
   $= 4 \times 25 \times 18$
   $= 100 \times 18$
   $= 1800$

   REMEMBER:
   $2 \times 250 = 500$
   $4 \times 250 = 1\,000$

   a) $2 \times 7 \times 25$

   b) $4 \times 84 \times 25$

   c) $2 \times 29 \times 500$

   d) $4 \times 475 \times 25$

   e) $2 \times 36 \times 2 \times 250$

   f) $25 \times 2 \times 50 \times 4$

   g) $2 \times 2 \times 15 \times 250$

   h) $2 \times 853 \times 500$

   i) $4 \times 952 \times 25$

4.

Printer	Printing Rate
A	1 page every 2 seconds
B	90 pages per minute
C	2 pages every second
D	160 pages in 2 minutes

Which printer is the fastest? Explain how you know.

5.

Amount	Cost
First 20	32 cents for each mango
Next 20	25 cents for each mango
More than 40	17 cents for each mango

The chart shows the price a grocery store pays for mangos.
How much would the following amounts cost?

   a) 15 mangos

   b) 30 mangos

   c) 50 mangos

1. You can multiply a 3-digit number by a 2-digit number using the method you learned previously.

   Multiply.

   a)
   ```
         3   2
             2   1
         3   7   4
     ×       5   3
     ─────────────────
         1   1   2   2
     1   8   7   0
     ─────────────────
     1   9   8   2   2
   ```

   b)
   ```
         4   6   9
     ×       2   3
     ─────────────
   ```

   c)
   ```
         6   8   5
     ×       2   7
     ─────────────
   ```

2. Cross out any number that is <u>not</u> a multiple of 4.

   13   24   32   50   40   2   27

3. Write the odd multiples of 7 that are between 20 and 80.

   [ ]   [ ]   [ ]   [,]   [ ]

4. What is the fifth prime number? Explain how you know.

5. Multiply.

   a) 569 × 34   b) 792 × 87   c) 926 × 96   d) 5243 × 88

6. The Karakoran mountain range in Tibet pushes up 2 cm a year.
   How much higher will the range be in 500 years?

7. Each basket holds 47 apples each. There are 326 baskets.
   How many apples are there altogether?

8. What is the largest factor of 24 that is less than 24?

9. Hassim plays basketball every week for 136 minutes.
   He needs 1 350 minutes to get a job at the summer camp.
   If he plays for 7 weeks, will he have enough hours?

10. Find the missing digits.

   a)
   ```
      3 [ ] 4
    ×       3
    ─────────
      9   7   2
   ```

   b)
   ```
      7 [ ] 7
    ×       5
    ─────────
    3   8   8   5
   ```

   c)
   ```
      2   5   2
    ×       [ ]
    ─────────────
    1   0   0   8
   ```

Abdul has 16 apples. A tray holds 4. There are 4 trays.

What has been shared or divided into **sets** or **groups**?   *(Apples.)*

How many **sets** are there?   *(There are 4 sets of apples.)*

How many of the things being divided are in each **set**?   *(There are 4 apples in each set.)*

----

1. a)   What has been shared or divided into sets?
    _____

    How many sets? _____

    How many in each set? _____

    b)   What has been shared or divided into sets?
    _____

    How many sets? _____

    How many in each set? _____

2.

	What has been shared or divided into sets?	How many sets?	How many in each set?
a) 8 books for each student / 32 books / 4 students			
b) 4 flowers in each vase / 6 flower vases / 24 flowers			
c) 5 apples on each tray / 20 apples / 4 trays			
d) 3 trees in each row / 7 rows / 21 trees			

3. Using circles for <u>sets</u> and dots for <u>things</u>, draw a picture to show…

a) 6 sets
3 things in each set

b) 4 groups
5 things in each group

c) 2 sets
9 things in each set

Amanda has 16 cookies. There are two ways she can **share** (or divide) her cookies equally.

Method 1: She can decide how many <u>sets</u> (or <u>groups</u>) of cookies she wants to make.

Example:
Amanda wants to make 4 sets of cookies. She draws 4 circles. She then puts one cookie at a time into the circles until she has placed all 16 cookies.

Method 2: She can decide how many cookies she wants to put <u>in each set</u>.

Example:
Amanda wants to put 4 cookies in each set. She counts out 4 cookies. She keeps counting out sets of 4 cookies until she has placed all 16 cookies into sets.

---

1. Share **24** dots equally. How many dots are in each set?
   HINT: Place one dot at a time.

   a) 4 sets:

   There are _____ dots in each set.

   b) 6 sets:

   There are _____ dots in each set.

2. Share the shapes equally among the sets.
   HINT: Count the shapes first. Divide by the number of circles.

   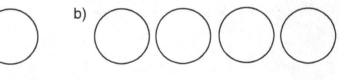

3. Share the squares equally among the sets.

4. Group the lines so that there are three lines in each set. Say how many sets there are.

   a) There are _____ sets.

   b) There are _____ sets

   c) There are _____ sets.

5. Group **18** candies so that…

   a) there are 9 candies in each set.

   b) there are 6 candies in each set.

6. In each question, fill in what you know. Write a question mark for what you don't know.

	What has been shared or divided into sets?	How many sets? or How many in each set?
a) Beth has 42 marbles. She puts 6 marbles in each jar.	marbles	There are 6 marbles in each set
b) 30 people in 6 cars.	people	There are 6 sets of people.
c) Jenny has 18 stickers. She gives them to her 2 sisters.		
d) Mike has 40 pictures. He puts 8 in each page of the album.		
e) 24 children are sitting at 3 tables.		
f) 35 flowers are in 5 vases.		

7. Divide the dots into sets.

   HINT: If you know the number of sets, start by drawing circles for sets. If you know the number of things in each set, fill one circle at a time with the correct number of dots.

   a) 21 dots; 3 sets

   b) 14 dots; 7 dots in each set

   _____ dots in each set

   _____ sets

   c) 36 dots; 9 dots in each set.

   d) 20 dots; 4 sets.

You can solve the division problem **12 ÷ 4 = ?** by skip counting on the number line.

If you divide 12 into sets of size 4, how many sets do you get? The number line shows that it takes three skips of size 4 to get 12.

$$4 + 4 + 4 = 12 \quad \text{so...} \quad 12 \div 4 = 3$$

- -

1. Use the number line to find the answer to the division statement. Be sure to draw arrows to show your skip counting.

a)

$8 \div 2 = $ _____

b)

$16 \div 8 = $ _____

2. What division statement does the picture represent?

a) _____

b) _____

3. You can also find the answer to a division question by skip counting on your fingers.

For instance, to find **45 ÷ 9**, count by 9s until you reach 45... the number of fingers you have up when you say "45" is the answer.

So 45 ÷ 9 = 5

Find the answers by skip counting on your fingers.

a) $35 \div 5 = $ _____   b) $12 \div 6 = $ _____   c) $32 \div 8 = $ _____   d) $21 \div 7 = $ _____   e) $45 \div 5 = $ _____

f) $36 \div 4 = $ _____   g) $25 \div 5 = $ _____   h) $42 \div 6 = $ _____   i) $27 \div 3 = $ _____   j) $16 \div 2 = $ _____

k) $36 \div 6 = $ _____   l) $35 \div 7 = $ _____   m) $18 \div 3 = $ _____   n) $21 \div 3 = $ _____   o) $40 \div 8 = $ _____

4. 24 flowers are in 6 bouquets. How many flowers in each bouquet? _____

5. 36 trees are in 9 rows. How many trees are in each row? _____

6. Amy uses 8 pencils in a month. How many months will she take to use 32 pencils? _____

Win-Chi wants to share 13 pancakes with 3 friends.
He sets out 4 plates, one for himself and one for each of his friends.
He puts one pancake at a time on a plate.

There is one pancake left over.

Thirteen pancakes cannot be shared equally into 4 sets.
Each person gets 3 pancakes, but *one* is left over.
This is the remainder.

13 ÷ 4 = 3 Remainder 1   OR   13 ÷ 4 = 3 R1   NOTE: R means "remainder"

----

1. Can you share 9 pancakes equally onto 2 plates?
   Show your work using dots for pancakes and circles for plates.

2. For each question, share the dots as equally as possible among the circles.

   a) 10 dots in 3 circles

   b) 17 dots in 4 circles

   ____ dots in each circle; ____ dots remaining   ____ dots in each circle; ____ dots remaining

3. Share the dots as equally as possible. Draw a picture and write a division statement.

   a) 13 dots in 3 circles   b) 19 dots in 3 circles   c) 36 dots in 5 circles

   13 ÷ 3 = 4 R1

   d) 33 dots in 4 circles   e) 43 dots in 7 circles

4. Eight friends want to share 25 apples among them.
   How many apples will each friend get?
   How many will be left over?

5. Three siblings have more than 5 and less than 13 animal posters.
   They share the posters evenly with no remainder.
   How many posters do they have? (Show all the possible answers.)

6. Find four different ways to share 19 cookies into equal groups so that one is left over.

Linda is preparing snacks for four classes.
She needs to divide 95 crackers into 4 groups.
She will use long division and a model to solve the problem.

1. Linda has written a division statement to solve a problem.
   How many groups does she want to make?
   How many tens blocks and how many ones would she need to model the problem?

   a) $2 \overline{) 53}$ b) $5 \overline{) 71}$ c) $4 \overline{) 95}$ d) $5 \overline{) 88}$

   groups _____   groups _____   groups _____   groups _____

   tens blocks _____   tens blocks _____   tens blocks _____   tens blocks _____

   ones _____   ones _____   ones _____   ones _____

2. How many tens blocks can be put in each group?

   a) $4 \overline{) 5\ 5}$ b) $5 \overline{) 9\ 7}$ c) $3 \overline{) 7\ 6}$ d) $3 \overline{) 8\ 9}$ e) $4 \overline{) 9\ 2}$

   f) $4 \overline{) 4\ 8}$ g) $5 \overline{) 9\ 7}$ h) $3 \overline{) 8\ 1}$ i) $7 \overline{) 8\ 5}$ j) $8 \overline{) 9\ 6}$

3. For each division statement, write how many groups have been made and how many tens blocks are in each group.

   a) $4 \overline{) 8\ 7}$ b) $3 \overline{) 9\ 4}$ c) $6 \overline{) 7\ 4}$ d) $2 \overline{) 9\ 8}$

   groups _____   groups _____   groups _____   groups _____

   number of tens in
   each group _____

   number of tens in
   each group _____

   number of tens in
   each group _____

   number of tens in
   each group _____

4. For each question, find how many tens have been placed by multiplying.

a)

How many groups? _____

How many tens? _____

How many tens in each group? _____

How many tens placed altogether? _____

b)

How many groups? _____

How many tens? _____

How many tens in each group? _____

How many tens placed altogether? _____

5. Use skip counting to find out how many tens can be placed in each group.
Then use multiplication to find out how many tens have been placed.

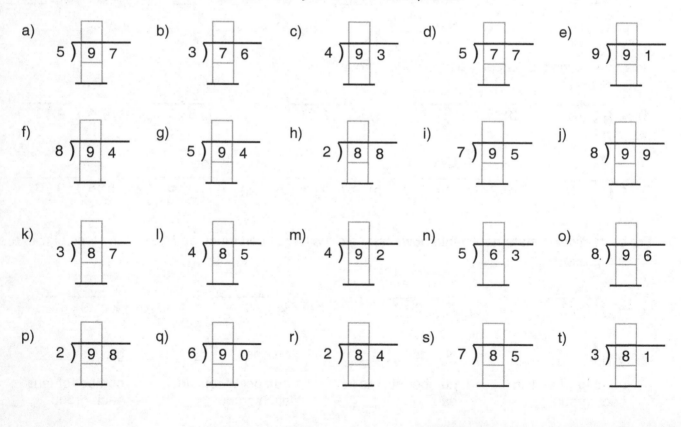

Step 3:

There are 9 tens blocks. Linda has placed 8.

She subtracts to find out how many are left over (9 − 8 = 1).

$$4 \overline{) 9\ 5}$$
$$-\ 8$$
$$\ \ \ 1$$
 with quotient 2

In the model:

So there is 9 − 8 = 1 left over.

6. For each question below, carry out the first <u>three</u> steps of long division.

a) 7) 9 7

b) 3) 7 4

c) 2) 6 3

d) 4) 7 3

e) 6) 8 9

f) 7) 8 5

g) 7) 8 4

h) 3) 8 7

i) 5) 7 1

j) 4) 5 2

Step 4:

There is one tens block left over and 5 ones. So there are 15 ones left over. Linda writes the 5 beside the 1 to show this.

$$4 \overline{) 9\ 5} \quad\longrightarrow\quad 4 \overline{) 9\ 5}$$
$$-\ 8 \qquad\qquad\quad -\ 8\ \downarrow$$
$$\ \ \ 1 \qquad\qquad\qquad 1\ 5$$
with quotient 2

There are this many ones still to place.

In the model:

There are still 15 ones to place in 4 groups.

7. For each question below, carry out the first <u>four</u> steps of long division.

a) 5) 7 5

b) 7) 8 7

c) 4) 9 3

d) 2) 7 3

e) 2) 7 4

f) 8) 9 7

g) 4) 7 6

h) 3) 9 4

i) 7) 9 1

j) 9) 9 4

Step 5:

Linda finds the number of ones he can put in each group by dividing 15 by 4.

$15 \div 4 = 3 \ R = \_\_\_$

In the model:

How can you figure out how many ones are left over?

8. For each question below, carry out the first <u>five</u> steps of long division.

a) 5) 9 4   b) 4) 8 7   c) 2) 7 5   d) 3) 5 1   e) 5) 7 2

f) 7) 8 5   g) 2) 9 5   h) 8) 9 6   i) 3) 9 2   j) 2) 9 3

Steps 6 and 7:

There are 3 ones in each group... and there are 4 groups.

So there are 12 ones altogether in the groups (4 × 3 = 12).

There were 15 ones so there are 3 ones left over (15 – 12 = 3)

In the model:

*There are 12 ones in the groups so there are 3 ones left: **15 – 12 = 3***

The division statement and the model both show that she can give each class 23 crackers with three left over.

9. For each question below, carry out <u>all seven</u> steps of long division.

a) 4) 6 5   b) 6) 7 8   c) 3) 8 4   d) 3) 7 5   e) 3) 9 6

Number Sense 1

f) 4) 7 1

g) 5) 8 4

h) 8) 9 6

i) 7) 8 5

j) 9) 9 5

k) 6) 6 9

l) 4) 7 7

m) 9) 9 4

n) 5) 6 8

o) 6) 9 9

10. Alan put 99 sandwiches on platters of 8. How many sandwiches are left over?

11. How many weeks are in 84 days?

12. Elson arranges 97 books into 7 rows.

   How many rows can he make and how many books are left over?

13. Mita spent $91 to rent a canoe for a week.

   How much did the canoe cost each day?

14.

Saran divides 59 cherries equally among 4 friends

Wendy divides 74 cherries equally among 5 friends.

Who will have more cherries left over?

1. Find 313 ÷ 2 by drawing a base ten model and by long division.

   Step 1: Draw a base ten model of 313.

   Draw your model here:

   Step 2: Divide the hundreds blocks into 2 equal groups.

   number of hundreds in each group

   number of hundreds placed

   number of hundreds left over

   remaining hundreds, tens, and ones

   Step 3: Exchange the leftover hundreds block for 10 tens.

   number of tens left over

   regroup a hundred as 10 tens

   Step 4: Divide the tens blocks into two equal groups.

   number of tens in each group

   number of tens placed

   number of tens left over

   remaining tens and ones

   Step 5: Exchange the leftover tens block for 10 ones.

   number of ones left over

   regroup a ten for 10 ones

Steps 6 and 7:   Divide the ones into 2 equal groups.

2. Divide.

a)   5) 7 8 6

b)   3) 8 3 5

c)   6) 8 7 5

d)   8) 9 9 5

3. In each question below, there are fewer hundreds than the number of groups.
   Write a "0" in the hundreds position to show that no hundreds can be placed in equal groups.
   Then perform the division as if the hundreds had automatically been exchanged for tens.

a)   8) 3 4 6   → 0 4 3 — *4 tens can be placed in each group.*
      − 3 2 ← *32 tens have been placed.*
        2 6
      − 2 4   *2 tens are left over.*
          2

b)   5) 4 7 2

c)   9) 2 9 9

d)   7) 3 6 7

4. Divide.

   a) 3) 115   b) 4) 341   c) 8) 425   d) 6) 379   e) 9) 658

   f) 5) 1525   g) 5) 7523   h) 3) 5213   i) 4) 1785   j) 7) 2213

5. Karen swims 4 laps of a pool.
   Altogether she swims 144 metres. How long is the pool?

6. The perimeter of a six-sided park is 732 km.
   How long is each side of the park?

1. How many pennies would each friend receive if you divided 3 000 pennies among ...

    a) 10 friends? _____   b) 100 friends? _____   c) 1 000 friends? _____

2. Continue the pattern.

    a) 3 000 000 ÷ 10 = <u> 300 000 </u>

    3 000 000 ÷ 100 = _____

    3 000 000 ÷ 1 000 = _____

    3 000 000 ÷ 10 000 = _____

    b) 2 700 000 ÷ 10 = _____

    2 700 000 ÷ 100 = _____

    2 700 000 ÷ 1 000 = _____

    2 700 000 ÷ 10 000 = _____

3. Describe any patterns you see in the question 2.

4. Under which deal do you pay less for each magazine?

52 Issues	52 Issues
First 4 issues free!	First 12 issues free!
$3 for each issue afterwards	$4 for each issue after that

5. Make up two division questions using the numbers in the chart.

Number of animal stickers in a pack	Price of a pack
8	96 cents
6	78 cents
7	91 cents

In the questions below, you will have to interpret what the remainder means.

> *Example:* Lars wants to put 87 hockey cards into a scrapbook. Each page holds 6 cards.
> How many pages will he need?   **87 ÷ 6 = 14 R3**
> Lars will need **15** pages (because he needs a page for the three leftover cards).

6. 4 people can sleep in a tent.
    How many tents are needed for 58 people?

7. 6 friends share 83 stickers.
    How many stickers does each friend receive?

8. A school cafeteria uses 7 loaves of bread each week.
    In how many weeks and days will the cafeteria use 98 loaves of bread?

9. Esther is moving to a new apartment.
    On each trip her car can carry 6 loads of boxes.
    How many trips will she need to make to move 75 boxes?

Number Sense 1

Answer the following questions in your notebook.

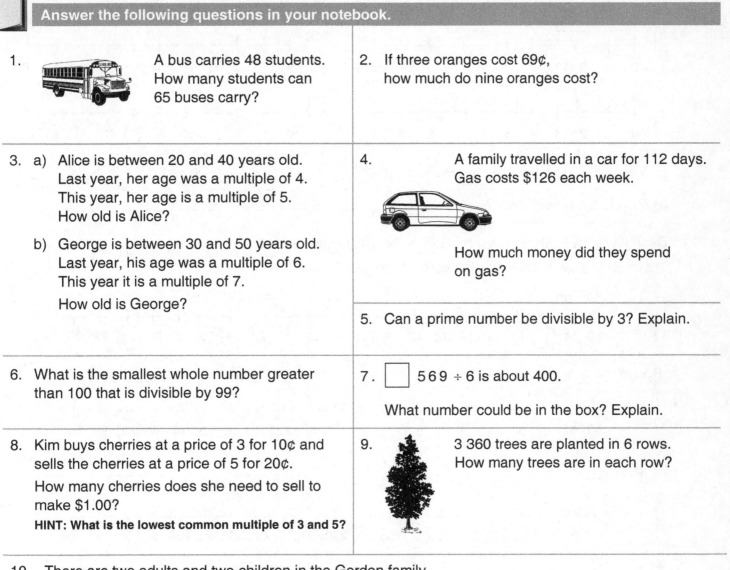

1. A bus carries 48 students. How many students can 65 buses carry?

2. If three oranges cost 69¢, how much do nine oranges cost?

3. a) Alice is between 20 and 40 years old. Last year, her age was a multiple of 4. This year, her age is a multiple of 5. How old is Alice?

   b) George is between 30 and 50 years old. Last year, his age was a multiple of 6. This year it is a multiple of 7. How old is George?

4. A family travelled in a car for 112 days. Gas costs $126 each week.

   How much money did they spend on gas?

5. Can a prime number be divisible by 3? Explain.

6. What is the smallest whole number greater than 100 that is divisible by 99?

7. ☐ 5 6 9 ÷ 6 is about 400.

   What number could be in the box? Explain.

8. Kim buys cherries at a price of 3 for 10¢ and sells the cherries at a price of 5 for 20¢.

   How many cherries does she need to sell to make $1.00?

   HINT: What is the lowest common multiple of 3 and 5?

9. 3 360 trees are planted in 6 rows. How many trees are in each row?

10. There are two adults and two children in the Gordon family.

    The ticket price for a play was $12.50 for adults and $8.50 for children.

    How much money did the family have to pay for the tickets?

    If they received $8 in change, what amount did they pay with?

11. ➢ Choose a number less than 10 and greater than 0.

    ➢ If the number is even, halve it and add one. If the number is odd, double it.

    ➢ Again, if the new number is even, halve it and add one. If the new number is odd, double it.

    a) Continue the number snake for the example. What happens?

    b) Investigate which one-digit number makes the longest snake.

    c) Try starting a number snake with a two-digit number. What happens?

    Example:
    9
    9 → 18
    9 → 18 → 10

1. Draw an arrow to the 0 or 10 to show whether the circled number is closer to **0 or 10**.

a)

```
←————————————————————————————————
  0   1   2  ③   4   5   6   7   8   9  10
```

b)

```
  0   1   2   3   4   5   6   7  ⑧   9  10
```

c)

```
  0   1  ②   3   4   5   6   7   8   9  10
```

d)

```
  0   1   2   3   4   5  ⑥   7   8   9  10
```

2. a) Which one-digit numbers are closer to i) 0? _____ ii) 10? _____

   b) Why is 5 a special case? _____

3. Draw an arrow to show which multiple of ten you would round to.
   Then round each number to the nearest tens.

   a)

```
←————————————————————————————————————————————————————
 10  11 ⑫ 13  14  15  16  17  18  19  20  21  22 ㉓ 24  25  26  27 ㉘ 29  30
```

   Round to _____10_____   _____   _____

   b)

```
 60  61  62  63  64  65  66 ⑥⑦ 68  69  70  71  72 ⑦③ 74  75  76  77 ⑦⑧ 79  80
```

   Round to   _____   _____   _____

   c)

```
250 251 252 253 ㉕④ 255 256 ㉕⑦ 258 259 260 261 262 263 264 265 266 267 ㉖⑧ 269 270
```

   Round to _____ _____   _____

4. Circle the correct answer.

   a) 21 is closer to 20 or 30   b) 12 is closer to 10 or 20

   c) 38 is closer to 30 or 40   d) 75 is closer to 70 or 80

   e) 252 is closer to 250 or 260   f) 586 is closer to 580 or 590

5. Draw an arrow to show whether the circled number is closer to 0 or 100.

   a)

```
  0  10  20  30  40  50  60 ⑦⓪ 80  90 100
```

   b)

```
  0  10  20  30 ④⓪ 50  60  70  80  90 100
```

6. Is 50 closer to 0 or to 100? Why is 50 a special case?

Number Sense 1

7. Circle the correct answer.

   a) 70 is closer to: 0 or 100   b) 30 is closer to: 0 or 100

   c) 60 is closer to: 0 or 100   d) 10 is closer to: 0 or 100

8. Show the approximate position of each number on the line. What multiple of 100 would you round to?

   a) 642   b) 684   c) 793   d) 701

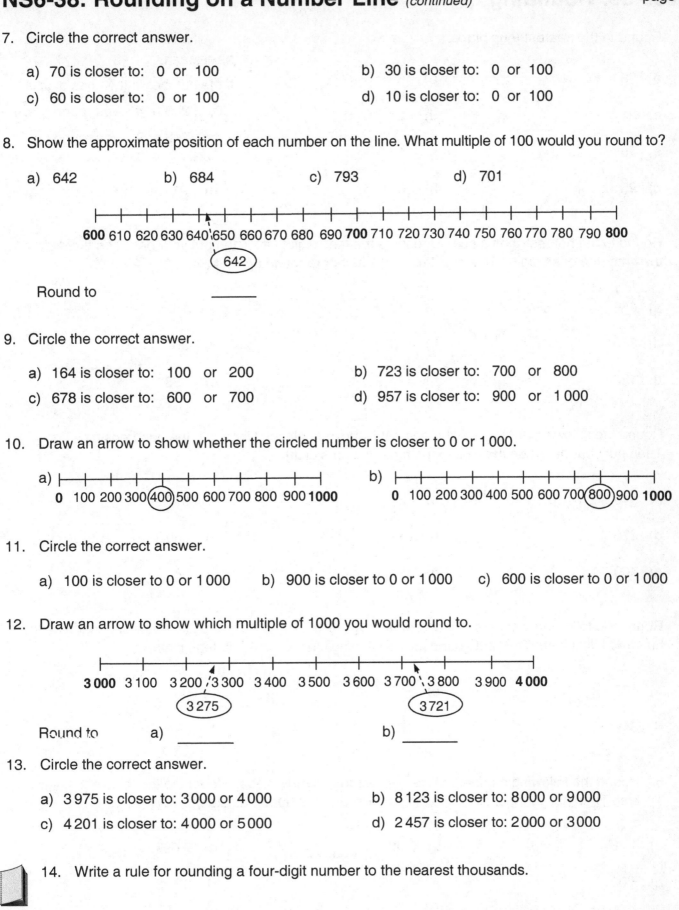

   Round to   _____

9. Circle the correct answer.

   a) 164 is closer to: 100 or 200   b) 723 is closer to: 700 or 800

   c) 678 is closer to: 600 or 700   d) 957 is closer to: 900 or 1 000

10. Draw an arrow to show whether the circled number is closer to 0 or 1 000.

11. Circle the correct answer.

   a) 100 is closer to 0 or 1 000   b) 900 is closer to 0 or 1 000   c) 600 is closer to 0 or 1 000

12. Draw an arrow to show which multiple of 1000 you would round to.

   Round to   a) _____   b) _____

13. Circle the correct answer.

   a) 3 975 is closer to: 3 000 or 4 000   b) 8 123 is closer to: 8 000 or 9 000

   c) 4 201 is closer to: 4 000 or 5 000   d) 2 457 is closer to: 2 000 or 3 000

14. Write a rule for rounding a four-digit number to the nearest thousands.

1. Round to the nearest <u>tens</u> place.

a) 38 [ ]   b) 46 [ ]

REMEMBER:

If the number in the ones digit is:

   0, 1, 2, 3 or 4 – you round <u>down</u>

   5, 6, 7, 8 or 9 – you round <u>up</u>

c) 21 [ ]   d) 62 [ ]

e) 79 [ ]   f) 81 [ ]

g) 25 [ ]   h) 36 [ ]   i) 91 [ ]

2. Round to the nearest <u>tens</u> place. Underline the tens digit first. Then put your pencil on the digit to the right (the ones digit). This digit tells you whether to round up or down.

a) 65̲6 [660]   b) 273 [ ]   c) 152 [ ]

d) 355 [ ]   e) 418 [ ]   f) 566 [ ]

g) 128 [ ]   h) 467 [ ]   i) 338 [ ]

3. Round the following numbers to the nearest <u>hundreds</u> place. Underline the hundreds digit first. Then put your pencil on the digit to the right (the tens digit).

a) 3̲40 [300]   b) 490 [ ]   c) 570 [ ]

d) 270 [ ]   e) 160 [ ]   f) 360 [ ]

g) 460 [ ]   h) 840 [ ]   i) 980 [ ]

4. Round the following numbers to the nearest <u>hundreds</u> place. As in the last question, underline the hundreds digit first. Then put your pencil on the digit to the right (the tens digit).

a) 167 [ ]   b) 347 [ ]   c) 567 [ ]

d) 349 [ ]   e) 873 [ ]   f) 291 [ ]

5. Round the following numbers to the nearest <u>thousands</u> place. Underline the thousands digit first. Then put your pencil on the digit to the right (the hundreds digit).

a) 4̲ 787 [5 000]   b) 3 092 [ ]   c) 7 697 [ ]

d) 5 021 [ ]   e) 2 723 [ ]   f) 8 538 [ ]

6. Underline the digit you wish to round to. Then say whether you would round up or down.

a) *hundreds*

| 7 | 3 | 2 | 5 |

round up
~~round down~~ (circled)

b) *hundreds*

| 4 | 1 | 2 | 7 |

round up
round down

c) *tens*

| 4 | 9 | 6 | 3 |

round up
round down

d) *thousands*

| 8 | 3 | 8 | 6 | 4 |

round up
round down

e) *ten thousands*

| 4 | 6 | 5 | 2 | 3 |

round up
round down

f) *ten thousands*

| 1 | 2 | 5 | 5 | 9 |

round up
round down

7. Complete the two steps from Question 6. Then follow the two steps below.

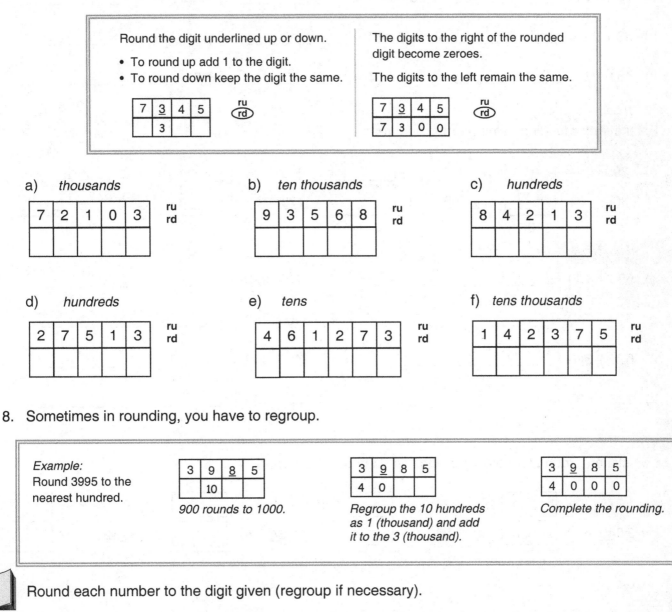

Round the digit underlined up or down.

- To round up add 1 to the digit.
- To round down keep the digit the same.

| 7 | 3 | 4 | 5 | ru (rd)
| | 3 | | |

The digits to the right of the rounded digit become zeroes.

The digits to the left remain the same.

| 7 | 3 | 4 | 5 | ru (rd)
| 7 | 3 | 0 | 0 |

a) *thousands*

| 7 | 2 | 1 | 0 | 3 | ru rd

b) *ten thousands*

| 9 | 3 | 5 | 6 | 8 | ru rd

c) *hundreds*

| 8 | 4 | 2 | 1 | 3 | ru rd

d) *hundreds*

| 2 | 7 | 5 | 1 | 3 | ru rd

e) *tens*

| 4 | 6 | 1 | 2 | 7 | 3 | ru rd

f) *tens thousands*

| 1 | 4 | 2 | 3 | 7 | 5 | ru rd

8. Sometimes in rounding, you have to regroup.

Example:
Round 3995 to the nearest hundred.

| 3 | 9 | 8 | 5 |
| | 10 | | |

900 rounds to 1000.

| 3 | 9 | 8 | 5 |
| 4 | 0 | | |

Regroup the 10 hundreds as 1 (thousand) and add it to the 3 (thousand).

| 3 | 9 | 8 | 5 |
| 4 | 0 | 0 | 0 |

Complete the rounding.

Round each number to the digit given (regroup if necessary).

a) 3 293   *tens*

b) 5 921   *hundreds*

c) 9 723   *thousands*

d) 13 975   *tens*

e) 23 159   *hundreds*

f) 999 857   *ten thousands*

g) 395 321   *hundred thousands*

NS6-40: Estimating Sums and Differences

1. Estimate the sums and differences.

$\approx$ ⟵ Mathematicians use this symbol to mean **"approximately equal to."**

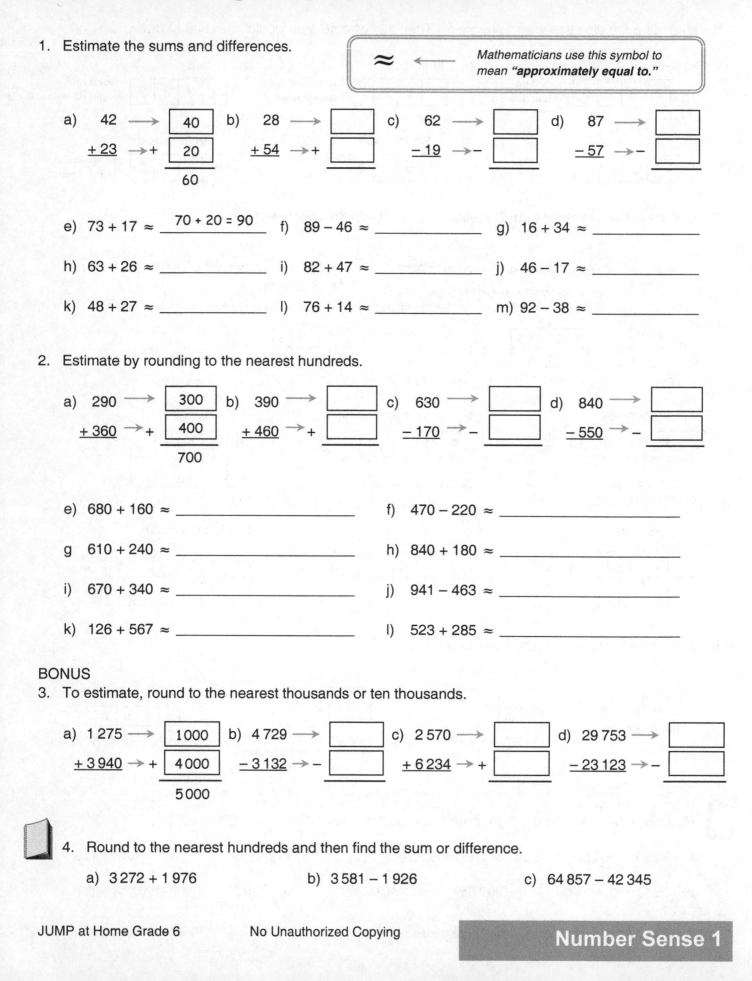

a) 42 ⟶ | 40 |
   + 23 ⟶ + | 20 |
   ‾‾‾‾‾‾
       60

b) 28 ⟶ | |
   + 54 ⟶ + | |

c) 62 ⟶ | |
   − 19 ⟶ − | |

d) 87 ⟶ | |
   − 57 ⟶ − | |

e) 73 + 17 ≈ _70 + 20 = 90_   f) 89 − 46 ≈ _____   g) 16 + 34 ≈ _____

h) 63 + 26 ≈ _____   i) 82 + 47 ≈ _____   j) 46 − 17 ≈ _____

k) 48 + 27 ≈ _____   l) 76 + 14 ≈ _____   m) 92 − 38 ≈ _____

2. Estimate by rounding to the nearest hundreds.

a) 290 ⟶ | 300 |
   + 360 ⟶ + | 400 |
   ‾‾‾‾‾‾
       700

b) 390 ⟶ | |
   + 460 ⟶ + | |

c) 630 ⟶ | |
   − 170 ⟶ − | |

d) 840 ⟶ | |
   − 550 ⟶ − | |

e) 680 + 160 ≈ _____   f) 470 − 220 ≈ _____

g   610 + 240 ≈ _____   h) 840 + 180 ≈ _____

i) 670 + 340 ≈ _____   j) 941 − 463 ≈ _____

k) 126 + 567 ≈ _____   l) 523 + 285 ≈ _____

BONUS
3. To estimate, round to the nearest thousands or ten thousands.

a) 1 275 ⟶ | 1000 |
   + 3 940 ⟶ + | 4000 |
   ‾‾‾‾‾‾
       5 000

b) 4 729 ⟶ | |
   − 3 132 ⟶ − | |

c) 2 570 ⟶ | |
   + 6 234 ⟶ + | |

d) 29 753 ⟶ | |
   − 23 123 ⟶ − | |

4. Round to the nearest hundreds and then find the sum or difference.

   a) 3 272 + 1 976   b) 3 581 − 1 926   c) 64 857 − 42 345

Answer the following questions in your notebook.

1. The population of Saskatchewan is 995 000 and the population of New Brunswick is 750 500.

   Estimate the difference in the two populations.

   Saskatchewan   **New Brunswick**

2. The population of Newfoundland is 520 200 and the population of Prince Edward Island is 137 900.

   Estimate the total population of the two provinces.

   Newfoundland   **Prince Edward Island**

3. Round 628 315 to the nearest:
   a) tens
   b) hundreds
   c) thousands
   d) ten thousands

4. Estimate the products by rounding to the leading digits.
   a) 32×75
   b) 492×81
   c) 307×12
   d) 2759×812

5. Estimate the following total amounts.
   a) 6 tapes at $4.99 a tape
   b) 5 pies at $3.12 a pie
   c) 8 books at $7.87 a book

6. Jacques multiplied a 1-digit number by a 3-digit number. The product was about 1 000.

   Describe three different pairs of numbers he might have multiplied.

7. The populations of New Brunswick and Nova Scotia are listed in an almanac as 750 000 and 936 900.

   What digit do you think these numbers have been rounded to? Explain.

   Nova Scotia

8. There are 1 483 beads in a jar.

   It takes 58 beads to make a bracelet.

   Sandra estimates that she can make 30 bracelets.

   Is her estimate reasonable? Explain.

9. A supermarket sold 472 apples, 783 oranges, 341 pears, and 693 bananas.
   a) How many pieces of fruit did they sell in all?
   b) Use estimation to check your solution. Explain your estimation strategy.

10. To estimate the difference 1 875 – 1 432, should you round the numbers to the nearest thousands or the nearest hundreds? Explain.

Answer the following questions in your notebook.

1. Predict which range each product or quotient will lie in before you perform the calculation.

A. 1 to 10	**B.** 11 to 100	**C.** 101 to 500	**D.** 501 to 1 000	**E.** above 1 000

   a) 37×25 b) $4\,279 \div 70$ c) $13\,200 \div 600$ d) 45×87

2. Which method of estimation will work best for each calculation below? Justify your answers.

   • Rounding   • Front-end estimation (round both numbers down to the leading digit)
   • Rounding one number up and one number down

   a) $657 + 452$ b) $891 + 701$ c) $425 + 375$ d) $395 - 352$

   For which question does neither method work well?

3. Use any method of estimation you choose to judge whether the answer is reasonable.
   Then perform the calculation to check if the answer is correct.

   a) $3\,875 + 2\,100 = 8\,257$ b) $37 \times 435 = 1\,285$ c) $9\,352 - 276 = 9\,076$

4. Some calculations are easy because ...

You can group numbers that add to 10 or 100.	You can do the calculation in steps.	You don't have to regroup.
$4\,\overline{7} + 3\,\overline{3} + 5\,\overline{40} + 3\,\overline{60}$	$100 - 23$ $= 100 - 20 - 3$	$3 \times 213 = 639$

   Which calculations below could you do mentally? Describe your method.
   For the harder calculations, say how you would estimate.

   a) $3\,875 - 1\,325$ b) $800 - 53$ c) 876×9 d) $7\,521 + 9\,859$

   e) 532×3 f) $321 + 587 + 413 + 379$ g) $42\,000 \div 70$

5. Write a number that could be rounded to:

   a) 1 000 or 1 400.

   b) 6 000 or 5 900 or 5 870.

6. How would you estimate ...

   a) the length of a row of 10 000 loonies?

   b) the number of seconds in a year?

Temperature is recorded on a scale that includes **negative** and **positive** whole numbers.

These numbers are called **integers**.

Negative integers indicate a
temperature <u>below</u> zero.

Positive integers indicate a
temperature <u>above</u> zero.

1. Write an integer for each days temperature.
   How much did the temperature change from day to day?
   (If the temperature fell, write a negative sign in front of your answer)

	Sunday	Monday	Tuesday	Wednesday	Thursday
Temperature (°c)	− 5	+ 15			
Change in temperature					

2.

   a) Mark the numbers on the number line.
      A: − 5   **B:** + 2   **C:** − 7   **D:** + 5   **E:** − 3

   b) How many spaces apart are the numbers?

      i) − 5 and − 4: _____ ii) − 2 and + 3: _____ iii) + 6 and + 8: _____

   c) How many negative numbers are greater than (ie. to the right of) − 4? _____

3. Leela recorded the winter temperatures shown in the chart.
   How much did the temperature change ...

   a) from Monday to Tuesday? _____

   b) from Tuesday to Wednesday? _____

   c) from Wednesday to Thursday? _____

Monday	Tuesday	Wednesday	Thursday
+ 5°C	− 2°C	− 7°C	+ 1°C

4. The chart shows the average temperature on the planets.

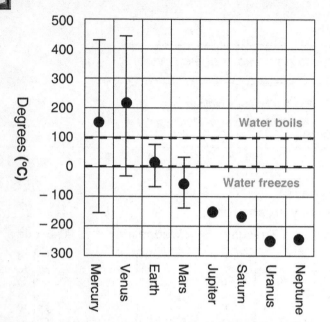

a) Which planet has the lowest temperature?

b) How much lower is the temperature on Uranus than on Jupiter?

c) The **range** of a set of numbers is the difference between the highest and lowest numbers.

   What is the range of temperatures on Mercury?

5. The number line below shows the approximate dates when animals were first domesticated.

a) Which type of animal was domesticated first?

b) How many years after cows were domesticated were cats domesticated?

c) How many years after horses were domesticated were rabbits domesticated?

d) Pick two animals. How many years after the first animal was the second animal domesticated?

6. Mackerel live about 200 m below sea level.
   Gulper eels live at 1 000 m below sea level.
   Write integers for the depths where the animals live.
   How far below the mackerel does the gulper eel live?

7. How many negative integers are greater than –6?

8. Why are –3 and +3 closer to each other than –4 and +4?

Number Sense 1

Many problems in mathematics and science have more than one solution.

If a problem involves two quantities, you can be sure you haven't missed any possible solutions if you list the values of one of the quantities in increasing order.

Example:

Find all the ways you can make 35¢ with dimes and nickels. Start with no dimes, then 1 dime, and so on up to 3 dimes (4 would be too many).

Then, count on by 5s to 35 to find out how many nickels you need to make 35¢.

Step 1:

dimes	nickels
0	
1	
2	
3	

Step 2:

dimes	nickels
0	7
1	5
2	3
3	1

----

1. Fill in the amount of pennies, nickels, dimes or quarters you need to…

a) Make 17¢

nickels	pennies
0	
1	
2	
3	

b) Make 45¢

dimes	nickels
0	
1	
2	
3	
4	

c) Make 23¢

nickels	pennies
0	
1	
2	
3	
4	

d) Make 32¢

dimes	pennies
0	
1	
2	
3	

e) Make 65¢

quarters	nickels
0	
1	
2	

f) Make 85¢

quarters	nickels

2.

quarters	nickels
0	
1	
2	

Ben wants to find all the ways he can make 60¢ using quarters and nickels. He lists the number of quarters in increasing order. Why did he stop at 2 quarters?

_____

_____

3. Make a chart to show all the ways you can make the given amount.

a) 90¢ using dimes and nickels

b) 125¢ using quarters and dimes

Example:

Alana wants to find all pairs of numbers that multiply to give 15.

There are no numbers that will multiply by 2 or 4 to give 15, so Alana leaves those rows in her chart blank.

The numbers in the last row of the chart are the same as those in the third row so Alana knows she has found all pairs.

$1 \times 15 = 15$ $\qquad$ $3 \times 5 = 15$

1st Number	2nd Number
1	15
2	---
3	5
4	---
5	3

----

4. Find all pairs of numbers that multiply to give the number in bold.

a) **6**

First Number	Second Number

b) **8**

First Number	Second Number

5.

quarters	dimes
0	
1	
2	

Alicia wants to find all the ways she can make 70¢ using quarters and dimes.

One of the entries on her chart won't work. Which one is it?

6. Find all the ways to make the amounts using quarters and dimes.
NOTE: Some entries on your chart may not work.

a) 80¢

quarters	dimes
0	
1	
2	

b) 105¢

quarters	dimes

7. Find all the widths and lengths of a rectangle with perimeter 12 units.

Width	Length
1	

8. Make a chart to find all the pairs of numbers that multiply to give.

a) 12 $\qquad$ b) 14 $\qquad$ c) 20 $\qquad$ d) 24

1. In the sequences below, the step or gap between the numbers increases or decreases.
   Can you see a pattern in the way the gap changes?

   Use the pattern to extend the sequence.

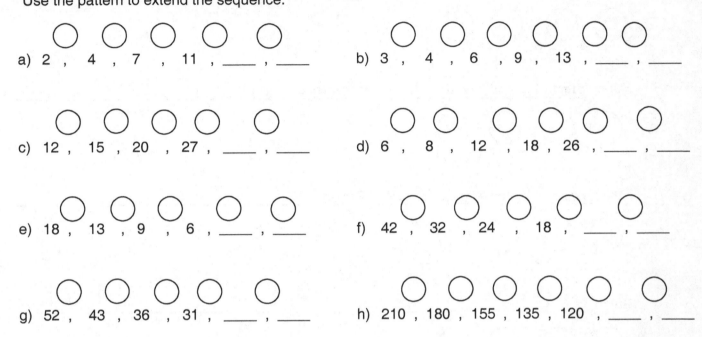

a) 2 , 4 , 7 , 11 , ___ , ___

b) 3 , 4 , 6 , 9 , 13 , ___ , ___

c) 12 , 15 , 20 , 27 , ___ , ___

d) 6 , 8 , 12 , 18 , 26 , ___ , ___

e) 18 , 13 , 9 , 6 , ___ , ___

f) 42 , 32 , 24 , 18 , ___ , ___

g) 52 , 43 , 36 , 31 , ___ , ___

h) 210 , 180 , 155 , 135 , 120 , ___ , ___

2. Complete the T-table for Figure 3 and Figure 4. Then use the pattern in the gap to predict the number of triangles needed for Figures 5 and 6.

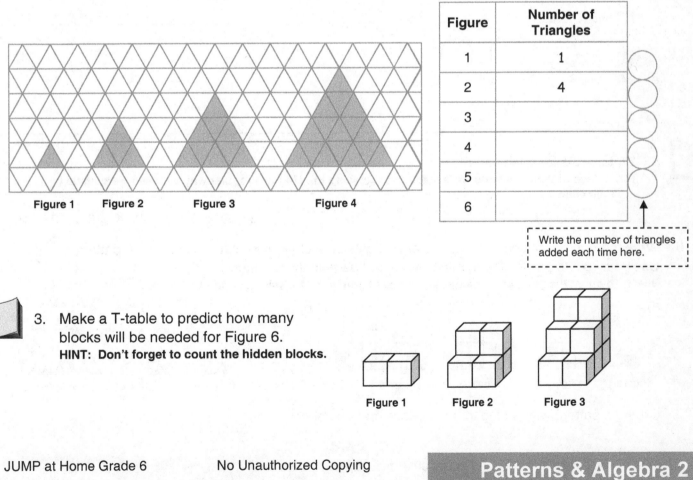

Figure	Number of Triangles	
1	1	
2	4	
3		
4		
5		
6		

Figure 1   Figure 2   Figure 3   Figure 4

Write the number of triangles added each time here.

3. Make a T-table to predict how many blocks will be needed for Figure 6.
   HINT: Don't forget to count the hidden blocks.

Figure 1   Figure 2   Figure 3

4. In each sequence below, the **step** changes in a regular way (it increases, decreases, or increases and decreases). Write a rule for each pattern.

a) 2 , 4 , 8 , 14 , 22
   (+2) (+4) (+6) (+8)

   Rule: ___Start at 2. Add 2, 4, 6 ... (the step increases by 2).___

b) 7 , 11 , 9 , 13 , 11
   (+4) (−2) (+4) (−2)

   Rule : ___Start at 7. Add 4, then subtract 2. Repeat.___

c) 2 , 3 , 5 , 8 , 12
   ◯ ◯ ◯ ◯

   Rule: _____

d) 5 , 7 , 4 , 6 , 3
   ◯ ◯ ◯ ◯

   Rule: _____

e) 34 , 33 , 30 , 25 , 18
   ◯ ◯ ◯ ◯

   Rule: _____

5. Write a rule for each pattern.
    HINT: Two of these patterns were made by increasing the step in a regular way, and two were made by multiplication.

    a) 2 , 5 , 10 , 17   b) 2 , 4 , 8 , 16   c) 1 , 3 , 9 , 27   d) 4 , 6 , 10 , 16

6. Write the number of shaded squares or triangles in each figure. Write a rule for the pattern. Use your rule to predict the number of shaded parts in the 5th figure.
    HINT: To count the number of triangles in the last figure in b), try skip counting by 3s.

a)   b)

Figure 1   Figure 2   Figure 3   Figure 4   Figure 1   Figure 2   Figure 3   Figure 4

7. Create a pattern with a step that increases and decreases.

Answer the following questions in your notebook.

1. The dots show how many people can sit along each side of a table.

Number of Tables	Number of People	

a) Draw a picture to show how many people could sit at 4 and 5 tables. Then, fill in the T-table.

b) Describe the pattern in the number of people. How does the step change?

c) Extend the pattern to find out how many people could sit at 8 tables.

2. a) The Ancient Greeks investigated numbers that could be arranged in geometric shapes.

1   3   6   10

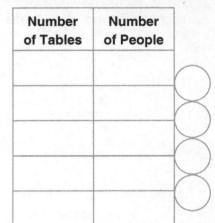

The first four **triangular** numbers are shown here to the left.

   i) Find the 5th and 6th triangular numbers by drawing a picture.

   ii) Describe the pattern in the triangular numbers. How does the step change?

   iii) Find the 8th triangular number by extending the pattern you found in ii).

b) Repeat steps i) to iii) with the **square** numbers.

1   4   9   16

3. One of the most famous sequences in mathematics is the **Fibonacci sequence**, shown below.

a) Find the gap between terms, then use the pattern in the gap to continue the sequence.

1 , 1 , 2 , 3 , 5 , 8 , 13 , 21 , ____ , ____

b) What pattern do you see in the number of odd and even numbers in the Fibonacci sequence?

c) Sum the first 4 odd Fibonacci numbers. Then sum the first 2 even numbers. What do you notice?

d) Sum the first six odd Fibonacci numbers and the first three even numbers. What to you notice?

1. Use addition or multiplication to complete the following charts.

a)

Years	Weeks
1	52
2	
3	
4	

b)

Years	Days
1	365
2	
3	

c)

Hours	Seconds
1	3600
2	
3	
4	

2. Water drains from two tanks at the rate shown in the chart below. Describe the pattern in the numbers in each column.

Which tank do you think will empty first?

Minutes	Tank 1	Tank 2
1	500 L	500 L
2	460 L	490 L
3	420 L	470 L
4	380 L	440 L

3. a) How much fuel will be left in the airplane after 25 minutes?

    b) How far from the airport will the plane be after 30 minutes?

    c) How much fuel will be left in the airplane when it reaches the airport?

Minutes	Litres of Fuel	km from Airport
0	1200	525
5	1150	450
10	1100	375

4. Halley's Comet returns to Earth every 76 years. It was last seen in 1986.

    a) How many times will the comet be seen in the 2000s?

    b) When was the first time Halley's Comet was seen in the 1900s?

5. Use multiplication to find the first few products. Look for a pattern.
    Use the pattern you've described to fill in the rest of the numbers.

a) $37 \times 3 =$ _____

        $37 \times 6 =$ _____

        $37 \times 9 =$ _____

        $37 \times 12 =$ _____

        _____ $=$ _____

b) $9 \times 2\,222 =$ _____

        $9 \times 3\,333 =$ _____

        $9 \times 4\,444 =$ _____

        $9 \times 5\,555 =$ _____

        _____ $=$ _____

6.   Using a calculator, can you discover any patterns like the ones in Question 5?

Patterns & Algebra 2

PA6-22: Equations

1. In a word problem an empty box can stand for an unknown quantity.
   Find the missing number in each problem and write it in the box.

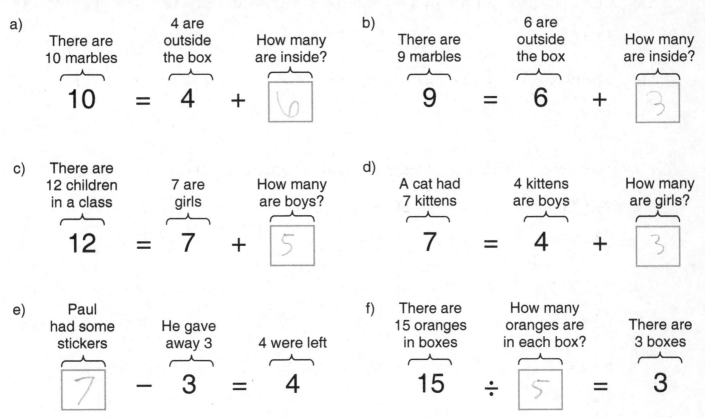

a)
There are 10 marbles | 4 are outside the box | How many are inside?

$$10 = 4 + \boxed{6}$$

b)
There are 9 marbles | 6 are outside the box | How many are inside?

$$9 = 6 + \boxed{3}$$

c)
There are 12 children in a class | 7 are girls | How many are boys?

$$12 = 7 + \boxed{5}$$

d)
A cat had 7 kittens | 4 kittens are boys | How many are girls?

$$7 = 4 + \boxed{3}$$

e)
Paul had some stickers | He gave away 3 | 4 were left

$$\boxed{7} - 3 = 4$$

f)
There are 15 oranges in boxes | How many oranges are in each box? | There are 3 boxes

$$15 \div \boxed{5} = 3$$

2. Find the number that makes each equation true (by guessing and checking) and write it in the box.

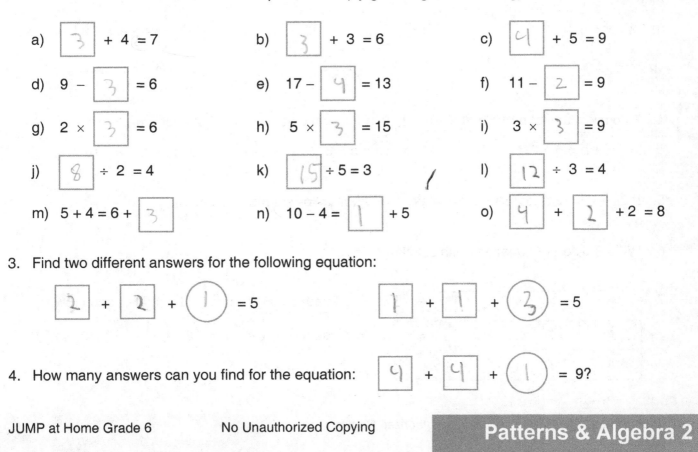

a) $\boxed{3} + 4 = 7$

b) $\boxed{3} + 3 = 6$

c) $\boxed{4} + 5 = 9$

d) $9 - \boxed{3} = 6$

e) $17 - \boxed{4} = 13$

f) $11 - \boxed{2} = 9$

g) $2 \times \boxed{3} = 6$

h) $5 \times \boxed{3} = 15$

i) $3 \times \boxed{3} = 9$

j) $\boxed{8} \div 2 = 4$

k) $\boxed{15} \div 5 = 3$

l) $\boxed{12} \div 3 = 4$

m) $5 + 4 = 6 + \boxed{3}$

n) $10 - 4 = \boxed{1} + 5$

o) $\boxed{4} + \boxed{2} + 2 = 8$

3. Find two different answers for the following equation:

$$\boxed{2} + \boxed{2} + \bigcirc\!\!\!1 = 5 \qquad \boxed{1} + \boxed{1} + \bigcirc\!\!\!3 = 5$$

4. How many answers can you find for the equation: $\boxed{4} + \boxed{4} + \bigcirc\!\!\!1 = 9$?

No Unauthorized Copying   **Patterns & Algebra 2**

1. What number does the letter represent?

a) $x + 3 = 9$

   $x = \boxed{}$

b) $A - 3 = 5$

   $A = \boxed{}$

c) $n + 5 = 11$

   $n = \boxed{}$

d) $6x = 18$

   $x = \boxed{}$

e) $y + 5 = 17$

   $y = \boxed{}$

f) $3n = 15$

   $n = \boxed{}$

g) $b \div 2 = 8$

   $b = \boxed{}$

h) $4x = 20$

   $x = \boxed{}$

i) $z - 2 = 23$

   $z = \boxed{}$

j) $m - 2 = 25$

   $m = \boxed{}$

2. What number does the box or the letter "n" represent? (Guess and check.)

a) $2 \times \square + 3 = 9$

   $\square = \boxed{}$

b) $5 \times \square - 2 = 8$

   $\square = \boxed{}$

c) $3 \times \square + 5 = 14$

   $\square = \boxed{}$

d) $2 \times \square - 5 = 3$

   $\square = \boxed{}$

e) $7 \times \square + 2 = 16$

   $\square = \boxed{}$

f) $n + 5 = 4 + 10$

   $n = \boxed{}$

g) $n - 2 = 12 - 4$

   $n = \boxed{}$

h) $4n + 1 = 13$

   $n = \boxed{}$

i) $5n + 2 = 27$

   $n = \boxed{}$

3. Find x.

a) $x + x = 8$

   $x = \underline{}$

b) $x + x + x = 12$

   $x = \underline{}$

c) $x + x + x = 24$

   $x = \underline{}$

4. Find all values of a and b (that are whole numbers) that make the equation true.

a) $a + b = 6$

b) $a \times b = 6$

c) $6 - a = b$

5. If $2a + 6 = 12$ and $2b + 6 = 14$, explain why b must be greater than a.

6. Write 3 different equations with solution 5.

7.

A	A	A	12
A	B	B	14
A	B	C	10

The shaded column shows the total of each row.

For instance $A + A + A = 12$

Find A, B, and C.

A **variable** is a letter or symbol (such as **x**, **n**, or **h**) that represents a number.

In the product of a number and a variable, the multiplication sign is usually dropped.

> $3 \times T$ is written $3T$, and $5 \times z$ is written $5z$.

---

1. Write a numerical expression for the cost of renting a kayak …

   a) 2 hours: __5 x 2 = 10__   b) 4 hours: _____   c) 7 hours: _____

   Rent a kayak
   $5 for each hour

2. Write an expression for the distance a car would travel at …

   a) Speed: 70 km per hour
      Time: 3 hours

      Distance: _____ km

   b) Speed: 40 km per hour
      Time: 2 hours

      Distance: _____ km

   c) Speed: 100 km per hour
      Time: h hours

      Distance: _____ km

3. Write an algebraic expression for the cost of renting a sailboat for …

   a) h hours: _____ or _____   b) t hours: _____ or _____

   c) x hours: _____ or _____   d) n hours: _____ or _____

   Rent a sailboat
   $7 per hour

4. Write an equation that tells you the relationship between the numbers in column A and column B.

a)

A	B
1	5
2	6
3	7

b)

A	B
1	3
2	6
3	9

c)

A	B
1	8
2	9
3	10

d)

A	B
1	5
2	10
3	15

e)

A	B
1	8
2	16
3	24

   __A + 3 = B__   __2 × A = B__   _____   _____   _____

5. Replace the letter in x in $x + 5 = 9$ with any other letter.
   Does the equation still give the same solution?
   Explain.

6. Write an equation for each problem. (Use a variable for the unknown)

   a) In a class of 28 students, 15 are girls.
      How many students are boys?

   b) Ramona had 48 stamps but gave some away.
      She kept 24. How many did she give away?

1. For each set of points, write a list of ordered pairs, and then complete the T-table.

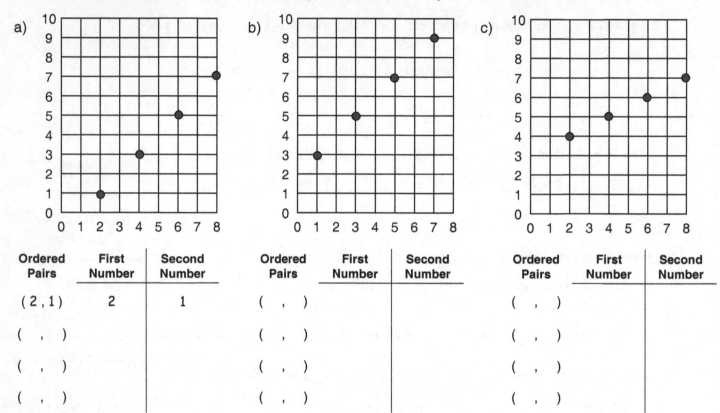

a)

Ordered Pairs	First Number	Second Number
(2 , 1)	2	1
(,)		
(,)		
(,)		

b)

Ordered Pairs	First Number	Second Number
(,)		
(,)		
(,)		
(,)		

c)

Ordered Pairs	First Number	Second Number
(,)		
(,)		
(,)		
(,)		

2. Mark four points on the line segments. Then write a list of ordered pairs, and complete the T-table.

a)

b)

c)

a)

Ordered Pairs	First Number	Second Number
(1 , 3)	1	3
(,)		
(,)		
(,)		

b)

Ordered Pairs	First Number	Second Number
(,)		
(,)		
(,)		
(,)		

c)

Ordered Pairs	First Number	Second Number
(,)		
(,)		
(,)		
(,)		

3. Write a list of ordered pairs based on the T-table provided. Mark the ordered pairs on the graph and connect the points to form a line.

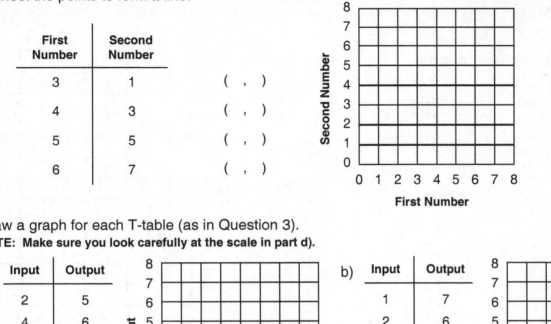

First Number	Second Number	
3	1	(,)
4	3	(,)
5	5	(,)
6	7	(,)

4. Draw a graph for each T-table (as in Question 3).
   NOTE: Make sure you look carefully at the scale in part d).

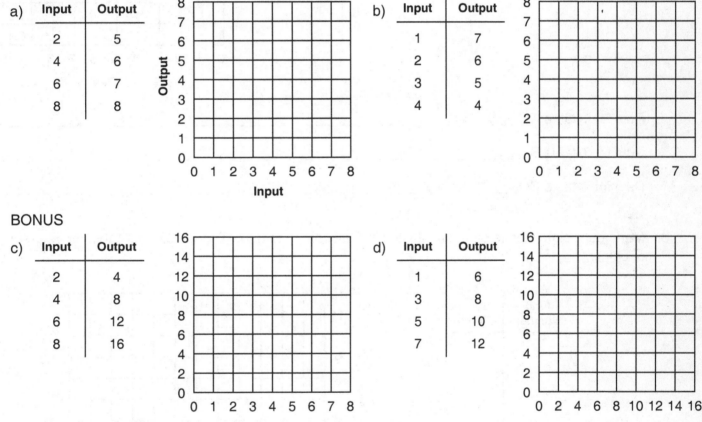

a)
Input	Output
2	5
4	6
6	7
8	8

b)
Input	Output
1	7
2	6
3	5
4	4

BONUS

c)
Input	Output
2	4
4	8
6	12
8	16

d)
Input	Output
1	6
3	8
5	10
7	12

5. Draw a coordinate grid (like those above) on grid paper and plot the following ordered pairs:
   (1 , 2), (3 , 5), (5 , 8), and (7 , 11).

6. On grid paper, make a T-table and graph for the following rules.
   a) Multiply by 2 and subtract 1
   b) Multiply by 4 and subtract 3
   c) Divide by 2 and add 3

7. Make a T-table for each set of points on the coordinate grid.
   Write a rule for each T-table that tells you how to calculate the output from the input.
   (See the rules in Question 6.)

Graph A		**Graph B**		**Graph C**	
Input	Output	Input	Output	Input	Output

Rule for T-table A: _____

Rule for T-table B: _____

Rule for T-table C: _____

8. Mark <u>four</u> points that lie on a straight line in the coordinate grid. Then, make a T-table for your set of points.

First Number	**Second Number**

Answer these questions in your notebook.

1.

The graph shows the cost of making a long distance telephone call.

a) If you talked for 2 minutes, how much would you pay?

b) What is the cost for a minute call?

c) How much would you pay to talk for 10 minutes?

d) If you paid 6 dollars, how long would you be able to talk for?

e) How much would you pay to talk for 30 seconds?

2.

The graph shows the distance Kathy travelled on a cycling trip.

a) How far had Kathy cycled after 2 hours?

b) How far had Kathy travelled after 6 hours?

c) Did Kathy rest at all on her trip? How do you know?

d) When she was cycling, did Kathy always travel at the same speed?

3.

Ben and Tom run a 120 m race.

a) How far from the start was Tom after 10 seconds?

b) How far from the start was Ben after 15 seconds?

c) Who won the race? By how much?

d) How much of a head start did Ben have?

e) How many seconds from the start did Tom overtake Ben?

4.

The graph shows the cost of renting a bike from Mike's store.

a) How much would you pay to rent the bike for:
   i) 2 hours?   ii) 4 hours?   iii) 3 hours?

b) How much do you pay for the bike before you have even ridden it?

c) Dave's store charges $3.50 an hour for a bike. Whose store would you rent from if you wanted the bike for 3 hours? Explain.

Answer the following questions in your notebook.

1. The picture below shows how many chairs can be placed at each arrangement of tables.

   a) Make a T-table and state a rule that tells the relationship between the number of tables and the number of chairs.

   b) How many chairs can be placed at 12 tables?

2. Andy has $10 in his bank account.
   He saves 25 dollars each month.
   How much does he have in his account after 10 months?

3. A recipe calls for 5 cups of flour for every 6 cups of water.
   How many cups of water will be needed for 25 cups of flour?

4. Raymond is 400 km from home on Wednesday morning.
   He cycles 65 km toward home each day.
   How far away from home is he by Saturday evening?

5. Every 6th person who arrives at a book sale receives a free calendar.
   Every 8th person receives a free book.
   Which of the first 50 people receive a book and a calendar?

6. Anna's basket holds 24 apples and Emily's basket holds 30 apples.
   They each collected less than 150 apples.
   How many baskets did they collect if they collected the same number of apples?

7. a) How many shaded squares will be on the perimeter of the 10th figure? How do you know?

   b) How many white squares will be in a figure that has a shaded perimeter of 32 squares?

8. Gerome wants to rent a hockey rink for 6 hours. Which is the cheapest way to rent the rink:
   (i) pay a fee of $60 for the first hour and $35 for each hour after that? or (ii) pay $45 each hour?

Patterns & Algebra 2

9.   What strategy would you use to find the 72nd shape in this pattern? What is the shape?

10. Paul shovelled sidewalks for 4 days.
     Each day, he shovelled 3 more sidewalks than the day before.
     He shovelled 30 sidewalks altogether.
     How many sidewalks did he shovel on each of the days? **Guess and check!**

11. Make a chart with three columns to show:
     - the number of edges along a side of the figure,
     - the number of small triangles in the figure,
     - the perimeter of the figure.

     Describe the pattern in each column and any relationships between the columns of the chart.

12. The picture shows how the temperature
     changes at different heights over a mountain.

     a)   Does the temperature increase or decrease
          at greater heights?

     b)   What distance does the arrow represent
          in real life?

     c)   Measure the length of the arrow.
          What is the scale of the picture?

          _____ cm = _____ m

     d)   Do the numbers in the sequence of temperatures decrease by the same amount each time?

     e)   If the pattern in the temperature continued, what would the temperature be at:

          (i) 3000 m?   (ii) 4000 m?

13. Marlene says she will need 27 blocks to make Figure 7.
     Is she right?
     Explain.

Fractions name equal parts of a whole.

The pie is cut into 4 equal parts. 3 parts out of 4 are shaded.

$\frac{3}{4}$ of a pie is shaded.

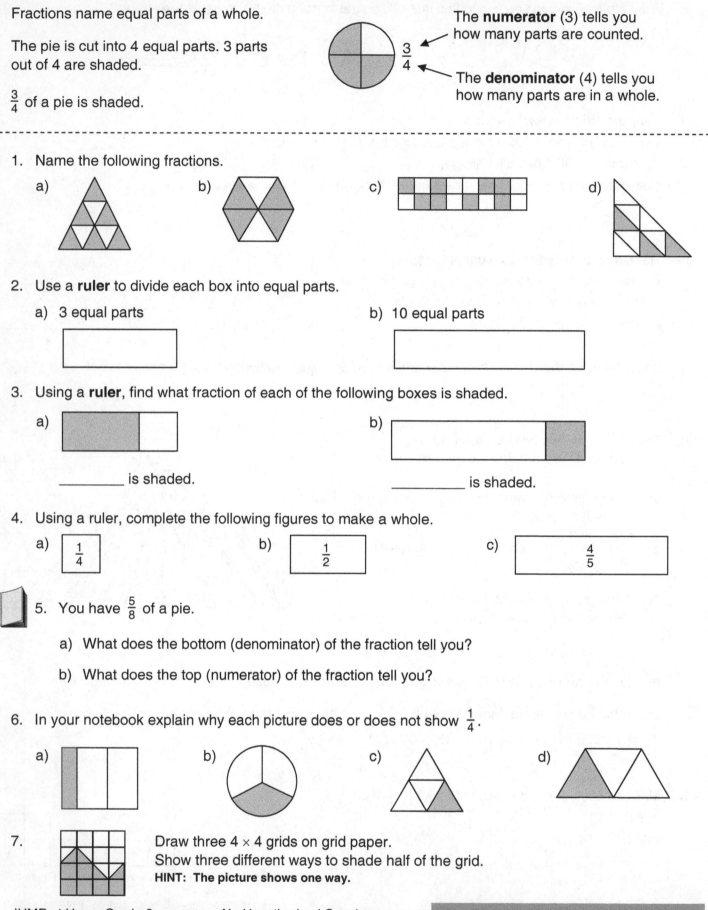

The **numerator** (3) tells you how many parts are counted.

$\frac{3}{4}$

The **denominator** (4) tells you how many parts are in a whole.

---

1. Name the following fractions.

   a)   b)   c)   d)

2. Use a **ruler** to divide each box into equal parts.

   a) 3 equal parts   b) 10 equal parts

3. Using a **ruler**, find what fraction of each of the following boxes is shaded.

   a)   b)

   _____ is shaded.   _____ is shaded.

4. Using a ruler, complete the following figures to make a whole.

   a) $\frac{1}{4}$ b) $\frac{1}{2}$ c) $\frac{4}{5}$

5. You have $\frac{5}{8}$ of a pie.

   a) What does the bottom (denominator) of the fraction tell you?

   b) What does the top (numerator) of the fraction tell you?

6. In your notebook explain why each picture does or does not show $\frac{1}{4}$.

   a)   b)   c)   d)

7. Draw three 4 × 4 grids on grid paper.
   Show three different ways to shade half of the grid.
   HINT: The picture shows one way.

Fractions can name parts of a set: $\frac{3}{5}$ of the figures are pentagons, $\frac{1}{5}$ are squares and $\frac{1}{5}$ are circles.

1. Fill in the blanks.

   a)

   _____ of the figures are pentagons.

   _____ of the figures are shaded.

   b)

   _____ of the figures are squares.

   _____ of the figures are shaded.

2. Fill in the blanks.

   a) $\frac{4}{7}$ of the figures are _____

   b) $\frac{2}{7}$ of the figures are _____

   c) $\frac{1}{7}$ of the figures are _____

   d) $\frac{5}{7}$ of the figures are _____

3. Describe this picture in two different ways using the fraction $\frac{3}{5}$.

4. A hockey team wins 6 games, loses 4 games, and ties one game.
   What fraction of the games did the team …

   a) win? _____   b) lose? _____   c) tie? _____

5. A box contains 2 blue marbles, 3 red marbles, and 4 yellow marbles.

   What fraction of the marbles are **not** blue? _____

6. The chart shows the number of children with each given hair colour in a class.

Hair Colour	Black	Brown	Red	Blonde
Number of Children	5	5	1	3

What fraction of children in the class has hair that is ...

a) red? ☐ b) black? ☐ c) blonde? ☐ d) brown? ☐

7. There are 23 children in a class.
Each child chose to do a science project on animals or on plants.
The chart shows the number who chose each topic.

a) Fill in the missing numbers in the chart.

b) What fraction of the children chose to study ...

animals? ☐   plants? ☐

c) What fraction of the girls chose to study ...

animals? ☐   plants? ☐

	Animals	Plants
Boys	7	4
Girls		
Children	12	

8. What fraction of the **squares** are on the **outside** of the figure? _____

9. Write a **fraction** for each statement below.

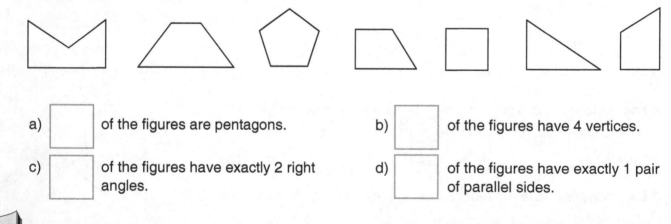

a) ☐ of the figures are pentagons.

b) ☐ of the figures have 4 vertices.

c) ☐ of the figures have exactly 2 right angles.

d) ☐ of the figures have exactly 1 pair of parallel sides.

10. Write two fractions statements for the figures in Question 9 above. Justify your answer.

Number Sense 2

1. 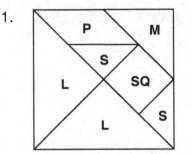 In a tangram ...

- 2 small triangles (**S**) cover a medium triangle (**M**)
- 2 small triangles (**S**) cover a square (**SQ**)
- 2 small triangles (**S**) cover a parallelogram (**P**)
- 4 small triangles (**S**) cover a large triangle (**L**)

What fraction of each shape is covered by a <u>single</u> small triangle?

a)

b)

c)

d)

e)

f)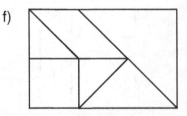

2. What fraction of each shape is shaded? Explain how you know.

a)

b)

c)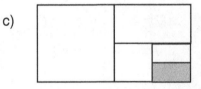

3. What fraction of the trapezoid is covered by a <u>single</u> small triangle?

Show your work.

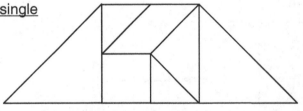

4. If ▓ = red and ⠿ = blue, approximately what fraction of each flag is shaded red? Explain.

a)

CHILE

b)

CANADA

c)

FRANCE

d)

SWITZERLAND

1. Imagine moving the shaded pieces from pies A and B into pie plate C. Show how much of pie C would be filled and then write a fraction for pie C.

$$\frac{1}{4} \qquad + \qquad \frac{2}{4} \qquad = \qquad \underline{}$$

2. Imagine pouring the liquid from cups A and B into cup C.
    Shade the amount of liquid that would be in C.
    Then complete the addition statements.

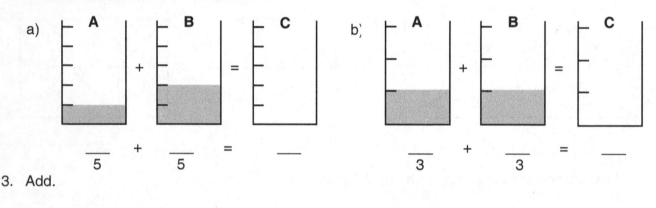

$$\frac{}{5} \qquad + \qquad \frac{}{5} \qquad = \qquad \underline{} \qquad\qquad \frac{}{3} \qquad + \qquad \frac{}{3} \qquad = \qquad \underline{}$$

3. Add.

    a) $\frac{3}{5} + \frac{1}{5} =$ b) $\frac{2}{4} + \frac{1}{4} =$ c) $\frac{3}{7} + \frac{2}{7} =$ d) $\frac{5}{8} + \frac{2}{8} =$

    e) $\frac{3}{11} + \frac{7}{11} =$ f) $\frac{5}{17} + \frac{9}{17} =$ g) $\frac{11}{24} + \frac{10}{24} =$ h) $\frac{18}{57} + \frac{13}{57} =$

4. Show how much pie would be left if you took away the amount shown. Then complete the fraction statement.

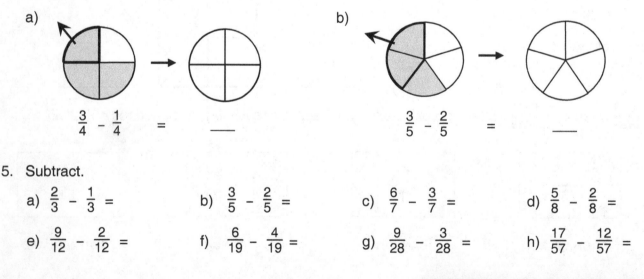

$$\frac{3}{4} \;-\; \frac{1}{4} \;=\; \underline{} \qquad\qquad\qquad \frac{3}{5} \;-\; \frac{2}{5} \;=\; \underline{}$$

5. Subtract.

    a) $\frac{2}{3} - \frac{1}{3} =$ b) $\frac{3}{5} - \frac{2}{5} =$ c) $\frac{6}{7} - \frac{3}{7} =$ d) $\frac{5}{8} - \frac{2}{8} =$

    e) $\frac{9}{12} - \frac{2}{12} =$ f) $\frac{6}{19} - \frac{4}{19} =$ g) $\frac{9}{28} - \frac{3}{28} =$ h) $\frac{17}{57} - \frac{12}{57} =$

1. What fraction has a greater numerator, $\frac{2}{6}$ or $\frac{5}{6}$? _____

   Which fraction is greater? _____

   Explain your thinking: _____

   _____

2. Circle the greater fraction in each pair.

   a) $\frac{5}{17}$ or $\frac{11}{17}$ b) $\frac{3}{17}$ or $\frac{4}{17}$ c) $\frac{11}{25}$ or $\frac{6}{25}$ d) $\frac{57}{115}$ or $\frac{43}{115}$

3. Two fractions have the same <u>denominators</u> (bottoms) but different <u>numerators</u> (tops). How can you tell which fraction is greater?

   _____

4. Write the fractions in order from least to greatest.

   a) $\frac{4}{5}$, $\frac{1}{5}$, $\frac{3}{5}$ [   ]   b) $\frac{9}{10}$, $\frac{2}{10}$, $\frac{1}{10}$, $\frac{5}{10}$ [   ]

5. Circle the greater fraction in each pair.

   a) $\frac{1}{7}$ or $\frac{1}{6}$ b) $\frac{8}{8}$ or $\frac{8}{9}$ c) $\frac{7}{300}$ or $\frac{7}{200}$

6. Fraction A and Fraction B have the same <u>numerators</u> (tops) but different <u>denominators</u> (bottoms). How can you tell which fraction is greater?

   _____

7. Write the fractions in order from least to greatest.

   a) $\frac{1}{9}$, $\frac{1}{4}$, $\frac{1}{17}$ [   ]   b) $\frac{2}{11}$, $\frac{2}{5}$, $\frac{2}{7}$, $\frac{2}{16}$ [   ]

8. Circle the greater fraction in each pair.

   a) $\frac{2}{3}$ or $\frac{2}{9}$ b) $\frac{7}{17}$ or $\frac{11}{17}$ c) $\frac{6}{288}$ or $\frac{6}{18}$

9. Which fraction is greater, $\frac{1}{2}$ or $\frac{1}{100}$? Explain your thinking.

10. Is it possible for $\frac{2}{3}$ of a pie to be bigger than $\frac{3}{4}$ of another pie? Show your thinking with a picture.

NS6-49: Mixed Fractions

William and Jessie ate three and three quarter pies altogether (or $3\frac{3}{4}$ pies).

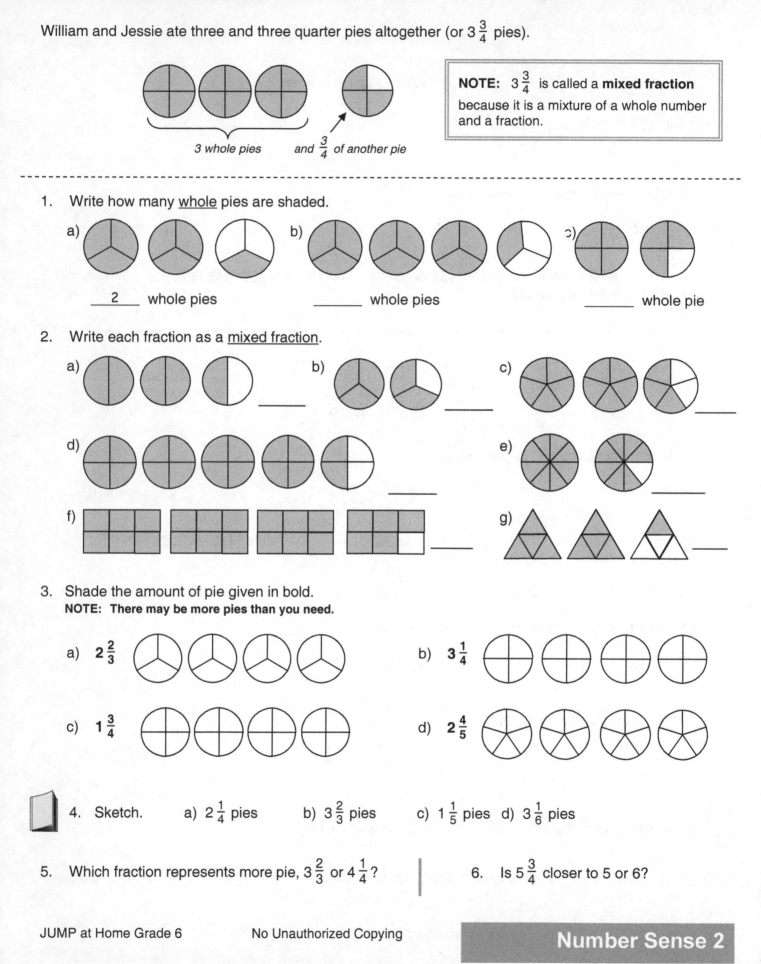

3 whole pies   and $\frac{3}{4}$ of another pie

NOTE: $3\frac{3}{4}$ is called a **mixed fraction** because it is a mixture of a whole number and a fraction.

1. Write how many <u>whole</u> pies are shaded.

a) _____2_____ whole pies

b) _____ whole pies

c) _____ whole pie

2. Write each fraction as a <u>mixed fraction</u>.

a) _____

b) _____

c) _____

d) _____

e) _____

f) _____

g) _____

3. Shade the amount of pie given in bold.
   NOTE: There may be more pies than you need.

a) $2\frac{2}{3}$

b) $3\frac{1}{4}$

c) $1\frac{3}{4}$

d) $2\frac{4}{5}$

4. Sketch.   a) $2\frac{1}{4}$ pies   b) $3\frac{2}{3}$ pies   c) $1\frac{1}{5}$ pies   d) $3\frac{1}{6}$ pies

5. Which fraction represents more pie, $3\frac{2}{3}$ or $4\frac{1}{4}$?

6. Is $5\frac{3}{4}$ closer to 5 or 6?

NS6-50: Improper Fractions

Huan-Yue and her friends ate **9** quarter-sized pieces of pizza.

$$\frac{9}{4} = 2\frac{1}{4}$$

improper fraction   *mixed fraction*

Altogether they ate $\frac{9}{4}$ pizzas.

When the numerator of a fraction is larger than the denominator, the fraction represents *more than a whole*. Such fractions are called **improper fractions**.

----

1. Write these fractions as <u>improper</u> fractions.

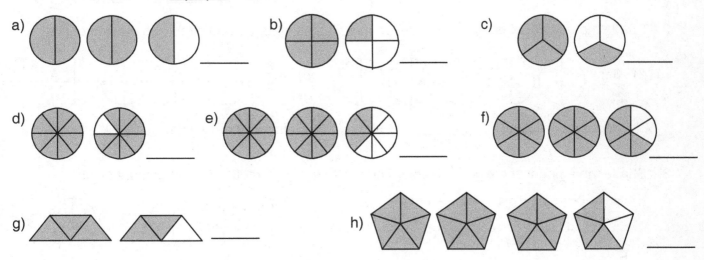

2. Shade one piece at a time until you have shaded the amount of pie given in bold.

a) $\frac{5}{2}$ b) $\frac{9}{4}$

c) $\frac{10}{3}$ d) $\frac{8}{4}$

3. Sketch.   a) $\frac{9}{4}$ pies   b) $\frac{7}{3}$ pies   c) $\frac{9}{2}$ pies   d) $\frac{7}{6}$ pies

4. Which fraction represents more pie? $\frac{7}{4}$ or $\frac{9}{4}$? How do you know?

5. Which fractions are more than a whole? How do you know?   a) $\frac{5}{7}$ b) $\frac{9}{8}$ c) $\frac{13}{11}$

Number Sense 2

NS6-51: Mixed and Improper Fractions

1. Write these fractions both as <u>mixed</u> fractions and as <u>improper</u> fractions.

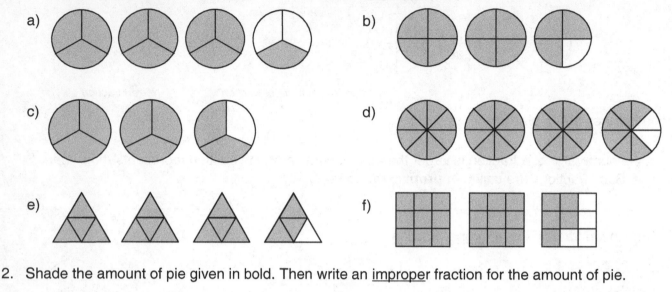

a)

b)

c)

d)

e)

f)

2. Shade the amount of pie given in bold. Then write an <u>improper</u> fraction for the amount of pie.

a) $3\frac{1}{2}$

Improper Fraction: _____

b) $3\frac{3}{4}$

Improper Fraction: _____

3. Shade the amount of pie given in bold. Then write a <u>mixed</u> fraction for the amount of pie.

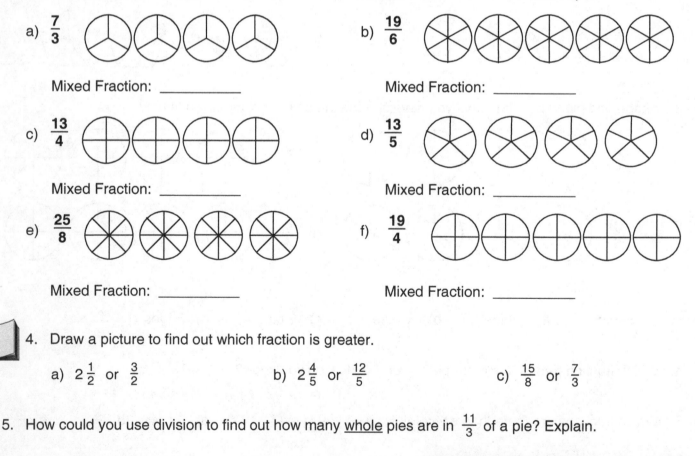

a) $\frac{7}{3}$

Mixed Fraction: _____

b) $\frac{19}{6}$

Mixed Fraction: _____

c) $\frac{13}{4}$

Mixed Fraction: _____

d) $\frac{13}{5}$

Mixed Fraction: _____

e) $\frac{25}{8}$

Mixed Fraction: _____

f) $\frac{19}{4}$

Mixed Fraction: _____

4. Draw a picture to find out which fraction is greater.

a) $2\frac{1}{2}$ or $\frac{3}{2}$

b) $2\frac{4}{5}$ or $\frac{12}{5}$

c) $\frac{15}{8}$ or $\frac{7}{3}$

5. How could you use division to find out how many <u>whole</u> pies are in $\frac{11}{3}$ of a pie? Explain.

NS6-52: Mixed Fractions (Advanced)

There are 4 quarter pieces in 1 pie.

There are 8 (2 × 4) quarters in 2 pies.

There are 12 (3 × 4) quarters in 3 pies.

How many quarter pieces are in $3\frac{3}{4}$ pies?

$3\frac{3}{4}$

12 pieces (3 × 4)   + 3 extra pieces

So there are 15 quarter pieces altogether.

---

1. Find the number of **halves** in each amount.

   a) 1 pie = _____ halves

   b) 2 pies = _____ halves

   c) 4 pies = _____ halves

   d) $3\frac{1}{2}$ pies = _____ halves

   e) $4\frac{1}{2}$ pies = _____ halves

   f) $5\frac{1}{2}$ pies = _____

2. Find the number of **thirds** in each amount.

   a) 1 pie = _____ thirds

   b) 2 pies = _____ thirds

   c) 4 pies = _____ thirds

   d) $1\frac{1}{3}$ pies = _____ thirds

   e) $2\frac{2}{3}$ pies = _____

   f) $5\frac{2}{3}$ pies = _____

3. A box holds 4 cans.

   a) 2 boxes hold _____ cans

   b) $2\frac{1}{4}$ boxes hold _____ cans

   c) $3\frac{3}{4}$ boxes hold _____ cans

4. A box holds 6 cans.

   a) $2\frac{1}{6}$ boxes hold _____ cans

   b) $2\frac{5}{6}$ boxes hold _____ cans

   c) $3\frac{1}{6}$ boxes hold _____ cans

5. Write the following mixed fractions as improper fractions.

   a) $2\frac{1}{3} = \frac{}{3}$

   b) $5\frac{1}{2} = \frac{}{2}$

   c) $4\frac{2}{3} = \frac{}{3}$

   d) $6\frac{1}{4} = \frac{}{4}$

6. Envelopes come in packs of 6.
   Alice used $2\frac{5}{6}$ packs.
   How many envelopes did she use? _____

7. Baseball cards come in packs of 8. How many cards are in $3\frac{1}{2}$ packs? _____

8. Maia and her friends ate $2\frac{3}{4}$ pizzas. How many quarter-sized pieces did they eat? _____

9.

   $\frac{1}{3}$ cup   **A**

   $\frac{1}{6}$ cup   **B**

   Cindy needs $2\frac{2}{3}$ cups of flour.

   a) How many scoops of cup A would she need? _____

   b) How many scoops of cup B would she need? _____

How many whole pies are there in $\frac{13}{4}$ pies?

There are 13 pieces altogether, and each pie has 4 pieces.
So you can find the number of whole pies by dividing 13 by 4: **13 ÷ 4 = 3 remainder 1**

There are 3 whole pies and 1 quarter left over, so: $\frac{13}{4} = 3\frac{1}{4}$

----

1. Find the number of whole pies in each amount by dividing.

   a) $\frac{4}{2}$ pies = _____ whole pies   b) $\frac{6}{2}$ pies = _____ whole pies   c) $\frac{12}{2}$ pies = _____ whole pies

   d) $\frac{6}{3}$ pies = _____ whole pies   e) $\frac{15}{3}$ pies = _____ whole pies   f) $\frac{8}{4}$ pies = _____ whole pies

2. Find the number of whole and the number of pieces remaining by dividing.

   a) $\frac{5}{2}$ pies = ___2___ whole pies and ___1___ half pies = ___$2\frac{1}{2}$___ pies

   b) $\frac{11}{3}$ pies = _____ whole pies and _____ thirds = _____ pies

   c) $\frac{10}{3}$ pies = _____ whole pies and _____ thirds = _____ pies

   d) $\frac{9}{2}$ pies = _____ whole pies and _____ half pies = _____ pies

3. Write the following improper fractions as mixed fractions.

   a) $\frac{3}{2}$ =   b) $\frac{9}{2}$ =   c) $\frac{8}{3}$ =   d) $\frac{15}{4}$ =   e) $\frac{22}{5}$ =

4. Write a mixed and improper fraction for the number of litres.

   1 L

5. Write a mixed and improper fraction for the length of the rope.

   1 m

6. Which is greater: $\frac{7}{3}$ or $\frac{5}{2}$? How do you know?

7. Between which two whole numbers is $\frac{7}{4}$?

8. How much greater than a whole is ...   a) $\frac{10}{7}$?   b) $\frac{6}{5}$?   c) $\frac{4}{3}$?   d) $\frac{11}{10}$?

NS6-54: Equivalent Fractions

Aidan shades $\frac{2}{6}$ of the squares in an array:

He then draws heavy lines around the squares to group them into 3 equal groups:

He sees that $\frac{1}{3}$ of the squares are shaded.

The pictures show that two sixths are equal to one third: $\frac{2}{6} = \frac{1}{3}$

Two sixths and one third are **equivalent fractions**.

----

1. Group the squares to make an equivalent fraction.

   a)

   $\frac{6}{10} = \frac{}{5}$

   b)

   $\frac{4}{6} = \frac{}{3}$

   c)

   $\frac{10}{12} = \frac{}{6}$

2. Write three equivalent fractions for the amount shaded here.

   _____   _____   _____

3. Group the buttons to make an equivalent fraction.

   a)

   $\frac{4}{6} = \frac{}{}$

   b)

   $\frac{3}{6} = \frac{}{}$

   c)

   $\frac{2}{6} = \frac{}{}$

   d)

   $\frac{6}{9} = \frac{}{}$

   e)

   $\frac{6}{10} = \frac{}{}$

4. Cut each pie into smaller pieces to make an equivalent fraction.

   a)

   $\frac{2}{3} = \frac{}{6}$

   b)

   $\frac{2}{3} = \frac{}{9}$

   c)

   $\frac{3}{4} = \frac{}{12}$

5. a) Draw lines to cut the pies into …

   4 pieces   6 pieces   8 pieces

   b) Then fill in the numerators of the equivalent fractions.

   $\frac{1}{2} = \frac{}{4} = \frac{}{6} = \frac{}{8}$

6. Draw shaded and unshaded circles (as in Question 3). Group the circles to show …

   a) six eighths is equivalent to three quarters

   b) four fifths is equivalent to eight tenths

Number Sense 2

NS6-55: Models of Equivalent Fractions

Anne makes a model of $\frac{2}{5}$ using 15 squares as follows:

First she makes a model of $\frac{2}{5}$ using shaded and unshaded squares (leaving space between the squares).

Step 1: ▣ ▣ ☐ ☐ ☐

$\frac{2}{5}$ of the squares are shaded. She then adds squares one at a time until she has placed 15 squares.

Step 2: ▣▣ ▣▣ ☐☐ ☐☐ ☐☐

Step 3: ▣▣▣ ▣▣▣ ☐☐☐ ☐☐☐ ☐☐☐

From the picture, Anne can see that $\frac{2}{5}$ of a set of 15 squares is equivalent to $\frac{6}{15}$ of the set.

---

1. Draw a model of $\frac{2}{3}$ using 12 squares.
   The question is started for you.

   HINT: Place the extra squares beside the ones already drawn, one square at a time.

   ▣ ▣ ☐

2. Draw a model of $\frac{3}{5}$ using 10 squares.

   HINT: Start by making a model of $\frac{3}{5}$.

3. Draw a model of $\frac{3}{4}$ using 8 squares.

4. $\frac{5}{6}$ of a pizza is covered in olives ◉.

   $\frac{1}{3}$ of the pizza is covered in mushrooms ⬆.

   Each piece has a topping. Complete the picture.

   How many pieces are covered in olives **and** mushrooms? _____

5. If box C was cut into 12 pieces, how many pieces would you shade to make a fraction equivalent to A and B?

   A   B   C

JUMP at Home Grade 6   No Unauthorized Copying   **Number Sense 2**

Dan has 6 cookies. He wants to give $\frac{2}{3}$ of his cookies to
his friends. To do so, he shares the cookies equally onto 3 plates:

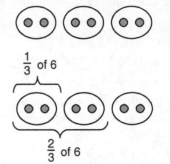

There are 3 equal groups, so each group is $\frac{1}{3}$ of 6.

There are 2 cookies in each group, so $\frac{1}{3}$ of 6 is 2.

There are 4 cookies in two groups, so $\frac{2}{3}$ of 6 is 4.

$\frac{1}{3}$ of 6

$\frac{2}{3}$ of 6

---

1. Write a fraction for the amount of dots shown. The first one has been done for you.

a) $\boxed{\dfrac{3}{4}}$ of 8

b) $\boxed{}$ of 15

2. Fill in the missing numbers.

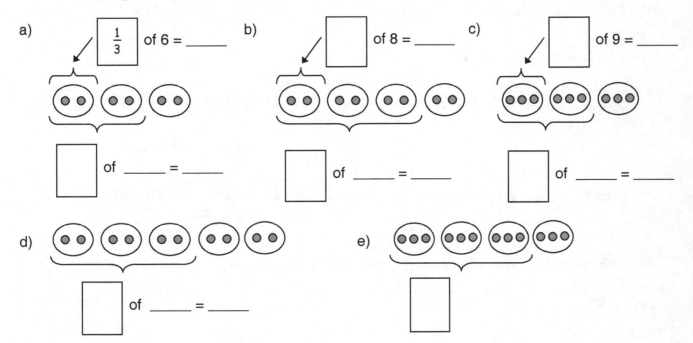

a) $\boxed{\dfrac{1}{3}}$ of 6 = _____

$\boxed{}$ of _____ = _____

b) $\boxed{}$ of 8 = _____

$\boxed{}$ of _____ = _____

c) $\boxed{}$ of 9 = _____

$\boxed{}$ of _____ = _____

d) $\boxed{}$ of _____ = _____

e) $\boxed{}$

3. Draw a circle to show the given amount. The first one has been done for you.

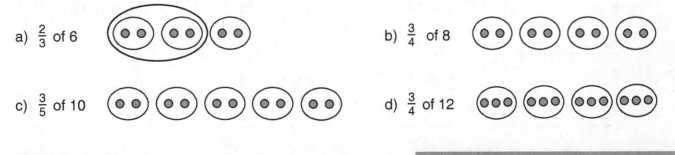

a) $\frac{2}{3}$ of 6

b) $\frac{3}{4}$ of 8

c) $\frac{3}{5}$ of 10

d) $\frac{3}{4}$ of 12

4. Fill in the correct number of dots in each circle, then draw a larger circle to show the given amount.

    a) $\frac{2}{3}$ of 12   ◯ ◯ ◯   b) $\frac{2}{3}$ of 9   ◯ ◯ ◯

5. Find the fraction of the whole amount by sharing the cookies equally.
    HINT: Draw the correct number of plates then place the cookies one at a time. Then circle the correct amount.

    a) Find $\frac{1}{4}$ of 8 cookies.   b) Find $\frac{1}{2}$ of 10 cookies.

    $\frac{1}{4}$ of 8 is _____ $\frac{1}{2}$ of 10 is _____

    c) Find $\frac{2}{3}$ of 6 cookies.   d) Find $\frac{3}{4}$ of 12 cookies.

    $\frac{2}{3}$ of 6 is _____ $\frac{3}{4}$ of 12 is _____

6. Andy finds $\frac{2}{3}$ of 12 as follows:

    Step 1   He finds $\frac{1}{3}$ of 12 by dividing 12 by 3:   (●●●●) (●●●●) (●●●●)

              12 ÷ 3 = 4 (4 is $\frac{1}{3}$ of 12)

    Step 2   Then he multiplies the result by 2:   (●●●●) (●●●●) (●●●●)

              4 × 2 = 8 (8 is $\frac{2}{3}$ of 12)

    Find the following amounts using Andy's method.

    a) $\frac{2}{3}$ of 9   b) $\frac{3}{4}$ of 8   c) $\frac{2}{3}$ of 15   d) $\frac{2}{5}$ of 10

    _____   _____   _____   _____

    e) $\frac{3}{5}$ of 25   f) $\frac{2}{7}$ of 14   g) $\frac{1}{6}$ of 18   h) $\frac{1}{2}$ of 12

    _____   _____   _____   _____

    i) $\frac{3}{4}$ of 12   j) $\frac{2}{3}$ of 21   k) $\frac{3}{8}$ of 16   l) $\frac{3}{7}$ of 21

    _____   _____   _____   _____

7. a)   Shade $\frac{2}{5}$ of the boxes.   b)   Shade $\frac{2}{3}$ of the boxes.   c)   Shade $\frac{3}{4}$ of the boxes.

8. a)   Shade $\frac{1}{4}$ of the boxes. Draw stripes in $\frac{1}{6}$ of the boxes.

   b)   Shade $\frac{1}{3}$ of the boxes. Draw stripes in $\frac{1}{6}$ of the boxes. Put dots in $\frac{1}{8}$ of the boxes.

9. 15 children are on a bus. $\frac{3}{5}$ are girls. How many girls are on the bus? _____

10. A kilogram of lichees costs $8. How much would $\frac{3}{4}$ of a kilogram cost? _____

11. Gerald has 12 apples. He gives away $\frac{3}{4}$ of the apples.

    a) How many apples did he give away? _____   b) How many did he keep? _____

12.   Shade $\frac{1}{3}$ of the squares.

      Draw stripes in $\frac{1}{6}$ of the squares.

      How many squares are blank?

13. Evelyn has 20 marbles.
    $\frac{2}{5}$ are blue. $\frac{1}{4}$ are yellow. The rest are green.
    How many are green?

14. Ed started studying at 9:10. He studied for $\frac{2}{3}$ of an hour.
    At what time did he stop studying?

15. Marion had 36 stickers.
    She kept $\frac{1}{6}$ for herself and divided the rest evenly among 5 friends.
    How many stickers did each friend get?

16. Which is longer: 17 months or $1\frac{3}{4}$ years?

17. Linda had 12 apples.
    She gave $\frac{1}{4}$ of them to Nandita. She gave 2 to Amy.
    She says that she has half left. Is she correct?

Number Sense 2

A fraction is reduced to **lowest terms** when the only whole number that will divide into its numerator and denominator is the number 1. $\frac{2}{4}$ is *not* in lowest terms (because 2 divides into 2 and 4) but $\frac{1}{2}$ is in lowest terms.

You can reduce a fraction to lowest terms by dividing a set of counters representing the fraction into equal groups. (You may have to group counters several times before the fraction is in lowest terms.)

<u>Step 1</u>: Count the number of counters in each group.

<u>Step 2</u>: Divide the numerator and denominator of the fraction by the number of counters in each group.

1. Reduce these fractions by grouping.

   a) $\frac{2}{4} = \frac{}{2}$

   b) $\frac{3}{9} = \frac{}{3}$

   c) $\frac{4}{6} = \frac{}{3}$

2. Show how you would reduce the fractions by dividing.

   a) $\dfrac{2 \div}{4 \div} = \underline{}$

   b) $\dfrac{3 \div}{9 \div} = \underline{}$

   c) $\dfrac{4 \div}{6 \div} = \underline{}$

3. Reduce the fractions below by dividing.

   a) $\frac{2}{10} = \frac{}{}$

   b) $\frac{2}{6} = \frac{}{}$

   c) $\frac{2}{8} = \frac{}{}$

   d) $\frac{2}{12} = \frac{}{}$

   e) $\frac{3}{9} = \frac{}{}$

   f) $\frac{3}{15} = \frac{}{}$

   g) $\frac{4}{12} = \frac{}{}$

   h) $\frac{6}{9} = \frac{}{}$

   i) $\frac{4}{6} = \frac{}{}$

   j) $\frac{10}{15} = \frac{}{}$

   k) $\frac{20}{25} = \frac{}{}$

   l) $\frac{8}{12} = \frac{}{}$

4. The pie chart show how the children in a Grade 6 class get to school.
   What fraction of the children …

   a) walk to school? $\boxed{\dfrac{}{}}$

   b) take the bus? $\boxed{\dfrac{}{}}$

   c) skateboard? $\boxed{\dfrac{}{}}$

   d) cycle? $\boxed{\dfrac{}{}}$

1.

A   **B**

How many pieces are in pie A? _____

How many pieces are in pie B? _____

Find the LCM of the number of
pieces in pies A and B: **LCM =** _____

Cut pie A and pie B into this many pieces.

How many pieces did you cut each piece
of pie A into? _____

How many pieces did you cut each piece
of pie B into? _____

2.

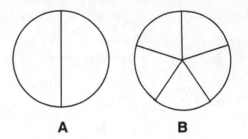

A   **B**

How many pieces are in pie A? _____

How many pieces are in pie B? _____

Find the LCM of the number of
pieces in pies A and B: **LCM =** _____

Cut pie A and pie B into this many pieces.

How many pieces did you cut each piece
of pie A into? _____

How many pieces did you cut each piece
of pie B into? _____

3.

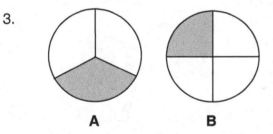

A   **B**

Write the name of each fraction.

A - _____   B - _____

Find the LCM of the number of
pieces in pies A and B: **LCM =** _____

Cut each pie into the same number of pieces,
given by the LCM.

Now write a new name for each fraction.

A - _____   B - _____

4.

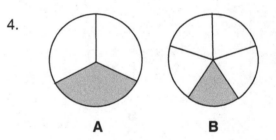

A   **B**

Write the name of each fraction.

A - _____   B - _____

Find the LCM of the number of
pieces in pies A and B: **LCM =** _____

Cut each pie into the same number of pieces,
given by the LCM.

Now write a new name for each fraction.

A - _____   B - _____

5.

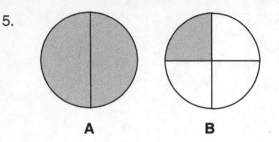

A   B

Write the name of each fraction.

A - _____ B - _____

Find the LCM of the number of pieces in pies A and B: **LCM** = _____

Cut each pie into the same number of pieces, given by the **LCM**.

Now write a new name for each fraction.

A - _____ B - _____

6.

A   B

Write the name of each fraction.

A - _____ B - _____

Find the LCM of the number of pieces in pies A and B: **LCM** = _____

Cut each pie into the same number of pieces, given by the **LCM**.

Now write a name for each fraction.

A - _____ B - _____

7.

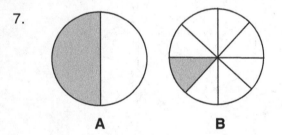

A   B

Write the name of each fraction.

A - _____ B - _____

Find the LCM of the number of pieces in pies A and B: **LCM** = _____

Cut each pie into the same number of pieces, given by the LCM.

Now write a new name for each fraction.

A - _____ B - _____

8.

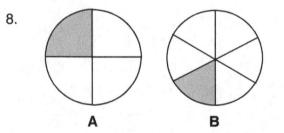

A   B

Write the name of each fraction.

A - _____ B - _____

Find the LCM of the number of pieces in pies A and B: **LCM** = _____

Cut each pie into the same number of pieces, given by the LCM.

Now write a new name for each fraction.

A - _____ B - _____

NS6-59: Comparing and Ordering Fractions

Use the fraction strips below to answer Questions 1 to 3.

1. Fill in the missing numbers on the fraction strips above. Then write > (greater than) or < (less than) between each pair of numbers below.

   a) $\frac{2}{3}$ ☐ $\frac{3}{5}$ b) $\frac{3}{4}$ ☐ $\frac{1}{2}$ c) $\frac{2}{5}$ ☐ $\frac{3}{4}$ d) $\frac{3}{4}$ ☐ $\frac{4}{5}$

2. Circle the fractions that are greater than $\frac{1}{3}$.

   $\frac{3}{5}$ $\frac{2}{5}$ $\frac{1}{2}$

3. Circle the fractions that are greater than $\frac{1}{2}$.

   $\frac{2}{3}$ $\frac{2}{5}$ $\frac{3}{4}$

4. Turn each fraction into an equivalent fraction so that both fractions have the same denominator (by finding the LCM of both denominators). Then write =, <, or > between the two fractions.

   a) $\frac{5 \times 1}{5 \times 2}$ ☐ $\frac{7}{10}$ b) $\frac{1}{2}$ ☐ $\frac{3}{10}$ c) $\frac{3}{4}$ ☐ $\frac{7}{8}$ d) $\frac{11}{20}$ ☐ $\frac{2}{5}$

   $\frac{5}{10}$ [<] $\frac{7}{10}$ ☐   ☐   ☐

   e) $\frac{2}{3}$ ☐ $\frac{4}{5}$ f) $\frac{1}{2}$ ☐ $\frac{2}{3}$ g) $\frac{3}{4}$ ☐ $\frac{2}{3}$ h) $\frac{2}{3}$ ☐ $\frac{6}{9}$

   ☐   ☐   ☐   ☐

   i) $\frac{3}{4}$ ☐ $\frac{4}{5}$ j) $\frac{1}{7}$ ☐ $\frac{5}{21}$ k) $\frac{17}{35}$ ☐ $\frac{3}{5}$ l) $\frac{4}{5}$ ☐ $\frac{5}{6}$

   ☐   ☐   ☐   ☐

     Number Sense 2

1. Write the fractions in order from least to greatest.

   HINT: First write each fraction with the same denominator.

   a) $\frac{1}{2}$ $\frac{2}{5}$ $\frac{3}{10}$

   $\boxed{\frac{5}{10}}$ $\boxed{\frac{4}{10}}$ $\boxed{\frac{3}{10}}$

   $\frac{3}{10}$ $\frac{2}{5}$ $\frac{1}{2}$

   b) $\frac{1}{3}$ $\frac{5}{6}$ $\frac{1}{2}$

   $\boxed{\frac{4}{12}}$ $\boxed{\frac{10}{12}}$ $\boxed{\frac{6}{12}}$

   $\frac{4}{12}$ $\frac{6}{12}$ $\frac{10}{12}$

   c) $\frac{5}{8}$ $\frac{1}{2}$ $\frac{3}{4}$

   $\boxed{\frac{10}{16}}$ $\boxed{\frac{8}{16}}$ $\boxed{\frac{12}{16}}$

   $\frac{1}{2}$ $\frac{5}{8}$ $\frac{3}{4}$

2. Write the fractions in the boxes in order from least to greatest.

   $\boxed{0}$ $\boxed{\frac{1}{10}}$ $\boxed{\frac{1}{5}}$ $\boxed{\frac{3}{10}}$ $\boxed{\frac{2}{5}}$ $\boxed{\frac{1}{2}}$ $\boxed{\frac{3}{5}}$ $\boxed{\frac{\triangledown}{10}}$ $\boxed{\frac{4}{5}}$ $\boxed{\frac{9}{10}}$ $\boxed{1}$

   $\frac{1}{10}$ $\frac{2}{5}$ $\frac{9}{10}$ $\frac{4}{5}$ $\frac{3}{5}$ $\frac{3}{10}$ $\frac{1}{5}$ $\frac{1}{2}$ $\frac{7}{10}$

3. Equivalent fractions are said to be in the same **family**. Write two fractions in the same family as the fraction in each triangle.

   a) $\frac{1}{2}$

   $\frac{5}{10}$ $\frac{50}{100}$ $\frac{25}{50}$ $\frac{7}{14}$

   b) $\frac{1}{3}$

   c) $\frac{3}{4}$

   d) $\frac{2}{5}$

4. In each question, circle the <u>pair</u> of fractions that are in the same family.

   a) $\frac{1}{2}$ $\frac{4}{6}$ $\frac{5}{10}$

   b) $\frac{2}{3}$ $\frac{4}{6}$ $\frac{1}{4}$

   c) $\frac{3}{15}$ $\frac{16}{20}$ $\frac{4}{5}$

5. Fill in the missing fractions in the sequence.
   HINT: Give all the fractions the same denominator.

   $\frac{1}{6}$ $\frac{1}{3}$ $\frac{1}{2}$ $\boxed{}$ $\frac{5}{6}$ $\boxed{}$

6. Explain how you know $\frac{1}{3}$ is greater than $\frac{1}{8}$.

7. Find 2 fractions from the fraction family of $\frac{4}{12}$ with numerators smaller than 4.

8. Find 5 fractions from the fraction family of $\frac{12}{24}$ with numerators smaller than 12.

9. A recipe for soup calls for $\frac{2}{3}$ of a can of tomatoes.

   A recipe for spaghetti sauce calls for $\frac{5}{6}$ of a can.

   Which recipe uses more tomatoes?

Answer the following questions in your notebook.

1. Anne had 1 hour for lunch.

   She played for $\frac{3}{5}$ of an hour and read for $\frac{1}{10}$ of an hour.

   a) How many minutes did she have left to eat lunch?

   b) What fraction of an hour was this?

2. a) What fraction of the walls were painted green?

   b) What colour was used to paint one fifth of the walls?

   c) What colour was used to paint one half of the walls?

Colour	Number of Walls Painted
White	10
Yellow	5
Blue	4
Green	1

3. Charles left for school at 7:10 am. He walked for $\frac{2}{5}$ of an hour to his friend's house, and then another $\frac{3}{5}$ of an hour to school. At what time did he arrive at school?

4. The pie chart shows the times of day when a lizard is active.

    Awake but Inactive

   Asleep

   Awake and Active

   a) What fraction of the day is the lizard…

      i) awake but inactive   ii) asleep   iii) awake and active

   b) How many hours a day is the lizard…

      i) awake but inactive   ii) asleep   iii) awake and active

5. John, Brian, Eldad, and Ahmed bought some pizzas.
   They ate the following fractions
   of a pizza (in no particular order): $\frac{2}{10}$, $\frac{2}{5}$, $\frac{7}{10}$, $\frac{6}{5}$

   There were 5 slices left over.

   a) How many pizzas did they buy?

   b) • Eldad ate $\frac{1}{5}$ of a pizza.

      • Ahmed ate $\frac{7}{10}$, which was 3 more slices than Brian.

      • John ate more than one pizza.

      How much pizza did each boy eat?

6. A box holds 9 cans. The box is $\frac{2}{3}$ full.

   How many cans are in the box?

NS6-62: Decimal Hundredths

Fractions with denominators that are multiples of ten (tenths, hundredths) commonly appear in units of measurement.

REMEMBER:

3. 7 5

ones | tenths | hundredths

- A millimetre is a tenth of a centimetre (10 mm = 1 cm)
- A centimetre is a tenth of a decimetre (10 cm = 1 dm)
- A decimetre is a tenth of a metre (10 dm = 1 m)
- A centimetre is a hundredth of a metre (100 cm = 1 m)

Decimals are short forms for fractions: .73 has 7 tenths (= 700 hundredths) plus 3 more hundredths.

---

1. Write a fraction and a decimal for each picture.

a)   b)   c)

2. Convert the fraction to a decimal. Then shade.

a) $\dfrac{39}{100}$ =

b) $\dfrac{65}{100}$ =

c) $\dfrac{7}{100}$ =

3. The picture shows a floor plan of a zoo. Write a fraction and a decimal for each shaded part:

Key:

▨ reptiles

▩ birds

⠿ amphibians

☐ paths

▨ _____ _____

▩ _____ _____

⠿ _____ _____

☐ _____ _____

4. Make your own floor plan for a zoo. Write a fraction and a decimal for each shaded part:

☐ _____

☐ _____

☐ _____

☐ _____

☐ _____

☐ _____

☐ _____

☐ _____

NS6-63: Tenths and Hundredths

1. Draw lines around the columns to show tenths as in a). Then, write a fraction and a decimal to represent the number of shaded squares.

a)

47 hundredths = 4 tenths ___ hundredths

$\frac{47}{100}$ = . _4_ _7_ ___

b)

___ hundredths = ___ tenths ___ hundredths

$\frac{}{100}$ = . ___ ___

c)

___ hundredths = ___ tenths ___ hundredths

$\frac{}{100}$ = . ___ ___

d)

___ hundredths = ___ tenths ___ hundredths

$\frac{}{100}$ = . ___ ___

2. Fill in the blanks.

    a) 43 hundredths = ___ tenths ___ hundredths

    $\frac{43}{100}$ = . _4_ _3_ ___

    b) 28 hundredths = ___ tenths ___ hundredths

    $\frac{}{100}$ = . ___ ___

    c) 66 hundredths = ___ tenths ___ hundredths

    $\frac{}{100}$ = . ___ ___

    d) 84 hundredths = ___ tenths ___ hundredths

    $\frac{}{100}$ = . ___ ___

    e) 9 hundredths = ___ tenths ___ hundredths

    $\frac{}{100}$ = . ___ ___

    f) 30 hundredths = ___ tenths ___ hundredths

    $\frac{}{100}$ = . ___ ___

3. Describe each decimal in two ways.

    a) .52 = _5_ tenths _2_ hundredths

        = ___52 hundredths___

    b) .55 = ___ tenths ___ hundredths

        = _____

    c) .40 = ___ tenths ___ hundredths

        = _____

    d) .23 = ___ tenths ___ hundredths

        = _____

    e) .02 = ___ tenths ___ hundredths

        = _____

    f) .18 = ___ tenths ___ hundredths

        = _____

               Number Sense 2

1. Fill in the chart below. The first one has been done for you.

Drawing	Fraction	Decimal	Equivalent Decimal	Equivalent Fraction	Drawing
	$\frac{4}{10}$	0.4	0.40	$\frac{40}{100}$	

2. Write a fraction for the number of <u>hundredths</u>. Then count the shaded columns and write a fraction for the number of <u>tenths</u>.

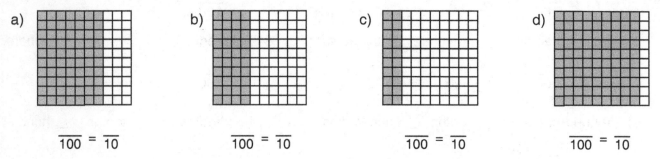

a) $\overline{100}$ = $\overline{10}$ b) $\overline{100}$ = $\overline{10}$ c) $\overline{100}$ = $\overline{10}$ d) $\overline{100}$ = $\overline{10}$

3. Fill in the missing numbers. **REMEMBER:** $\frac{10}{100} = \frac{1}{10}$

a) $.5 = \frac{5}{10} = \overline{100} = .\_\_$ b) $.\_ = \frac{3}{10} = \overline{100} = .30$ c) $.\_ = \frac{9}{10} = \overline{100} = .90$

d) $.\_ = \frac{8}{10} = \overline{100} = .\_\_$ e) $.\_ = \overline{10} = \frac{40}{100} = .\_\_$ f) $.\_ = \overline{10} = \frac{70}{100} = .\_\_$

g) $.\_ = \frac{4}{10} = \overline{100} = .\_\_$ h) $.\_ = \frac{6}{10} = \overline{100} = .\_\_$ i) $.3 = \overline{10} = \overline{100} = .\_\_$

A **dime** is **one tenth** of a dollar. A **penny** is one **hundredth** of a dollar.

1. Express the value of each decimal in four different ways.

a) .64

6 dimes 4 pennies

6 tenths 4 hundredths

64 pennies

64 hundredths

b) .72

_____

_____

_____

_____

c) .43

_____

_____

_____

_____

d) .04

_____

_____

_____

_____

2. A **decimetre** is **one tenth** of a metre. A **centimetre** is a **hundredth** of a metre.
Express the value of each measurement in four different ways.

a) .28 m

2 decimetres 8 centimetres

_____

_____

_____

b) .13 m

_____

_____

_____

_____

3. Express the value of each decimal in 4 different ways.
HINT: First add a zero in the hundredths place.

a) .6 ____ dimes ____ pennies

____ tenths ____ hundredths

____ pennies

____ hundredths

b) .8 ____ dimes ____ pennies

____ tenths ____ hundredths

____ pennies

____ hundredths

4. Express the value of each decimal in four different ways. Then circle the greater number.

a) .27 ____ dimes ____ pennies

____ tenths ____ hundredths

____ pennies

____ hundredths

b) .3 ____ dimes ____ pennies

____ tenths ____ hundredths

____ pennies

____ hundredth

5. George says .63 is greater than .8 because 63 is greater than 8. Can you explain his mistake?

1. Fill in the missing numbers.

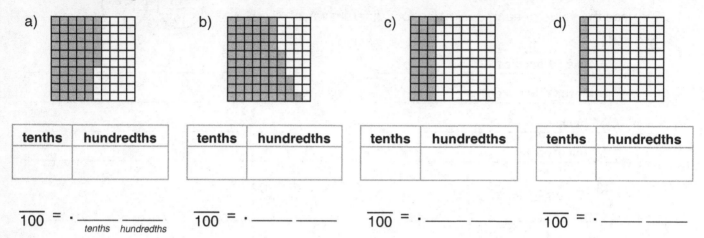

a)		b)		c)		d)	
tenths	hundredths	tenths	hundredths	tenths	hundredths	tenths	hundredths

$\overline{100}$ = . ___ ___ $\overline{100}$ = . ___ ___ $\overline{100}$ = . ___ ___ $\overline{100}$ = . ___ ___
     tenths hundredths

2. Write the following decimals as fractions.

a) $.3 = \overline{10}$ b) $.5 = \overline{10}$ c) $.8 = \overline{10}$ d) $.2 = \overline{10}$ e) $.1 = \overline{10}$

f) $.34 = \overline{100}$ g) $.39 = \overline{100}$ h) $.77 = \overline{100}$ i) $.86 = \overline{100}$ j) $.61 = \overline{100}$

k) .7 =   l) .34 =   m) .06 =   n) .4 =   o) .04 =

p) .6 =   q) .46 =   r) . 25 =   s) .93 =   t) .06 =

3. Change the following fractions to decimals.

a) $\frac{2}{10} = .$ ___   b) $\frac{4}{10} = .$ ___   c) $\frac{3}{10} = .$ ___   d) $\frac{9}{10} = .$ ___

e) $\frac{93}{100} = .$ ___ ___   f) $\frac{78}{100} = .$ ___ ___   g) $\frac{66}{100} = .$ ___ ___   h) $\frac{5}{100} = .$ ___ ___

4. Circle the equalities that are incorrect.

a) $.36 = \frac{36}{100}$ b) $.9 = \frac{9}{100}$ c) $.6 = \frac{6}{10}$ d) $\frac{27}{100} = .27$ e) $\frac{3}{100} = .03$

f) $.75 = \frac{74}{100}$ g) $.40 = \frac{40}{10}$ h) $.75 = \frac{75}{100}$ i) $.08 = \frac{8}{100}$ j) $.03 = \frac{3}{10}$

5. Write as a decimal.

a) 8 tenths 2 hundredths =   b) 0 tenths 9 hundredths =

6. Write .46 as a fraction in lowest terms. Explain how you found your answer.

A hundreds block may be used to represent a whole. 10 is one tenth of 100, so a tens block represents one tenth of the whole. 1 is one hundredth of 100, so a ones block represents one hundredth of the whole.

2 wholes   3 tenths   4 hundredths

ones   hundredths

$2\frac{34}{100} = 2.34$

tenths

NOTE: A mixed fraction can be written as a decimal.

1. Write a mixed fraction and a decimal for the base ten models below.

a)

b)

c)

d)

e)

2. Draw a base ten model for the following decimals.

a) 3.21

b) 1.62

3. Write a decimal and a mixed fraction for each of the pictures below.

a)

b)

4. Write a decimal for each of the mixed fractions below.

a) $1\frac{32}{100} =$

b) $2\frac{71}{100} =$

c) $8\frac{7}{10} =$

d) $4\frac{27}{100} =$

e) $3\frac{7}{100} =$

f) $17\frac{8}{10} =$

g) $27\frac{1}{10} =$

h) $38\frac{5}{100} =$

5. Which decimal represents a greater number?
   Explain your answer with a picture.

a) 6 tenths or 6 hundredths?

b) .8 or .08?

c) 1.02 or 1.20?

This number line is divided into tenths. The number represented by Point A is $2\frac{3}{10}$ or 2.3.

1. Write a fraction or a mixed fraction for each point.

A: _____ B: _____ C: _____ D: _____

E: _____ F: _____ G: _____ H: _____

2. Mark each point with an "X" and label the point with the correct letter.

A. 1.3   **B.** 2.7   **C.** .70   **D.** 1.1

E. $2\frac{1}{10}$

F. one and three tenths   **G.** nine tenths   **H.** one and one tenth   **I.** two decimal nine

3. Write the name of each point as a decimal in words.

A. _____   B. _____   C. _____

4. Mark the decimals on the number lines.

a) **0.6**   b) **1.2**

BONUS

5. Mark the following fractions and decimals on the number line.

A. .72   **B.** $\frac{34}{100}$ **C.** .05   **D.** $\frac{51}{100}$

NS6-69: Comparing and Ordering Fractions and Decimals

1.

a) Write a decimal for each point marked on the number line. (The first decimal is written for you.)

b) Which decimal is equal to one half? $\frac{1}{2}$ =

2. Use the number line in Question 1 to say whether each decimal is closer to "zero," "a half," or "one."

a) .3 is closer to _____

b) .7 is closer to _____

c) .8 is closer to _____

d) .9 is closer to _____

e) .1 is closer to _____

f) .2 is closer to _____

3.

Use the number lines above to compare the numbers given. Write < (less than) or > (greater than) between each pair of numbers.

a) 0.7 ☐ $\frac{3}{4}$

b) 0.4 ☐ $\frac{7}{10}$

c) 0.8 ☐ $\frac{1}{2}$

d) 0.2 ☐ $\frac{1}{4}$

e) 0.4 ☐ $\frac{1}{2}$

f) 0.35 ☐ $\frac{1}{4}$

g) 0.07 ☐ $\frac{1}{2}$

h) $\frac{3}{4}$ ☐ .65

4. Which whole number is each decimal or mixed fraction closest to: "zero," "one," "two," or "three"?

a) 2.4 is closest to _____

b) 2.8 is closest to _____

c) $1\frac{3}{10}$ is closest to _____

NS6-70: Ordering Fractions and Decimals

1. Write the numbers in order by first changing each decimal to a fraction with a denominator of 10.
   NOTE: Show your work beside each number.

   a) 0.6 $\frac{6}{10}$ 0.7 0.4 b) 1.2 $1\frac{2}{10}$ 3.7 3.5 c) 4.7 4.5 $4\frac{3}{10}$

   _____   _____   _____

2. Ali says: "To compare .6 and .42, I add a zero to .6:

   .6 = 6 tenths = 60 hundredths = .60

   60 (hundredths) is greater than 42 (hundredths).

   So .6 is greater than .42."

   Add a zero to the decimal expressed in tenths. Then circle the greater number in each pair.

   a) .4   .32   b) .72   .8   c) .32   .2

3. Write each decimal as a fraction with denominator 100 by first adding a zero to the decimal.

   a) $.7 = \boxed{.70} = \boxed{\frac{70}{100}}$ b) $.9 = \boxed{} = \boxed{}$ c) $.1 = \boxed{} = \boxed{}$

4. Write the numbers in order from least to greatest by first changing all of the decimals to fractions with denominator 100.

   a) .3   .9   .45   b) $\frac{37}{100}$ .8   .32   c) 1.4 $1\frac{34}{100}$ 1.35

   $\boxed{\frac{30}{100}}$ $\boxed{}$ $\boxed{}$ $\boxed{}$ $\boxed{}$ $\boxed{}$ $\boxed{}$ $\boxed{}$ $\boxed{}$

   _____   _____   _____

5. Change $\frac{27}{10}$ to a mixed fraction by shading the correct number of pieces.

   Mixed Fraction: _____

6. Change the following improper fractions to mixed fractions.

   a) $\frac{25}{10}$ b) $\frac{37}{10}$ c) $\frac{86}{10}$ d) $\frac{60}{10}$ e) $\frac{186}{100}$ f) $\frac{175}{100}$

7. Change the following improper fractions to decimals by first writing them as mixed fractions.

   a) $\frac{35}{10} = 3\frac{5}{10} = 3.5$ b) $\frac{38}{10}$ c) $\frac{87}{10}$ d) $\frac{53}{10}$ e) $\frac{153}{100}$ f) $\frac{342}{100}$

8. Which is greater, $\frac{23}{10}$ or 2.4? Explain. | 9. Write 5 decimals greater than 1.32 and less than 1.4.

10. Shade $\frac{1}{2}$ of the squares. Write 2 fractions and 2 decimals for $\frac{1}{2}$.

Fractions: $\frac{1}{2}$ = $\frac{}{10}$ = $\frac{}{100}$

Decimals: $\frac{1}{2}$ = .____ = .____

11. Shade $\frac{1}{5}$ of the boxes. Write 2 fractions and 2 decimals for $\frac{1}{5}$.

Fractions: $\frac{1}{5}$ = $\frac{}{10}$ = $\frac{}{100}$

Decimals: $\frac{1}{5}$ = .____ = .____

12. Write equivalent fractions.

a) $\frac{2}{5}$ = $\frac{}{10}$ = $\frac{}{100}$ b) $\frac{3}{5}$ = $\frac{}{10}$ = $\frac{}{100}$ c) $\frac{4}{5}$ = $\frac{}{10}$ = $\frac{}{100}$

13. Shade $\frac{1}{4}$ of the squares. Write a fraction and a decimal for $\frac{1}{4}$ and $\frac{3}{4}$.

Fraction: $\frac{1}{4}$ = $\frac{}{100}$ Decimal: $\frac{1}{4}$ = .____

Fraction: $\frac{3}{4}$ = $\frac{}{100}$ Decimal: $\frac{3}{4}$ = .____

14. Circle the greater number.
HINT: First change all fractions and decimals to fractions with denominator 100.

a) $\frac{3}{4}$. 72   b) $\frac{1}{2}$ .53   c) $\frac{3}{5}$. 87

$\frac{75}{100}$

15. Write the numbers in order from least to greatest. Explain how you found your answer.

a) .8   .42 $\frac{3}{4}$ b) $\frac{1}{2}$ $\frac{4}{5}$ .35   c) $\frac{3}{5}$ .45 $\frac{1}{2}$

16. How does knowing that $\frac{1}{4}$ = 0.25 help you find the decimal form of $\frac{3}{4}$?

17. Explain how you know 0.65 is greater that $\frac{1}{2}$.

If a thousands cube is used to represent a whole number, then a hundreds block represents a tenth, a tens block represents a hundredth, and a ones block represents a thousandth of a whole.

REMEMBER:

tenths   thousandths

ones 6.146

hundredths

1 whole   1 tenth   1 hundredth   1 thousandth

----

1. Beside each number, write the place value of the underlined digit.

a) 3.2<u>7</u>4

b) 9.27<u>3</u>

c) 2.<u>5</u>37

d) 7.12<u>9</u>

e) <u>5</u>.214

f) 8.<u>9</u>78

2. Write the following numbers into the place value chart. The first one has been done for you.

	ones	tenths	hundredths	thousandths
a) 6.512	6	5	1	2
c) 7.03				
e) 1.763				
g) 6.38				
i) 5.813				

	ones	tenths	hundredths	thousandths
b) 6.354				
d) 1.305				
f) 0.536				
h) 8				
j) 0.13				

3. Write the following decimals as fractions.

a) .652 =

b) .372 =

c) .20 =

d) .002 =

4. Write each decimal in expanded form.

a) .237 = _2 tenths + 3 hundredths + 7 thousandths_

b) .325 = _____

c) 6.336 = _____

5. Write the following fractions as decimals.

a) $\frac{49}{100}$ =

b) $\frac{50}{100}$ =

c) $\frac{758}{1000}$ =

d) $\frac{25}{1000}$ =

6. Compare each pair of decimals by writing < or > in the box.
   HINT: Add zeroes wherever necessary to give each number the same number of digits after the decimal point.

a) .375 ☐ .378

b) .233 ☐ .47

c) .956 ☐ .1

d) .27 ☐ .207

e) .7 ☐ .32

f) .8 ☐ .516

Number Sense 2

1. Write a fraction for each shaded part. Then add the fractions, and shade your answer. The first one has been done for you.

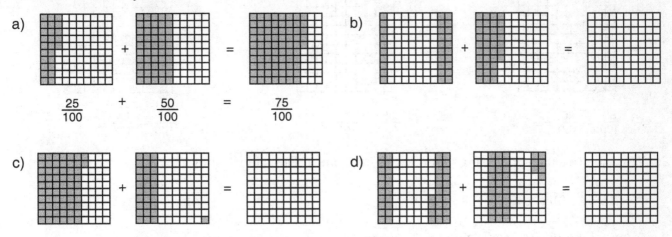

a)

$$\frac{25}{100} \quad + \quad \frac{50}{100} \quad = \quad \frac{75}{100}$$

b)

c)

d)

2. Write the decimals that correspond to the fractions in Question 1 above.

a) .25 + .50 = .75	b)
c)	d)

3. Add the decimals by lining up the digits. Be sure that your final answer is expressed as a decimal.

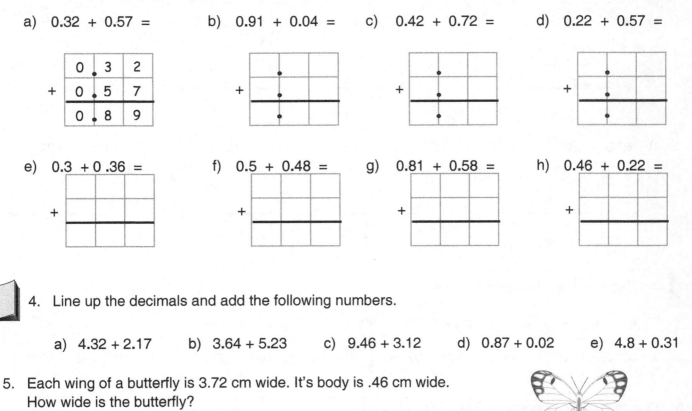

a) 0.32 + 0.57 =

	0	3	2
+	0	5	7
	0	8	9

b) 0.91 + 0.04 =

c) 0.42 + 0.72 =

d) 0.22 + 0.57 =

e) 0.3 + 0 .36 =

f) 0.5 + 0.48 =

g) 0.81 + 0.58 =

h) 0.46 + 0.22 =

4. Line up the decimals and add the following numbers.

   a) 4.32 + 2.17   b) 3.64 + 5.23   c) 9.46 + 3.12   d) 0.87 + 0.02   e) 4.8 + 0.31

5. Each wing of a butterfly is 3.72 cm wide. It's body is .46 cm wide. How wide is the butterfly?

6. Anne made punch by mixing .63 litres of juice with .36 litres of ginger ale. How many litres of punch did she make?

NS6-73: Subtracting Hundredths

1. Subtract by crossing out the correct number of boxes.

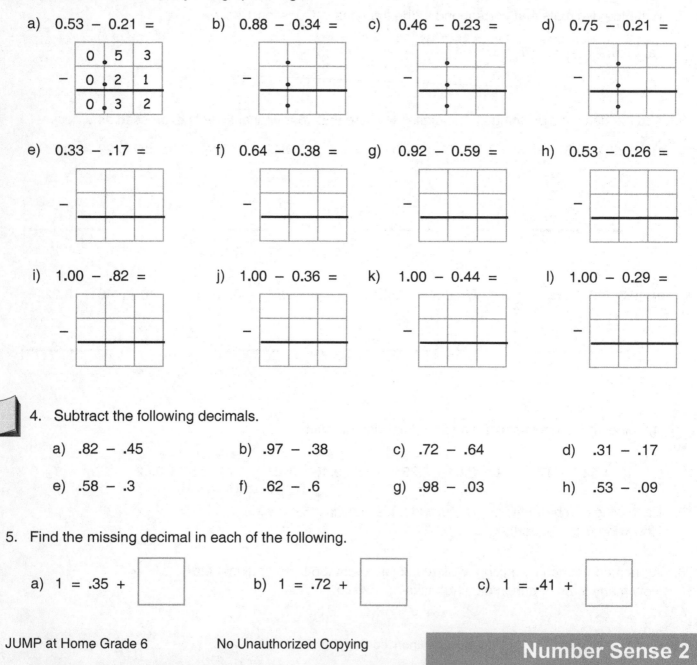

   a) $\frac{50}{100} - \frac{30}{100} =$ b) $\frac{38}{100} - \frac{12}{100} =$ c) $\frac{69}{100} - \frac{34}{100} =$

2. Write the decimals that correspond to the fractions in Question 1 above.

a) .50 - .30 = .20	b)	c)

3. Subtract the decimals by lining up the digits.

   a) 0.53 − 0.21 =

	0 .	5	3
−	0 .	2	1
	0 .	3	2

   b) 0.88 − 0.34 =   c) 0.46 − 0.23 =   d) 0.75 − 0.21 =

   e) 0.33 − .17 =   f) 0.64 − 0.38 =   g) 0.92 − 0.59 =   h) 0.53 − 0.26 =

   i) 1.00 − .82 =   j) 1.00 − 0.36 =   k) 1.00 − 0.44 =   l) 1.00 − 0.29 =

4. Subtract the following decimals.

   a) .82 − .45   b) .97 − .38   c) .72 − .64   d) .31 − .17

   e) .58 − .3   f) .62 − .6   g) .98 − .03   h) .53 − .09

5. Find the missing decimal in each of the following.

   a) 1 = .35 + ☐   b) 1 = .72 + ☐   c) 1 = .41 + ☐

JUMP at Home Grade 6   No Unauthorized Copying   **Number Sense 2**

1. Add by drawing a base ten model. Then, using the chart provided, line up the decimal points and add.
   NOTE: Use a hundreds block for a whole and a tens block for one tenth.

   a) 1.23 + 1.12

   b) 1.46 + 1.33

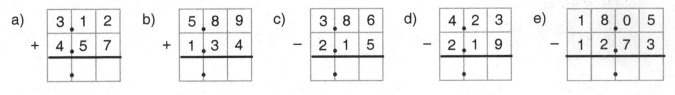

ones	tenths	hundredths
+		

ones	tenths	hundredths
+		

2. Draw a model of the greater number. Then subtract by crossing out blocks as shown in part a).

   a) 2.35 − 1.12 = 1.23

   b) 3.24 − 2.11

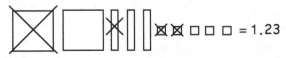 = 1.23

3. Add or subtract.

   a)
3	1	2
+ 4	5	7

   b)
5	8	9
+ 1	3	4

   c)
3	8	6
− 2	1	5

   d)
4	2	3
− 2	1	9

   e)
1	8	0	5
− 1	2	7	3

4. Subtract each pair of numbers by lining up the decimal points.

   a) 7.87 − 4.03   b) 9.74 − 6.35   c) 2.75 − .28   d) 28.71 − 1.4   e) 17.9 − 4.29

5. The average temperature in Jakarta is 30.33°C and, in Toronto, it is 11.9°C.
   How much warmer is Jakarta than Toronto?

6. Mercury is 57.6 million kilometres from the Sun.
   Earth is 148.64 million kilometres from the Sun.

   How much farther from the Sun is the Earth?

7. Continue the patterns.   a) .2,   .4,   .6, ____, ____, ____   b) .3,   .6,   .9, ____, ____, ____

If a hundreds block represents 1 whole,
then a tens block represents 1 tenth (or 0.1).

10 tenths make 1 whole:
10 × 0.1 = 1.0

----

1. Multiply the number of tens blocks by 10. Then show how many hundreds blocks you would have. The first one is done for you.

a)

10 × 0.2 = ___2___

b)

10 × 0.3 = _____

c)

10 × 0.6 = _____

2. Multiply.

a) 10 × .5 = ____   b) 10 × .7 = ____   c) 10 × 1.4 = ____   d) 10 × .9 = ____

e) 10 × 1.7 = ____   f) 1.6 × 10 = ____   g) 18.2 × 10 = ____   h) 17.3 × 10 = ____

i) 10 × 23.5 = ____   j) 10 × 1.72 = ____   k) 10 × 42.6 = ____   l) 5.36 × 10 = ____

3. To change from dm to cm, you multiply by 10 (there are 10 cm in 1 dm).

1 dm

$1 \text{ cm} = \frac{1}{10} \text{ dm} = 0.1 \text{ dm}$

Find the answers.

a) .6 dm = _____ cm   b) .8 dm = _____ cm   c) 1.6 dm = _____ cm

4. 10 × 3 can be written as a sum: 3 + 3 + 3 + 3 + 3 + 3 + 3 + 3 + 3 + 3.

   Write 10 × .3 as a sum and skip count by .3 to find the answer.

5. A dime is a tenth of a dollar (10¢ = $0.10).

   Draw a picture or use play money to show that 10 × $0.20 = $2.00.

NS6-76: Multiplying Decimals by 100 and 1000

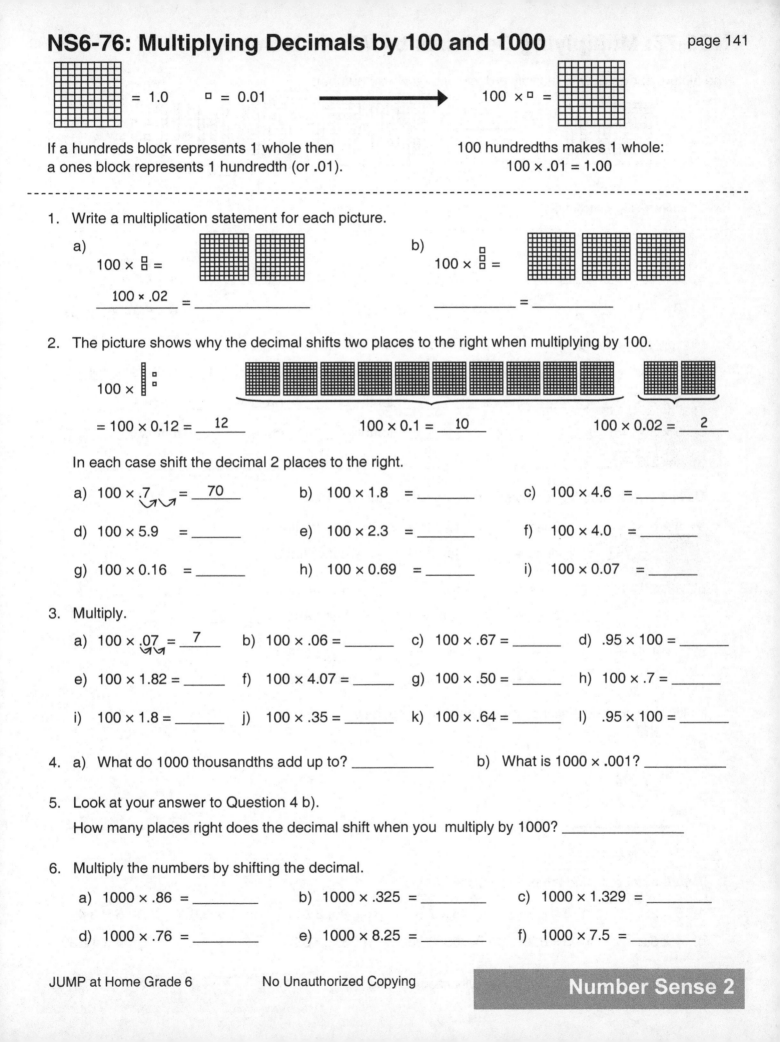

= 1.0   □ = 0.01   ⟶   100 × □ =

If a hundreds block represents 1 whole then
a ones block represents 1 hundredth (or .01).

100 hundredths makes 1 whole:
100 × .01 = 1.00

- -

1. Write a multiplication statement for each picture.

   a)
   $100 \times \begin{smallmatrix}□\\□\end{smallmatrix} =$

   ___100 × .02___ = _____

   b)
   $100 \times \begin{smallmatrix}□\\□\end{smallmatrix} =$

   _____ = _____

2. The picture shows why the decimal shifts two places to the right when multiplying by 100.

   $100 \times \begin{smallmatrix}|\\|\end{smallmatrix}\begin{smallmatrix}□\\□\end{smallmatrix}$

   = 100 × 0.12 = ___12___   100 × 0.1 = ___10___   100 × 0.02 = ___2___

   In each case shift the decimal 2 places to the right.

   a) 100 × .7 = ___70___   b) 100 × 1.8 = _____   c) 100 × 4.6 = _____

   d) 100 × 5.9 = _____   e) 100 × 2.3 = _____   f) 100 × 4.0 = _____

   g) 100 × 0.16 = _____   h) 100 × 0.69 = _____   i) 100 × 0.07 = _____

3. Multiply.

   a) 100 × .07 = ___7___   b) 100 × .06 = _____   c) 100 × .67 = _____   d) .95 × 100 = _____

   e) 100 × 1.82 = _____   f) 100 × 4.07 = _____   g) 100 × .50 = _____   h) 100 × .7 = _____

   i) 100 × 1.8 = _____   j) 100 × .35 = _____   k) 100 × .64 = _____   l) .95 × 100 = _____

4. a) What do 1000 thousandths add up to? _____   b) What is 1000 × .001? _____

5. Look at your answer to Question 4 b).

   How many places right does the decimal shift when you multiply by 1000? _____

6. Multiply the numbers by shifting the decimal.

   a) 1000 × .86 = _____   b) 1000 × .325 = _____   c) 1000 × 1.329 = _____

   d) 1000 × .76 = _____   e) 1000 × 8.25 = _____   f) 1000 × 7.5 = _____

The picture shows how to multiply a decimal by a whole number.

1.23   × 3 $3 \times 1.23 = 3.69$

HINT: Simply multiply each digit separately.

----

1. Multiply mentally.

   a) $2 \times 1.43 =$ _____   b) $3 \times 1.2 =$ _____   c) $5 \times 1.01 =$ _____   d) $4 \times 2.1 =$ _____

   e) $2 \times 5.34 =$ _____   f) $4 \times 2.1 =$ _____   g) $3 \times 3.12 =$ _____   h) $3 \times 4.32 =$ _____

2. Multiply by exchanging tenths for ones (the first one is done for you).

   a) 6×1.4 = __$6 \times 1 = 6$__ ones + __$6 \times 4 = 24$__ tenths = __8__ ones + __4__ tenths = __8.4__

   b) 3×2.5 = _____ ones + _____ tenths = _____ ones + _____ tenths = _____

   c) 3×2.7 = _____ ones + _____ tenths = _____ ones + _____ tenths = _____

   d) 4×2.6 = _____

3. Multiply by exchanging tenths for ones or hundredths for tenths.

   a) $3 \times 2.51 =$ _____ ones + _____ tenths + _____ hundredths

      = _____ ones + _____ tenths + _____ hundredths = _____

   b) $4 \times 2.14 =$ _____ ones + _____ tenths + _____ hundredths

      = _____ ones + _____ tenths + _____ hundredths = _____

   c) $5 \times 1.41 =$ _____ ones + _____ tenths + _____ hundredths

      = _____ ones + _____ tenths + _____ hundredths = _____

4. Multiply. In some questions you will have to regroup twice.

   a)   b)   c)   d)

   | 3 | 4 | 5 | | 7 | 6 | 2 | | 4 | 3 | 1 | | 3 | 2 | 5 |
   | × | | 3 | | × | | 4 | | × | | 6 | | × | | 3 |

5. In your notebook, find the products.

   a) 5×2.1 b) 3×8.3 c) 5×7.5 d) 9×2.81 e) 7×3.6 f) 6×3.4

   g) 4×3.2 h) 5×6.35 i) 6×3.95 j) 8×2.63 k) 3×31.21 l) 4×12.32

When you divide a decimal by 10 the decimal shifts <u>one place to the left</u>:

0 . 7 ÷ 10 = .07   7 . 0 ÷ 10 = .7

When you divide a decimal by 100 the decimal shifts <u>two places to the left</u>.

7 . 0 ÷ 100 = .07

Divide 1 whole into
10 equal parts –
each part is 1 tenth:
1.0 ÷ 10 = 0.1

Divide 1 tenth into
10 equal parts –
each part is 1 hundredth:
0.1 ÷ 10 = 0.01

Divide 1 whole into
100 equal parts –
each part is 1 hundredth:
1.0 ÷ 100 = 0.01

---

1. Complete the picture and write a division statement for each picture.

   a)   ÷ 10 =

   <u> 2.0 ÷ 10 </u> = <u> .2 </u>

   b)   ÷ 10 =

   <u>   </u> = <u>   </u>

   c)   ÷ 10 = □□□

   <u> .3 ÷ 10 </u> = <u>   </u>

   d)   ÷ 10 =

   <u>   </u> = <u>   </u>

   e)   ÷ 10 =

   <u>   </u> = <u>   </u>

2. Complete the picture and write a division statement (the first one is done for you).

   a)   ÷ 10 =

   <u> 2.3 ÷ 10 </u> = <u> .23 </u>

   b)   ÷ 10 =

   <u>   </u> = <u>   </u>

3. Shift the decimal one or two places to the left by drawing an arrow as shown in 3 a).
   HINT: If there is no decimal, add one to the right of the number first.

   a) 0.3 ÷ 10 = <u>.03 </u>   b) 0.5 ÷ 10 = _____   c) 0.7 ÷ 10 = _____   d) 1.3 ÷ 10 = _____

   e) 7.6 ÷ 10 = _____   f) 12.0 ÷ 10 = _____   g) 9 ÷ 10 = _____   h) 6 ÷ 10 = _____

   i) 42 ÷ 10 = _____   j) 17 ÷ 10 = _____   k) .9 ÷ 10 = _____   l) 27.3 ÷ 10 = _____

   m) 3.0 ÷ 100 = _____   n) 6.2 ÷ 100 = _____   o) .7 ÷ 100 = _____   p) 17.2 ÷ 100 = _____

4. Explain why 1.00 ÷ 100 = .01 using dollar coins as a whole.

5. A wall 3.5 m wide is painted with 100 stripes of equal width.
   How wide is each stripe?

6. 5 × 3 = 15 and 15 ÷ 5 = 3 are in the same fact family.
   Write a division statement in the same fact family as 10 × 0.1 = 1.0.

You can divide a decimal by a whole number by making a base ten model. Keep track of your work using long division. Use a hundreds block to represent 1 whole, a tens block to represent 1 tenth, and a ones block to represent 1 hundredth.

1 whole   1 tenth   □ 1 hundredth

----

1. Find **5.12 ÷ 2** by drawing a base ten model and by long division.

   Step 1: *Draw a base ten model of 5.12.*

   > Draw your model here:

   Step 2: *Divide the whole blocks into 2 equal groups.*

   - number of ones or units in each group
   - number of ones placed
   - number of ones left over

   remaining wholes, tenths and hundredths

   Step 3: *Exchange the left over whole blocks for 10 tenths.*

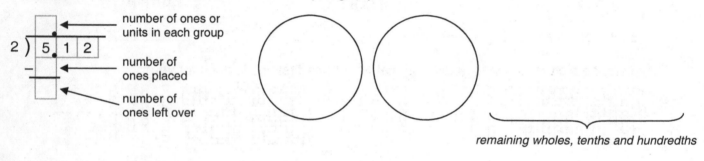

   - number of tenths to be placed

   regroup a whole as 10 tenths

   REMEMBER: *A whole is represented by a hundreds block.*

   Step 4: *Divide the tenths blocks into 2 equal groups.*

   - number of tenths in each group
   - number of tenths placed
   - number of tenths left over

   remaining tenths and hundredths

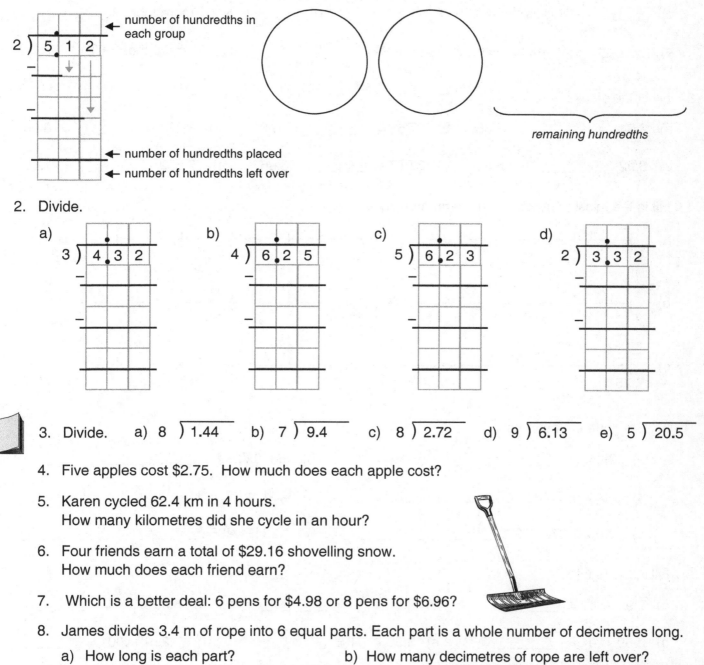

Step 5:   *Regroup the left over tenth block as 10 hundredths.*

← number of hundredths to be placed

exchange a tenth for 10 hundredths

Steps 6 and 7:   *Divide the hundredths into 2 equal groups.*

← number of hundredths in each group

remaining hundredths

← number of hundredths placed

← number of hundredths left over

2. Divide.

    a)   3) 4 . 3 2   b)   4) 6 . 2 5   c)   5) 6 . 2 3   d)   2) 3 . 3 2

3. Divide.   a) $8\,\overline{)\,1.44}$ b) $7\,\overline{)\,9.4}$ c) $8\,\overline{)\,2.72}$ d) $9\,\overline{)\,6.13}$ e) $5\,\overline{)\,20.5}$

4. Five apples cost $2.75. How much does each apple cost?

5. Karen cycled 62.4 km in 4 hours.
   How many kilometres did she cycle in an hour?

6. Four friends earn a total of $29.16 shovelling snow.
   How much does each friend earn?

7. Which is a better deal: 6 pens for $4.98 or 8 pens for $6.96?

8. James divides 3.4 m of rope into 6 equal parts. Each part is a whole number of decimetres long.

   a) How long is each part?   b) How many decimetres of rope are left over?

1. Fill in the blanks.

   a) .74 + .1 = _____

   b) .23 + .1 = _____

   c) .09   + .1 = _____

   d) .79 + .1 = _____

   e) .50 + .01 = _____

   f) 2.79 + .01 = _____

   g) 3.056 + .001 = _____

   h) 0.009 + .001 = _____

   i) 2.372 + .01 = _____

2. Fill in the blanks.

   a) _____ is .1 more than .4

   b) _____ is .1 more than 0.9

   c) _____ is .1 more than 3.25

   d) _____ is .01 more than .75

   e) _____ is .01 more than .79

   f) _____ is .001 more than .372

3. Fill in the blanks.

   a) 2.34 + _____ = 2.35

   b) 3.75 + _____ = 3.85

   c) 8.07 – _____ = 8.06

   d) 6.92 – _____ = 6.82

   e) 3.957 + _____ = 3.967

   f) 7.852 + _____ = 7.853

4. Fill in the missing numbers on the number lines.

   a)
   7.0   8.0

   b)
   3.15   3.25

   c)
   7.253   7.263

5. Continue the patterns.

   a) .3, .4, .5, _____, _____, _____

   b) 9.6, 9.7, 9.8 , _____, _____, _____

   c) 2.5, 2.6, 2.7, _____, _____, _____

   d) 4.34, 4.35, 4.36 _____, _____, _____

   e) 2.96, 2.97, 2.98, _____, _____, _____

   f) 1.234, 1.235 , _____, _____

6. Fill in the blanks.

   a) 7.9 + .1 = _____

   b) 2.9 + .1 = _____

   c) 6.95 + .1 = _____

   d) 2.69 + .01 = _____

   e) 3.99 + .01 = _____

   f) 7.299 + .001 = _____

NS6-81: Place Value and Rounding

1. Round to the nearest whole number.

    a) 26.408   b) 38.97   c) 59.962   d) 71.001

2. Round to the nearest tenth.

    a) 26.54   b) 47.946   c) 49.874   d) 38.96

3. Estimate by rounding to the nearest whole number.

    a) 94.7 ÷ 5.2

    Estimate.

    ☐ ÷ ☐ = ☐

    b) 2.96 × 8.147

    Estimate.

    ☐ × ☐ = ☐

    c) 4.51 × 0.86

    Estimate.

    ☐ × ☐ = ☐

4. Estimate by rounding each number to the nearest whole number. Use your estimate to say which answers are reasonable.

    a) 32.7 + 4.16 = 73.8   b) 0.7 × 8.3 = 5.81   c) 9.2 × 10.3 = 947.6

    d) 97.2 ÷ 0.9 = .8   e) 88.2 ÷ 9.8 = 9   f) 54.3 − 18.6 = 35.7

5. Calculate each answer from Question 4. Were your predictions correct?

6. 5.3 is said to be precise to the tenths. Any number from 5.25 to 5.34 could round it. What numbers could round to 7.2?

7. Which measurement would need to be taken to the nearest tenth?

    a) Height of a building (metres).
    b) Distance shot put is thrown in Olympic Games (metres).
    c) Length of the Canada/U.S. border (kilometres).

8. What amount is represented by the tenths digit?

    a) 3.54 m   b) 6.207 km   c) 4.69 dm

    d) 4.6 million   e) $17.46   f) 83.4 cm

The size of a unit of measurement depends on which unit has been selected as the <u>whole</u>.

A millimetre is a **tenth** of a centimetre,
but it is only a **hundredth** of a decimetre.
REMEMBER: A decimetre is 10 centimetres.

1 cm   1 mm

1 dm

----

1. Draw a picture in the space provided to show 1 tenth of each whole.

    a)

    1 whole   1 tenth

    b)

    1 whole   1 tenth

    c)

    1 whole   1 tenth

2. Write each measurement as a fraction and then as a decimal.

    a) 1 cm = $\frac{1}{10}$ dm = ___.1___ dm

    b) 100 mm = [ ] m = _____ m

    c) 1 mm = [ ] cm = _____ cm

    d) 16 mm = [ ] cm = _____ cm

    e) 77 mm = [ ] dm = _____ dm

    f) 83 cm = [ ] m = _____ m

3. Add the measurements by first changing the <u>smaller unit</u> into a decimal in the <u>larger unit</u>.

    a) 5 cm + 7.3 dm = __0.5 dm + 7.3 dm = 7.8 dm__

    b) 5 cm + 3.2 dm = _____

    c) 8 mm + 5.7 cm = _____

    d) 33 cm + 1.64 m = _____

    e) 685 cm + 12.3 m = _____

    f) 982 cm + 1.5 m = _____

4. Write a decimal for each description. Some questions have more than one answer.

    a) Between 4.31 and 4.34   [ ].[ ][ ]

    b) Between 2.60 and 2.70   [ ].[ ][ ]

    c) Between 13.75 and 13.8   [ ][ ].[ ][ ]

    d) Between 9.7 and 9.8   [ ][ ].[ ][ ]

    e) One tenth greater than 5.23   [ ].[ ][ ]

    f) One hundredth less than 4.00   [ ].[ ][ ]

5. Add.

   a) $4\,000 + 300 + 7 + 0.01 =$ _____

   b) $20\,000 + 300 + 30 + 0.2 + .04 =$ _____

   c) $300\,000 + 20\,000 + 5000 + 70 + 0.1 + 0.09 + 0.006 =$ _____

6. Write < or > to show which decimal is greater.

   a) 4.9 [ ] 4.6   b) 3.45 [ ] 3.35   c) 1.9 [ ] 1.26   d) 0.7 [ ] 0.524

7. Put a decimal in each number so that the digit **7** has the value $\frac{7}{10}$.

   a) 5 7 2   b) 1 0 7   c) 2 8 7 5 9   d) 7

8. Use the digits 5, 6, 7, and 0 to write a number between the given numbers.

   a) .567 < _____ < .576

   b) 5.607 < _____ < 5.760

9. Write three decimals between .3 and .5: _____ _____ _____

10. Write −, +, ×, or ÷ in the circle.

    a) 62.57 ( ) 10 = 72.57   b) 19.2 ( ) 10 = 192   c) 9 ( ) 10 = .9

11. Write the decimals in order from least to greatest. Explain your answer for c).

    a) .37 .275 .371   b) .007 .07 .7   c) 1.29 1.3 2.001

12. Use the number line to estimate which fraction lies in each range.

    ```
    |---+---+---+---+---+---+---+---+---+---|
    0  .1  .2  .3  .4  .5  .6  .7  .8  .9  1.0
    ```

    Fractions: $\frac{1}{2}$, $\frac{1}{3}$, $\frac{3}{4}$, $\frac{1}{10}$

    Ranges:

A	B	C	D	E
0 to .2	.2 to .4	.4 to .6	.6 to .8	.8 to 1.0

13. Is 6 a reasonable estimate for $8 \times .72$? Explain.

14. How do you know that 10×87.3 is 873 and not 8 730?

15. Charge 1.25 hours to a mixed fraction in lowest terms, then to a time in minutes.

Answer the following questions in your notebook.

1. Explain how you would change 5.47 m into cm.
   HINT: How many centimetres are in $\frac{47}{100}$ of a metre?

2. $0.68 means 6 dimes and 8 pennies.

   Why do we use the decimal notation for money?

   What is a dime a tenth of?

   What is a penny a hundredth of?

3. The wind speed in Vancouver was 26.7 km/h on Monday, 16.0 km/h on Tuesday and 2.4 km/h on Wednesday.

   What was the average wind speed over the 3 days?

4. The tallest human skeleton is 2.7 m high and the shortest is 60 cm high. What is the difference in the heights of the skeletons?

5.

Star	Distance from the Sun in light years
Alpha Centauri	4.3
Barnard's Star	6.0
L726-8	8.8
Sirius	9.5
61 Cigni	11.0

A light year is 9.5 trillion kilometres.
NOTE: This is the distance light travels in one year.

a) If you travelled from the Sun to Barnard's Star, how many trillion km would you have travelled?

b) Which star is just over twice as far from the Sun as Alpha Centauri?

6. Food moves through the esophagus at a rate of .72 km per hour.

   How many metres per hour is this?

7. Write the following prices in order from least to greatest.
   What is the difference between the highest and the lowest prices?
   HINT: Change all the prices to dollars per kilogram.

A: Cherries –
59¢ for each 100 g

B: Watermelon –
$3.90 for each kg

C: Strawberries –
$0.32 for each 100 g

D: Blueberries –
$3.99 for each 500 g

Number Sense 2

NS6-84: Unit Rates

A rate is a comparison of two quantities in different units.

In a **unit rate**, one of the quantities is equal to one.

For instance, "1 apple costs 30¢" is a unit rate.

30¢

----

1. Fill in the missing information.

   a) 17 km in 1 hour

      _____ km in 3 hours

   b) 1 book costs $4.95

      4 book costs _____

   c) 2 teachers for 75 students

      6 teachers for _____

   d) 5 mangoes cost $4.95

      1 mango costs _____

   e) 4 mangoes cost $12

      1 mango costs _____

   f) 6 pears cost $4.92

      1 pear costs _____

2. Find the unit rate.

   a) 4 kg of rice for 60 cups of water.

      1 kg of rice for _____ cups of water.

   b) 236 km in 4 hours.

      _____ km in 1 hr.

   c) 6 cans of juice cost $1.98

      1 can costs _____

3. Use a ruler to find out the height of each animal. (One centimetre represents 50 cm in real life.)

   a)
   Kangaroo
   Height of picture in cm: _____
   Height of animal in m: _____

   b)
   Height of picture in cm: _____
   Height of animal in m: _____
   Horse

   c)
   Height of picture in cm: _____
   Height of animal in m: _____

   Giraffe

4. Ron earns $66 babysitting for six hours. How much does he earn in an hour?

   _____

5. Tina earns $75 cutting lawns for 5 hours. How much does she earn in an hour?

   _____

JUMP at Home Grade 6   No Unauthorized Copying   **Number Sense 2**

A **ratio** is a comparison between two numbers.

1.

a) The ratio of moons to circles is _____ : _____

b) The ratio of triangles to moons is _____ : _____

c) The ratio of cylinders to squares is _____ : _____

d) The ratio of squares to circles is _____ : _____

e) The ratio of squares to moon is _____ : _____

f) The ratio of squares to figures is _____ : _____

2. Write the number of vowels compared to the number of consonants in the following words.

a) apple   _2_ : _3_

b) banana   ____ : ____

c) orange   ____ : ____

d) pear   ____ : ____

3. Write the ratio of the lengths.

	3		2		6		6		4		1		5	
A		B		C		D		E		F		G		H

a) AB to DE _____ : _____

b) BC to CD _____ : _____

c) EF to FG _____ : _____

d) EF to BC _____ : _____

e) AB to GH _____ : _____

f) CD to FG _____ : _____

4. To make punch, you need ...

- 4 L of ginger ale
- 2 L of orange juice
- 3 L of mango juice

What is the ratio of ginger ale to punch?

_____

5.

a) In the above pattern, what does the ratio 2 : 3 describe?

_____

b) What does the ratio 5 : 10 describe?

_____

6. Build a model or draw a picture that could be described by the ratio 3 : 4.

NS6-86: Equivalent Ratios

1. The picture shows that the ratio of apples to bananas on a grocery shelf is:

   8 apples to every 6 bananas

   OR

   4 apples to every 3 bananas.

   Group the fruit to show two equivalent ratios.

   a)

   _____ to every _____

   or _____ to every _____

   b)

   _____ to every _____

   or _____ to every _____

2. Starting with the ratio 2 triangles to every 3 squares, Talia created a sequence of equivalent ratios. Fill in the missing figures and ratios.

Triangles				
Squares				
Ratio	2 : 3			

3. Starting with the ratio given, write a sequence of five ratios that are all equivalent.

   a) 3 : 4 = 6 : 8 =   :   =   :   =   :

   b) 2 : 5 =

4. Find the missing terms.   a) 3 : 4 = _____ : 8   b) 5 : 7 = 10 : _____   c) 2 : 5 = _____ : 25

A recipe for granola calls for 2 cups of raisins for every 3 cups of oats.

How many cups of raisins will Eschi need for 12 cups of oats?

She writes a sequence of equivalent ratios to find out.

NOTE: She multiplies both terms in the ratio 2 : 3 by 2, then by 3, then by 4.

2 : 3 = 4 : 6 = 6 : 9 = 8 : 12

Eschi needs 8 cups of raisins.

---

5. Solve each problem by writing a sequence of equivalent ratios (as in the example above).

   a) A recipe calls for 5 cups of oats for every 3 cups of raisins.
       How many cups of oats are needed for 12 cups of raisins?

   b) 2 cm on a map represent 11 km.
       How many km do 8 cm on the map represent?

   c) Six bus tickets cost $5.
       How much will 18 tickets cost?

There are 3 boys for every 2 girls in a class of 20 children.

To find out how many boys are in the class, write a sequence of ratios.

$$3 \text{ boys} : 2 \text{ girls} = 6 \text{ boys} : 4 \text{ girls} = 9 \text{ boys} : 6 \text{ girls} = \underline{12 \text{ boys} : 8 \text{ girls}}$$

Stop when the terms of the ratio add to 20.

12 boys + 8 girls = 20 students. So there are 12 boys in the class.

1. Write a sequence of ratios to solve each problem. The first one is started for you.

a) There are 5 boys for every 4 girls in a class of 27 children.
   How many girls are in the class?

$$5 : 4 = 10 : 8 =$$

b) There are 3 red fish for every 5 blue fish in an aquarium.
   With 24 fish, how many fish are blue?

c) A recipe for punch calls for 3 L of orange juice for every 2 litres of mango juice.
   How many litres of orange juice are needed to make 15 litres of punch?

Five subway tickets cost $4. Kyle wants to know how much 20 tickets will cost. He writes the ratio of tickets to dollars as a fraction. Then, he finds an equivalent fraction by multiplying:

Step 1:	Step 2:	Step 3:	Step 4:
$\dfrac{4}{5} = \dfrac{?}{20}$	$\dfrac{4}{5} = \dfrac{}{20}$	$\dfrac{4}{5} \xrightarrow[\times 4]{\times 4} \dfrac{}{20}$	$\dfrac{4}{5} \xrightarrow[\times 4]{\times 4} \dfrac{16}{20}$

2. Solve the following ratios. Draw arrows to show what you multiply by.

a) $\dfrac{3}{4} \xrightarrow[\times 5]{\times 5} \dfrac{}{20}$

b) $\dfrac{1}{5} = \dfrac{}{25}$

c) $\dfrac{2}{5} = \dfrac{}{20}$

d) $\dfrac{6}{7} = \dfrac{}{35}$

e) $\dfrac{3}{4} = \dfrac{}{16}$

f) $\dfrac{2}{3} = \dfrac{}{12}$

g) $\dfrac{15}{25} = \dfrac{}{100}$

h) $\dfrac{5}{9} = \dfrac{}{45}$

BONUS

NOTE: Sometimes, in the questions below, the arrow may point from right to left.

3. a) $\dfrac{15}{} \xleftarrow[\times 5]{\times 5} \dfrac{3}{4}$

b) $\dfrac{10}{} = \dfrac{2}{5}$

c) $\dfrac{9}{} = \dfrac{3}{7}$

d) $\dfrac{10}{15} = \dfrac{}{3}$

e) $\dfrac{4}{5} = \dfrac{}{15}$

f) $\dfrac{2}{3} = \dfrac{}{9}$

g) $\dfrac{}{45} = \dfrac{2}{5}$

h) $\dfrac{}{20} = \dfrac{7}{10}$

In a pet shop, there are 3 cats for every 2 dogs. If there are 12 cats in the shop, how many dogs are there?

Solution:

Step 1:
Write, as a fraction, the ratio of the two things being compared.

$$\frac{3}{2}$$

Step 2:
Write, in words, what each number stands for.

cats $\frac{3}{2}$
dogs

Step 3:
On the other side of an equals sign, write the *same* words, on the *same* levels.

cats $\frac{3}{2}$ = —— cats
dogs   dogs

Step 4:
Re-read the question to determine which quantity (i.e. number of cats or dogs) has been given (in this case, cats) – then place that quantity on the proper level.

cats $\frac{3}{2}$ = $\frac{12}{\ \ }$ cats
dogs   dogs

Step 5:
Solve the ratio.

Solve the following questions in your notebook.

1. There are 2 apples in a bowl for every 3 oranges.
   If there are 9 oranges, how many apples are there?

2. Five bus tickets costs $3.
   How many bus tickets can you buy with $9?

3. A basketball team won 2 out of every 3 games they played. They played a total of 15 games.
   How many games did they win?
   NOTE: The quantities are "games won" and "games played."

4. To make fruit punch, you mix 1 litre of orange juice with 2 litres of pineapple juice.
   If you have 3 litres of orange juice, how many litres of pineapple juice do you need?

5. Nora can run 3 laps in 4 minutes.
   At that rate, how many laps could she run in 12 minutes?

6. The ratio of boys to girls in a class is 4:5.
   If there are 20 boys, how many girls are there?

7. 2 cm on a map represents 5 km in real life.
   If a lake is 6 cm long on the map, what is its actual size?

Tony can paint 3 walls in $\frac{1}{2}$ an hour. He wants to know how many walls he can paint in 5 hours.

He first changes the ratio $\frac{1}{2}$: 3 to a more convenient form by doubling both terms of the ratio.

$\frac{1}{2}$ hour : 3 walls = 1 hour : 6 walls

Then he multiplies each term by 5.

1 hour : 6 walls = 5 hours : 30 walls

Tony can paint 30 walls in 5 hours.

----

1. Change each ratio so the number on the left is a whole number.

a) $\frac{1}{2}$ hour : 2 km walked =

b) $\frac{1}{4}$ cup of flour : 2 cups of potatoes =

c) $\frac{1}{3}$ hour : 3 km rowed =

d) $\frac{1}{3}$ cup of raisins : 2 cups of oats =

e) 0.3 km : 1 litre of gas used =

f) 1.7 mL of ginger ale : 0.3 mL or orange juice =
   HINT: For this ratio, multiply each term by 10.

2. Solve each problem by changing the ratio into a more convenient form.

   a) Rhonda can ride her bike 3 km in $\frac{1}{4}$ of an hour. How far can she ride in 2 hours?

   b) A plant grows 3 cm in 4 days. How many days will it take to grow 6 cm?

3. How many equivalent ratios can you write for this array?

4. For each ratio below write an equivalent ratio with one term equal to 20.
   a) 4 : 6   b) 3 : 5   c) 4 : 5   d) 10 : 30

5. In a class of 30 students there are 10 girls. Explain why the ratio of girls to boys is 1 to 2.

NS6-90: Percents

A **percent** is a ratio that compares a number to 100.

The term percent means "out of 100" or "for every 100." For instance, 84% on a test means 84 out of 100.

You can think of percent as a short form for a fraction with 100 in the denominator, e.g. $45\% = \frac{45}{100}$

---

1. Write the following percents as fractions.

   a) 7%   b) 92%   c) 5%   d) 15%

   e) 50%   f) 100%   g) 2%   h) 7%

2. Write the following fractions as percents.

   a) $\frac{2}{100}$ b) $\frac{31}{100}$ c) $\frac{52}{100}$ d) $\frac{100}{100}$

   e) $\frac{17}{100}$ f) $\frac{88}{100}$ g) $\frac{2}{100}$ h) $\frac{1}{100}$

3. Write the following decimals as percents, by first turning them into fractions. The first one has been done for you.

   a) $.72 = \frac{72}{100} = 72\%$ b) .27   c) .04

4. Write the fraction as a percent by changing it to a fraction over 100. The first one has been done for you.

   a) $\frac{3}{5} \begin{smallmatrix} \times 20 \\ \times 20 \end{smallmatrix} = \frac{60}{100} = 60\%$ b) $\frac{2}{5}$

   c) $\frac{4}{5}$ d) $\frac{1}{4}$

   e) $\frac{3}{4}$ f) $\frac{1}{2}$

   g) $\frac{3}{10}$ h) $\frac{7}{10}$

   i) $\frac{17}{25}$ j) $\frac{7}{20}$

   k) $\frac{3}{25}$ l) $\frac{19}{20}$

   m) $\frac{23}{50}$ n) $\frac{47}{50}$

5. Write the following decimals as a percents. The first one has been done for you.

a) $.2 = \frac{2}{10} \overset{\times 10}{\underset{\times 10}{=}} \frac{20}{100} = 20\%$

b) .5

c) .7

d) .9

6. What percent of the figure is shaded?

a)

b)

c)

d)

7. Change the following fractions to percents by first reducing them to lowest terms.

a) $\frac{9}{15} \overset{\div 3}{\underset{\div 3}{=}} \frac{3}{5} = \frac{3}{5} \overset{\times 20}{\underset{\times 20}{=}} \frac{60}{100} = 60\%$

b) $\frac{12}{15}$

c) $\frac{3}{6}$

d) $\frac{7}{35}$

e) $\frac{21}{28}$

f) $\frac{18}{45}$

g) $\frac{12}{30}$

h) $\frac{10}{40}$

i) $\frac{20}{40}$

j) $\frac{16}{40}$

k) $\frac{60}{150}$

l) $\frac{45}{75}$

NS6-91: Visual Representations of Percents

1. Fill in the chart below. The first one has been done for you.

Drawing				
Fraction	$\frac{23}{100}$	$\frac{}{100}$	$\frac{45}{100}$	$\frac{}{100}$
Decimal	0._2_3_	0.__ __	0.__ __	0.81
Percent	23%	63%	____ %	____ %

Use a ruler for Questions 2 to 5.

2. Shade 50% of each box.

   a)

   b)

   c)

3. Shade 25% of each box.

   a)

   b)

4. The triangle is 50% of a parallelogram. Show what 100% might look like.

5. Colour 50% of the rectangle blue, 40% red, and 10% green.

6. a) Write a fraction for the part shaded: _____

   b) Write the fraction with a denominator of 100: _____

   c) Write a decimal and percent for the part shaded: _____ _____

Number Sense 2

7. Write a fraction and a percent for each division of the number line.

Fraction | 0 | | | | 1

Percent | 0% | | | |

8. Draw marks to show 25%, 50%, and 75% of the line segment.

a) ─────────────

b) ─────────────────

c) ──────────

d) ──────────────────────

9. Extend each line segment to show 100%.

a) | 50% |

b) | 25% |

c) | 20% |

d) | 75% |

e) 0%   60%

f) 0%   80%

g) 0%   10%

h) 0%   50%

10. Estimate the percent of the line segment represented by each mark.

a) 0%   ✗   100%

b) 0%   ✗   100%

11. Draw a <u>rough</u> sketch of a floor plan for a museum.

The different collections should take up the following amounts of space:

- Dinosaurs   40%
- Animals   20%
- Rocks and Minerals   10%
- Ancient Artefacts   20%

Washrooms should take up the final 10% of the floor space.

12. Asia covers 30% of the world's land mass.
    Using a globe, compare the size of Asia to the size of Australia.
    Approximately what percent of the world's land mass does Australia cover?

1. From the list below, choose the percent to which each fraction is closest.

| 10% | 25% | 50% | 75% | 100% |

a) $\frac{3}{5}$ _____   b) $\frac{4}{5}$ _____   c) $\frac{2}{5}$ _____   d) $\frac{2}{10}$ _____

e) $\frac{1}{10}$ _____   f) $\frac{4}{10}$ _____   g) $\frac{9}{10}$ _____   h) $\frac{4}{25}$ _____

i) $\frac{11}{20}$ _____   j) $\frac{16}{20}$ _____   k) $\frac{37}{40}$ _____   l) $\frac{1}{12}$ _____

2. Write <, > or = between the following pairs of numbers. The first one has been done for you.
   HINT: Change each pair of numbers to a pair of fractions with the same denominator.

a) $\frac{1}{2}$ ☐ 47%

$\frac{50 \times 1}{50 \times 2}$ ☐ $\frac{47}{100}$

$\frac{50}{100}$ > $\frac{47}{100}$

b) $\frac{1}{2}$ ☐ 53%

c) $\frac{1}{4}$ ☐ 23%

d) $\frac{3}{4}$ ☐ 70%

e) $\frac{2}{5}$ ☐ 32%

f) .27 ☐ 62%

g) .02 ☐ 11%

h) $\frac{1}{10}$ ☐ 10%

i) $\frac{19}{25}$ ☐ 93%

j) $\frac{23}{50}$ ☐ 46%

k) .9 ☐ 10%

l) $\frac{11}{20}$ ☐ 19%

3. Write each set of numbers in order from least to greatest by first changing each number to a <u>fraction</u>.

   a) $\frac{3}{5}$, 42% , .73   b) $\frac{1}{2}$, .73 , 80%

   c) $\frac{1}{4}$, .09 , 15%   d) $\frac{2}{3}$, 57% , .62

If you use a thousands cube to represent 1 whole, you can see that taking $\frac{1}{10}$ of a number is the same as dividing the number by 10 – the decimal shifts one place left.

$\frac{1}{10}$ of 1 = .1 $\frac{1}{10}$ of .1 = .01 $\frac{1}{10}$ of .01 = .001

----

1. Find $\frac{1}{10}$ of the following numbers by shifting the decimal.   Write your answers in the boxes provided.

   a) 4   b) 7   c) 32   d) 120   e) 3.8   f) 2.5

2. 10% is short for $\frac{1}{10}$. Find 10% of the following numbers.

   a) 9   b) 5.7   c) 4.05   d) 6.35   e) .06   f) 21.1

3. You can find percents that are multiples of 10 as follows.

   Example: Finding 30% of 21 is the same as finding 10% of 21
                       and multiplying the result by 3.

              <u>Step 1:</u>   10% of 21 = | 2.1 |

              <u>Step 2:</u>   3 × | 2.1 | = 6.3   →   so 30% of 21 = 6.3

   Find the percents using the method above.

   a) 40% of 15   b) 60% of 25   c) 90% of 2.3

   i)   10% of 15 = | | i)   10% of ____ = | | i)   10% of ____ = | |

   ii) 4 × | | = _____   ii) ____ × | | = _____   ii) ____ × | | = _____

   d) 60% of 35   e) 40% of 24   f) 20% of 1.3

   i)   10% of ____ = | | i)   10% of ____ = | | i)   10% of ____ = | |

   ii) ____ × | | = _____   ii) ____ × | | = _____   ii) ____ × | | = _____

35% is short for $\frac{35}{100}$. To find 35% of 27, Sadie finds $\frac{35}{100}$ of 27.

<u>Step 1:</u>   She multiplies 27 by 35.   <u>Step 2:</u>   She divides the result by 100.

	2	3
		2	7
×		3	5
	1	3	5
	8	1	0
	9	4	5

$945 \div 100 = 9.45$

So 35% of 27 is 9.45.

----

1. Find the following percents using Sadie's method.

    a) 45% of 32

   <u>Step 1:</u>   ×

   <u>Step 2:</u>

   _____ ÷ 100 =

   So _____ of _____ is _____.

    b) 28% of 63

   <u>Step 1:</u>   ×

   <u>Step 2:</u>

   _____ ÷ 100 =

   So _____ of _____ is _____.

2. Find the following percents using Sadie's method.

    a) 13% of 9   b) 52% of 7   c) 65% of 8   d) 78% of 9

    e) 23% of 42   f) 17% of 68   g) 37% of 80   h) 62% of 75

3. 25% is equal to $\frac{1}{4}$ and 75% is equal to $\frac{3}{4}$. Find ...

    a) 25% of 80   b) 25% of 280   c) 25% of 12   d) 75% of 20   e) 75% of 320

NS6-95: Percents: Word Problems

1. Find the missing percent of each child's stamp stamp collection that comes from other countries.
   HINT: **Change all fractions to percents.**

a) Anne's collection:

Canada	USA	Other
40%	$\frac{1}{2}$	
= 40%	= 50%	= 10%

b) Brian's collection:

Canada	England	Other
80%	$\frac{1}{10}$	

c) Juan's collection:

Mexico	USA	Other
$\frac{1}{2}$	40%	

d) Lanre's collection:

Canada	Nigeria	Other
22%	$\frac{3}{5}$	

e) Faith's collection:

Jamaica	Canada	Other
$\frac{3}{4}$	15%	

f) Carlo's collection:

France	Italy	Other
$\frac{3}{4}$	10%	

2. A painter spends $500.00 on art supplies. Complete the chart.

	Fraction of Money Spent	Percentage of Money Spent	Amount of Money Spent
Brushes			$50.00
Paint	$\frac{4}{10}$		
Canvas		50%	

3. Indra spent 1 hour doing homework. The chart shows the time she spent on each subject.

   a) Complete the chart.

   b) How did you find the amount of time spent on math?

Subject	Fraction of 1 hour	Percent of 1 hour	Decimal	Number of minutes
English	$\frac{1}{4}$		.25	15
Science	$\frac{1}{20}$	5%		
Math		50%		
French			.20	

4. Roger wants to buy a deck of cards that costs $8.00. The taxes are 15%. How much did he pay in taxes?

5. There are 15 boys and 12 girls in a class.
   $\frac{3}{4}$ of the girls have black hair, and 60% of the boys have black hair.
   How many children have black hair?

Number Sense 2

1. Write the number of girls (**g**), boys (**b**), and children (**c**) in each class.

   a)   There are 8 boys and 5 girls in a class.   **b:** _____   **g:** _____   **c:** _____

   b)   There are 4 boys and 7 girls in a class.   **b:** _____   **g:** _____   **c:** _____

   c)   There are 12 boys and 15 girls in a class.   **b:** _____   **g:** _____   **c:** _____

   d)   There are 9 girls in a class of 20 children.   **b:** _____   **g:** _____   **c:** _____

   e)   There are 7 boys in a class of 10 children.   **b:** _____   **g:** _____   **c:** _____

2. Write the number of boys, girls and children in each class.
   Then write the fraction of children who are boys and the fraction who are girls in the boxes provided.

   a)   There are 5 boys and 6 girls in a class.   **b:** ____ ☐   **g:** ____ ☐   **c:** _____

   b)   There are 15 children in the class. 8 are boys. **b:** ____ ☐   **g:** ____ ☐   **c:** _____

3. Write the fraction of children in the class who are boys and the fraction who are girls.

   a)   There are 5 boys and 12 children in the class.   **b:** ☐   **g:** ☐

   b)   There are 3 boys and 2 girls in the class.   **b:** ☐   **g:** ☐

   c)   There are 9 girls and 20 children in the class.   **b:** ☐   **g:** ☐

   d)   The ratio of boys to girls is 5:9 in the class.   **b:** ☐   **g:** ☐

   e)   The ratio of girls to boys is 7:8 in the class.   **b:** ☐   **g:** ☐

   f)   The ratio of boys to girls is 10:11 in the class.   **b:** ☐   **g:** ☐

4. From the information given, determine the number of girls and boys in each class.

   a)   There are 20 children in a class. $\frac{2}{5}$ are boys.   b)   There are 42 children. $\frac{3}{7}$ are girls.

   c)   There are 15 children.   d)   There are 24 children.
        The ratio of girls to boys is 3:2.   The ratio of girls to boys is 3:5.

Number Sense 2

Answer the following questions in your notebook.

5. Find the number of boys and girls in each classroom.

   a) In classroom A, there are 25 children: 60% are girls.

   b) In classroom B, there are 28 children. The ratio of boys to girls is 3 : 4.

   c) In classroom C, there are 30 children. The ratio of boys to girls is 1 : 2.

6. For each question below, say which classroom has more girls.

   a) In classroom A, there are 40 children. 60% are girls.

   In classroom B, there are 36 children. The ratio of boys to girls is 5 : 4.

   b) In classroom A, there are 28 children. The ratio of boys to girls is 5 : 2.

   In classroom B, there are 30 children. $\frac{3}{5}$ of the children are boys.

7. In the word "Whitehorse"…

   a) … what is the ratio of vowels to consonants?

   b) … what fraction of the letters are vowels?

   c) … what percent of the letters are consonants?

8. Look at the circle graph. Estimate the fraction of pets of each typed owned according and complete the chart.

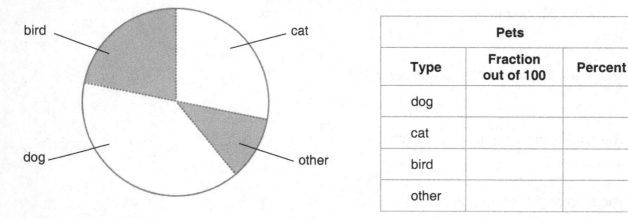

Pets		
Type	Fraction out of 100	Percent
dog		
cat		
bird		
other		

9. Write the amounts in order from least to greatest: $\frac{1}{20}$, 20% , 0.2. Show your work.

10. Kevin has 360 hockey cards.

    30% are Toronto Maple Leaf cards, and $\frac{1}{2}$ are Montreal Canadien cards. The rest are Vancouver Canuck cards.

    How many of each type of card does he have?

11. What percent of a metre stick is 37 cm? Explain.

Answer the following questions in your notebook.

1. *Meteorologists* study the weather.

   The world's highest temperature in the shade was recorded in Libya in 1932.

   The temperature reached 58°C.

   a) How long ago was this temperature recorded?

   b) On an average summer day in Toronto, the temperature is 30°C.
      How much higher was the temperature recorded in Libya?

   c) The lowest temperature recorded (in Antarctica) was – 89°C.
      What is the difference between the lowest and the highest temperatures recorded?

2. The Olympic women's high jump gold medal was earned with a jump of 2.06 m.
   The silver jump was 2.02 m.

   a) Round both jumps to the nearest tenth.

   b) Make up two jumps which would round to the same number
      (when rounded to the tenths).

   c) Why are Olympic high jumps measured so precisely?

3. Doctors study the body. Here are some facts a doctor might know.

   a) FACT: "The heart pumps about 0.06 L of blood with each beat."
      About how many times would the heart need to beat to pump a litre of blood?

   b) FACT: "All of the blood passes through the heart in a minute."
      How many times would the blood pass through the heart in a day?

   c) FACT: "Bones make up about 15% of the weight of the body."
      How much would the bones of a 62 kg person weigh?

   d) FACT: "The brain is 85% water."
      What fraction of the brain is not water?

   e) FACT: "The most common type of blood is Type O blood.

      45% of people have Type O blood."

      About how many children in a class of 24 kids would have Type O blood?

Answer the following questions in your notebook.

1. 98% of Antarctica is covered in ice.

   What fraction of Antarctica is not covered in ice?

2. A ball is dropped from a height of 100 m.

   Each time it hits the ground, it bounces $\frac{3}{5}$ of the height it fell from. How high did it bounce…

   a) on the first bounce?

   b) on the second bounce?

3. The peel of a banana weighs $\frac{1}{8}$ of the total weight of a banana.

   If you buy 4 kg of bananas at $0.60 per kg …

   a) how much do you pay for the peel?

   b) how much do you pay for the part you eat?

4. The price of a soccer ball is $8.00.
   If the price rises by $0.25 each year,

   How much will the ball cost in 10 years?

5. Janice earned $28.35 on Monday.
   On Thursday, she spent $17.52 for a shirt.
   She now has $32.23.
   How much money did she have before she started work Monday?

6. Anthony's taxi service charges $2.50 for the first kilometre and $1.50 for each additional km.
   If Bob paid $17.50 in total, how many km did he travel in the taxi?

7. There are three apartment buildings in a block.

   • Apartment A has 50 suites.

   • Apartment B has 50% more suites than Apartment A.

   • Apartment C has twice as many suites as Apartment B.

   a) How many suites do Apartment B and Apartment C have?

   b) How many suites do the three apartments have altogether?

area the amount of space occupied by the face or surface of an object

array an arrangement of things (for example, objects, symbols, or numbers) in rows and columns

base-10 materials materials used to represent ones (ones squares or cubes), tens (tens strips or rods), hundreds (hundreds squares or flats), and thousands (thousands cubes)

centimetre (cm) a unit of measurement used to describe length, height, or thickness

column things (for example, objects, symbols, numbers) that run up and down

composite number a number that has more than two factors

consecutive numbers numbers that occur one after the other on a number line

coordinate system a grid with labelled rows and columns, used to describe the location of a dot or object, for example the dot is at (A,3)

decimal a short form for tenths (for example, 0.2) or hundredths (for example, 0.02), and so on

decimetre (dm) a unit of measurement used to describe length, height, or thickness; equal to 10 cm

decreasing sequence a sequence where each number is less than the one before it

denominator the number on the bottom portion of a fraction; tells you how many parts are in a whole

diagonal things (for example, objects, symbols, or numbers) that are in a line from one corner to another corner

difference the "gap" between two numbers; the remainder left after subtraction

divide to find how many times one number contains another number

dividend in a division problem, the number that is being divided or shared

divisible by containing a number a specific number of times without having a remainder (for example, 15 is divisible by 5 and 3)

divisor in a division problem, the number that is divided into another number

equivalent fractions fractions that represent the same amount, but have different denominators (for example, $\frac{2}{3} = \frac{4}{6}$)

estimate a guess or calculation of an approximate number

expanded form a way to write a number that shows the place value of each digit (for example, 27 in expanded form can be written as 2 tens + 7 ones, or 20 + 7)

factor tree a diagram that uses branches (lines) to show prime factorization

factors whole numbers that are multiplied to give a product

fraction a number used to name a part of a set or a region

growing pattern a pattern in which each term is greater than the previous term

improper fraction a fraction that has a numerator that is larger than the denominator; this represents more than a whole

increasing sequence a sequence where each number is greater than the one before it

integer a whole number that is either positive, negative, or zero

kilometre (km) a unit of measurement for length; equal to 1000 cm

leading digit the first (non-zero) digit in a number

line graph a way to display data; often used to represent the relationship between two variables; has a vertical and a horizontal axis, labels, and data points connected by a line

litre (L) a unit of measurement to describe capacity; equal to 1000 mL

lowest common multiple (LCM) the least nonzero number that two numbers can divide into evenly (for example, 6 is the LCM of 2 and 3)

metre (m) a unit of measurement used to describe length, height, or thickness; equal to 100 cm

mililitre (mL) a unit of measurement used to describe capacity

millimetre (mm) a unit of measurement used to describe length, height, or thickness; equal to 0.1 cm

mixed fraction a mixture of a whole number and a fraction

model a physical representation (for example, using base-10 materials to represent a number)

multiple of a number that is the result of multiplying one number by another specific number (for example, the multiples of 5 are 0, 5, 10, 15, and so on)

multiply to find the total of a number times another number

number line a line with numbers marked at intervals, used to help with skip counting

numerator the number on the top portion of a fraction; tells you how many parts are counted

pattern (repeating pattern) the same repeating group of objects, numbers, or attributes

perfect square the result of a number multiplied by itself

perimeter the distance around the outside of a shape

prime factorization a number written as a product of prime numbers

prime number a number that has only two factors: itself and 1

product the result from multiplying two or more numbers together

quotient the result from dividing one number by another number

regroup to exchange one place value for another place value (for example, 10 ones squares for 1 tens strip)

remainder the number left over after dividing or subtracting (for example, $10 \div 3 = 3$ R1)

row things (for example, objects, symbols, or numbers) that run left to right

set a group of like objects

skip counting counting by a number (for example, 2s, 3s, 4s) by "skipping" over the numbers in between

square centimetre (cm2) a unit of measurement used to describe area

sum the result from adding two or more numbers together

term a number in a sequence

term number the position of a term in a sequence

T-table a chart used to compare two sequences of numbers

unit rate a comparison of two quantities where one quantity is equal to 1

variable a letter or symbol that represents a number

Venn diagram a diagram containing circles, used to organize items according to attributes; the parts of the circles that overlap represent items that share attributes

About the Authors

JOHN MIGHTON is a mathematician, author, and playwright. He completed a Ph.D. in mathematics at the University of Toronto and is currently a fellow of the Fields Institute for Mathematical Research. The founder of JUMP Math (www.jumpmath.org), Mighton also gives lectures to student teachers at York University and the Ontario Institute for Studies in Education, and invited talks and training sessions for parents and educators. He is the author of the *JUMP at Home* workbooks and the national bestsellers *The Myth of Ability* and *The End of Ignorance*. He has won the Governor General's Literary Award and the Siminovitch Prize for his plays.

DR. ANNA KLEBANOV received her B.Sc., M.Sc., Ph.D., and teaching certificate from the Technion – Israel Institute of Technology. She is the recipient of three teaching awards for excellence. She began her career at JUMP Math as a curriculum writer in 2007, working with Dr. John Mighton and Dr. Sindi Sabourin on JUMP Math's broad range of publications.

DR. SINDI SABOURIN received her Ph.D. in mathematics from Queen's University, specializing in commutative algebra. She is the recipient of the Governor General's Gold Medal Award from Queen's University and a National Sciences and Research Council Postdoctoral Fellowship. Her career with JUMP Math began in 2003 as a volunteer doing in-class tutoring, one-on-one tutoring, as well as working on answer keys. In 2006, she became a curriculum writer working on JUMP Math's broad range of publications.